THE TURTLE BAY COOKBOOK

THE
TURTLE BAY
COOKBOOK

A FEAST OF FLAVORS FROM
LATIN AMERICA AND THE CARIBBEAN

FEATURING RECIPES FROM
COASTAL MEXICO, CENTRAL AMERICA, AND THE CARIBBEAN

BY
MARIE PERUCCA-RAMÍREZ &
JULIO J. RAMÍREZ, C.E.C., A.A.C.

WHITEHAND PRESS ✸ CARMEL, CALIFORNIA

WriteHand Press
Carmel, CA 93923

Based on *El Cocodrilo's Cookbook*
Published in 1996 by Macmillan, New York, revised and expanded

Library of Congress Cataloging–in–Publication Data

Perucca–Ramírez, Marie.
The Turtle Bay cookbook: a feast of flavors from Latin America and the Caribbean
/ Marie Perucca–Ramírez and Julio J. Ramírez.

Includes bibliographical references and index.

ISBN 0-9641055-2-7
1. Cookery, Latin American. 2. Cookery, Caribbean. 3. Food, History–New World
4. Turtle Bay Taqueria
I. Ramírez, Julio J. II. Title.

First Edition, First Printing
Library of Congress Cataloging card Number 00-136013
Printed in Hong Kong through Global Interprint, Inc.

10 9 8 7 6 5 4 3 2 1

Cover Art by Marcia Perry
Book Design by Chiara Ramírez
Typesetting by Short But Sweet Graphics
Photography by Jesse Ramírez
Food Styling by Katie Klarin
Interior Illustrations by Liz Cano-Manning

FOREWORD

This cookbook is a collection of our favorite recipes from the Turtle Bay Taquerias, the Fishwife Seafood Restaurants, and the former El Cocodrilo Rotisserie and Seafood Grill. It's a celebration of the food of the American tropics—Mexico, Central America, and the Caribbean—with special emphasis on those food items that were originally cultivated here in the Western Hemisphere.

In keeping with our theme, we are dedicating this book to the rain forest—that unique biosphere that gave rise to, and continues to sustain, the traditional cultures of tropical America. Interspersed throughout this cookbook are mini-profiles of some of the creatures of the American rain forest, recognizing their important contribution to the equilibrium of their delicate environment. We are increasingly hopeful that, as our generation comes to appreciate and value this vast but fragile wilderness, we will be able to work together to protect the remaining rain forest from our own selfish interests. Knowing how interdependent we are with all other living species on this earth, we must strive to preserve and renew this living treasure for our children and the children who follow them. This could well be our generation's greatest contribution to the future of our planet.

ACKNOWLEDGMENTS

A heartfelt THANK YOU

to our partner JEFFERSON SEAY for making this project possible,

to LINDA LANDUCCI for her wise counsel and insightful critique of the original manuscript, and BARBARA CHRISTIAN for her sharp proofing skills,

to MARY JOSEPHINE MORTON CAIN for her encouragement in making this labor of love a reality,

to THE LATE CHEF AARON ARONSON for his culinary genius and inspired contributions to this book,

to THE KITCHEN STAFF at The Fishwife Seafood Restaurants and Turtle Bay Taquerias for the culinary alchemy they perform daily, transforming the gifts of the earth into gifts for the table,

to BOB SILVA and CAROL ATKINSON for the many roads we've traveled and the meals we've shared,

and to everyone involved in this project for their belief in and commitment to the philosophy and goals contained in this work.

MP-R & JJR

A special THANK YOU to MARIE MAGDALENO for assuming many of my restaurant responsibilities so that I could focus on the research and writing of this book.

MP-R

A LITTLE HISTORY

THE FISHWIFE SEAFOOD RESTAURANTS & TURTLE BAY TAQUERIAS

In 1985 Julio J. Ramírez and Marie Perucca-Ramírez opened The Fishwife Seafood Café in Seaside, California. The concept was simple: offer fresh, innovative, and healthful cuisine at reasonable prices.

Drawing on his expertise as an executive chef, and on their exploration of traditional cuisines in Latin America and the Caribbean, Julio and Marie developed a menu combining the fresh seafood and produce available on the Monterey Peninsula with herbs, spices, and recipes from Europe and the Americas.

Soon joined in this partnership by chef Jefferson Seay, the three restaurateurs developed a large and loyal local following. In 1986, the success of the café led them to open a larger restaurant next to Asilomar Beach in Pacific Grove: The Fishwife at Asilomar Beach. There, the restaurant's reputation for excellence has continued to grow along with its enthusiastic following. The Fishwife's dedication to its original concept has earned it numerous awards and recognition, including being consistently voted "Best Seafood Restaurant" on the Monterey Peninsula by locals (*Coast Weekly*: The Best of Monterey, 1989-2001; *Adventures in Dining*: Reader's Choice Awards). The Fishwife has been named among the list of Top Ten Restaurants on the Monterey Peninsula.

Following the success of their seafood restaurants, the partners wanted to open another restaurant with a similar focus on fresh, flavorful, healthful cuisine—but with a more global view. Drawing on the foods of Julio's childhood in Nicaragua and the talents of their kitchen crew, Ramírez, Perucca, and Seay created a Latin fusion cuisine which combined the spirit and flavor of tropical America with California technique and style. The resulting restaurant, El Cocodrilo Rotisserie & Seafood Grill, opened to rave reviews in October of 1990. The atmosphere at El Cocodrilo was casual and fun. The restaurant was decorated with masks, pottery, weavings, animal sculptures, and photographs of the American tropics; a vibrant rain forest mural covered the back wall. In honor of the crocodile, the restaurant's namesake, El Cocodrilo donated a percentage of its gross sales to support the Orinoco Crocodile Project in Venezuela.

In 1997, planning to travel and rest, the partners sold El Cocodrilo—but a trip to the Yucatán Peninsula convinced them that there was a cuisine that had to be offered here on the Monterey Peninsula. The result was Turtle Bay Taqueria. Opened at the end of 1997, Turtle Bay continues the Fishwife tradition of marrying tropical flavors with California style. Featuring the fresh cuisine of the Yucatán and coastal Mexico, Turtle Bay offers fresh fish, citrus-marinated meats, fresh fruit salsas, and spices and marinades imported from Mexico.

A second Taqueria in downtown Monterey opened in December of 1998. Turtle Bay Monterey features 14-foot palm trees, large colorful paintings of tropical wildlife—iguanas, fish, frogs, parrots—by local artist Marcia Perry, and an undersea tableau in etched glass by artist Lynn Owen. The March 2000 issue of *Sunset Magazine* named Turtle Bay one the "Great Taquerias of the West."

Both The Fishwife and Turtle Bay Restaurants are committed to promoting education in the community. Along with helping with school fund-raisers and mentoring students, the restaurants have established The New Millennium Scholarship. This scholarship is awarded to graduating high school seniors who want to make a positive contribution to our community and who have shown self-determination and willingness to overcome hardships to achieve their educational goals. A portion of the proceeds from the sale of this cookbook will help fund the New Millennium Scholarship.

TABLE OF CONTENTS

CHAPTER 3
FRESH SALSAS, CONDIMENTS, AND SPICES

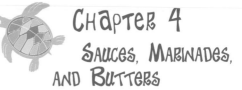

CHAPTER 4
SAUCES, MARINADES, AND BUTTERS

TABLE OF CONTENTS

 CHAPTER 5
APPETIZERS

 CHAPTER 6
SOUPS, CHOWDERS, AND GUMBOS

CHAPTER 7
SIDES AND SALADS

CHAPTER 8
ENTREES

TABLE OF CONTENTS

CHAPTER 9
DESSERTS

Table of Contents

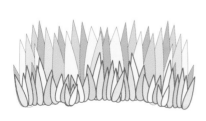

Chapter 1

Introduction

The sixteenth century marked the beginning of a great food exchange between two worlds. Over the millennia, civilizations thriving in both the Eastern and Western Hemispheres had developed distinctive agricultural inventories and culinary styles. Divided by great oceans, each hemisphere was arguably unaware of the other's existence. When the Europeans sailed to the lands in the west, these ocean barriers were breached and the civilizations of Europe, Asia, and Africa met those of North, Central, and South America. This multicultural encounter resulted in an exchange of foods and cooking techniques, enriching the cuisine of peoples on both sides of the world.

The Europeans had originally gone to the Americas with plans to conquer and colonize the lands and to convert the native populations to the Christian religion. They sought gold, land, power, and religious dominance; however, it was actually the humble plant seeds and cuttings that they sent back to the Old World, more than the shiploads of gold and silver, that proved to be the real treasure of the Americas. These foods, distributed by trade and travel to the far corners of the earth, became staples and cash crops for many peoples, enriching the diet of the entire planet.

Over time, each culture develops a signature style of cooking that becomes part of that group's uniqueness. The habitual use of certain key ingredients, flavorings, and cooking methods is what allows us to identify these cuisines by name, using such simple terms as "Chinese" and "Mexican." For members of a culture, the flavors and aromas of its traditional cuisine evoke memories of home. Though many of us are unaware of it, that sixteenth-century meeting of the Eastern and Western Hemispheres had a profound impact on many of these ethnic cuisines. With the dispersal of the food of the Americas throughout the world, foreign cultures accepted, adapted, and then adopted these new foods as their own. By combining the new exotic ingredients from the Americas with their traditional food inventory, the cooks of the past centuries created a multitude of fusion cuisines that survive today as regional and ethnic cuisines. Most people would be surprised to know that the key ingredients in many of the "traditional" cuisines of Europe, Africa, and Asia were introduced from the Americas only a few hundred years ago. The chiles in Szechwan and Thai cooking, the corn in Zimbabwean *sadza*, the tomatoes in Italian pasta sauces, the peanuts in Indian curries, the potatoes in Russian vodka and Irish stews, the chocolate and vanilla in Swiss confectionery are just a few examples.

Since the sixteenth century and the start of transoceanic travel, many food boundaries have been broken: trade, migration, and even war have carried the seeds of the world's agricultural larder to the furthest-flung cultures on earth. Sweet potatoes grow in China, prickly pears in South Africa, pineapples in Malaysia, peanuts and cocoa in Sudan, potatoes in Nepal, corn in Romania. Each of these cultures has adopted these new ingredients and made them their own. So the cuisine we identify today as Italian or Indian, Mexican or Moroccan, is actually in great part the outcome of that transoceanic food exchange that began with the European quest for colonies and trade routes in the Americas, a quest that resulted in the discovery and dissemination of the greatest bounty of the Americas: food. And while the dissemination went both ways—items such as dairy products, wheat, sugar, and rice were introduced into the cuisines of the New World—this book will focus on those foods which originated here in the Americas and went on to transform the cuisines of other countries around the world.

The Bounty of the Americas

Imagine...

When the Spanish conquistadors marched into the Aztec capital of Tenochtitlán in 1519, they were unprepared for the splendor and sophistication of this metropolis. Tenochtitlán, the religious and administrative center of a powerful empire, covered ten square miles and supported a population of perhaps three hundred thousand—several times larger than sixteenth-century London.

Try to imagine this city as seen through the eyes of an Old World traveler who is entering the city for the first time. Imagine

... a city of tall stone temples, elaborate ceremonial buildings, palaces, schools, orchards, and gardens;

... a city with wide, spacious roadways, canals, drawbridges, and aqueducts;

... a city alive with a bustling population of artists, architects, merchants, teachers, priests, royals, and workmen;

... a city standing at the center of trade routes which radiate out hundreds—even thousands—of miles throughout the Aztec empire and beyond;

... a city welcoming trade caravans traveling from distant lands, laden with the goods of two continents;

... a city boasting of a huge marketplace where the wealth of the Aztec empire and treasures from diverse cultures beyond are displayed for sale.

Now, imagine an immense open marketplace full of people, movement, and color. The marketplace is divided into sectors, depending on the wares of the merchants. There are

... sectors for goldsmiths and silversmiths who offer exquisitely crafted jewelry and tableware;

... sectors for feather workers who fashion the brilliant plumes of quetzals and macaws into capes, shields, headdresses, and ceremonial fans;

... sectors for fruit, vegetable, and condiment vendors;

... sectors for fishmongers who display fresh fish, and butchers who display dressed rabbit, wild duck, peccary and haunches of venison as well as live turkeys, dogs, iguanas, armadillos, and turtles;

... sectors for florists who offer brilliantly colored flowers and ornamental plants;

... sectors for merchants who exhibit fine cotton and other cloth;

... sectors for craftsmen who display fine leather goods, pottery, ceramics, and copperware;

... sectors for herbalists who offer over 1,000 medicinal and magical plants that can cure disease, induce hallucinations, and cast and ward off spells;

... sectors for beauty specialists who sell cosmetics;

... sectors for vendors of rope, cord, and thread;

... sectors for those who sell household pets, including multihued birds and chattering monkeys;

... and a sector for specialty items where, in one particularly popular stall, a man sells syrup-sweetened snow brought down from the peaks of a towering volcano.

Smell the tantalizing aromas wafting from the food vendors' stalls: the delicious scents of corn tortillas roasting on clay comals, herb-and-pepper spiced stews thickened with seeds or nuts simmering on open fires, steaming tamales, and barbacoa from smoking, stone-lined earthen pits.

Now stroll through the stalls of the fruit and vegetable merchants. Marvel at the multicolored baskets overflowing with papayas, chiles, pineapples, guavas, peanuts, vanilla beans, corn, pumpkins, plums, avocados, squash, varieties of beans, potatoes, sunflower seeds, sesame seeds, pine nuts, cactus fruit, tomatoes, tapioca, cocoa—the bounty of the Americas!

This was the New World that the Europeans entered with their voyages of discovery, beginning in the late fifteenth century. The uniquely rich and nourishing array of fruits and vegetables on display at the market place at Tenochtitlán represented the culmination of thousands of years of cultivation and development by New World agriculturists. The arrival of the Europeans would throw this world into social, political, and cultural chaos, for the Europeans had come to plunder, conquer, colonize, and convert. But while the thrones of Europe fought to fill their coffers with gold and silver, the real treasure of the Americas—her agricultural storehouse—was being dispersed in the form of seeds to the far corners of the earth. Through trade and migration, the seeds of the Americas were carried across the oceans to the savannas of Africa, the high desert of China, the steppes of Russia, and the valleys of Europe, enriching all the peoples of the world.

Early American Agriculture

The agricultural bounty displayed in the market place in Tenochtitlán in 1519 was the product of two continents, many cultures, and thousands of years of careful sorting and tending of seeds. There were two primary centers of agricultural innovation in the New World: south-central Mexico and the Yucatán Peninsula; and the Andes Mountains of Ecuador and Peru.

Around eight thousand years ago in Mexico, Meso-American peoples developed methods of primitive farming. These early agriculturists learned how to supplement their diet of wild plants and animals with plants which they cultivated themselves. Evidence found in a group of caves in Tamaulipas, Mexico, shows that between seven and five thousand years ago, early Americans had begun to domesticate summer squash for food and grow chile peppers for seasonings. They grew bottle gourds for both food and utilitarian purposes: they ate the young and tender fruit, and used the mature, hard-shelled gourds as water containers. The grain amaranth was also cultivated by the early Meso-Americans. The domestication of corn, around 2500 B.C., was a revolutionary development. Up until this time, the people had remained hunters and semi-agriculturalists—that is, nomadic. The domestication of corn provided the basis for settled life in Meso-America. From these early agriculturists, the Toltec, Maya, and Aztec civilizations arose. These peoples then hybridized corn to increase yields, and that, in turn, supported the growth of larger populations. They also cultivated beans, squash, chile peppers, avocados, potatoes, tobacco, and several species of cotton. Agricultural technology included irrigation canals; artificial gardens that floated on water; and moisture-retention tillage, which allowed dry farming on non-irrigated lands.

The diet of early Meso-Americans was nutritionally complete, though it included little meat. Corn supplied carbohydrates; squash and beans supplied vegetable proteins and nutrients; avocados provided essential fats and oils; and chiles supplied essential vitamins A and C. And because these early Americans soaked their corn in lime, the necessary calcium and niacin were added to their diet. While commoners' diets were simpler, Mexican nobles feasted on roasted turkey, quail, and casseroles of turkey prepared with chiles, tomatoes, and ground pumpkinseeds.

Anthropologists have found evidence that beans were being grown in the Andes as early as 5600 B.C. Farming provided the base on which the Inca and the predecessors of the Inca built their extraordinary civilizations. Approximately six thousand years ago, the early Andean farmers grew peanuts, white potatoes, and sweet potatoes. Of the hundreds of species of potatoes known today, many were developed by these prehistoric farmers. They also grew tomatoes, lima beans, chile, and squashes. Some evidence suggests that Andean farmers may even have domesticated corn more than five thousand years ago. The early Peruvian technology included stone hoes and digging sticks, irrigation systems, and the use of sea gull manure, *guano*, to fertilize the fields. Because of these advanced farming practices, the little valleys on the rainless coast of Peru were able to support dense and highly distinctive populations for thousands of years.

Beginning in the thirteenth century, the Inca began conquering and consolidating the various peoples and nations of the Andes. Under the Inca Empire, land was farmed communally. Crop yields were divided into three parts: one to sustain the local community; one to support the royal government of the Inca; and one to support the state religion—the worship of Inti—and its attendant priesthood. Surpluses were distributed to needy areas or stored against future need in government storehouses. To increase the land's productivity, government agencies collected and distributed *guano* fertilizer from the offshore islands of Peru, and sea gulls were declared protected by Inca law. As a result of the *guano*, Peruvian farmland yielded two crops a year. Stone walls were built to terrace whole mountainsides, and fertile land was collected and moved up the mountains to enrich the planting areas. Elaborate systems of ditches and sluices brought water to these fields. Some of these mountain irrigation systems were fifty to seventy-five miles long and are considered major feats of engineering even today. Many of these systems, in fact, are still in use. In desert regions, vast aqueducts were built to bring water from the mountains, as far as four hundred miles away, to form rich, productive oases.

Besides corn, potatoes, beans, chiles, and squashes, the early Peruvian diet also included pineapples, papayas, avocados, guinea pigs, *chicha* (corn beer), and ceremonial bread made from corn. Higher up in the Andes, where it was too cold for corn, quinoa, a high-protein grain, was grown. Llamas, domesticated thousands of years before and primarily raised as pack animals, also provided their owners with fertilizer, fuel, wool, and pelts. The animals were used as offerings for ritual sacrifice, and when they died of natural causes, they were eaten.

Many New World peoples profited from the agricultural innovations of the Andean and Meso-American agriculturists. Through trade, migration, and sometimes warfare, seeds and cuttings were dispersed throughout much of the hemisphere. On the settled islands of the Caribbean—Monserrat, for example—the original peoples dwelled in villages where they lived by fishing, hunting, and gathering. They maintained gardens in which they grew plants that had been originally domesticated primarily in South America and then improved over thousands of years by careful selection. Large cultivated plots included corn, peanuts, cassava, pineapples, sweet potatoes, papayas, peppers, squashes, guavas, avocados, and a variety of New World beans, as well as medicinal plants.

Along with improving their agricultural storehouse, early Americans also developed often unique ways of preparing and preserving their food items. These techniques evolved over the ages in response to the individual needs of each population.

Native American peoples had no large domestic animals to provide a ready source of cooking fat; their traditional cooking was relatively fat-free. Lard—and deep-frying as a cooking method—would be introduced by the Europeans along with the domestic pig. And while the early Americans did

have some plant oils available to them—peanut oil in South America, corn oil in Central America, and sunflower oil in North America—oil was not used extensively in cooking. The preferred methods of cooking included grilling and steaming. Leaves were often used by the Maya to wrap foods for underground pit cooking. Achiote (annatto) seeds, sea salt, and chiles were used to flavor fish and meats such as pheasant and venison. The central Mexicans used corn husks to wrap tamales for steaming. Comals—flat clay griddles—were used to cook tortillas. North American coastal peoples developed the clambake: hot stones were placed in a cooking pit and layers of seaweed were alternated with corn, potatoes, clams, and lobsters. The Caribs developed *boucan*, a style of barbecue in which meat was salted and then smoke-dried on green-wood lattices built over a fire.

Jerky (from the Quechua word *charqui*) was developed by the Incas as a means of preserving the meat of game animals. Deboned and defatted meat was cut into slices one-quarter-inch thick and then dipped into brine or rubbed with salt. The meat was then rolled up in the animal's hide for ten to twelve hours until the moisture was drawn out of the meat by the salt. The meat was then hung in the sun to dry in the cool, dehydrating breezes of the Andean altiplano. Finally, the finished product, jerky, was tied up in convenient bundles.

Pemmican (from the Cree word for fat) was made from drying thinly sliced, lean meat—usually from a large game animal such as a buffalo—over a fire or in the sun and wind. After drying, the meat was pounded to shreds and mixed thoroughly with an almost equal quantity of melted fat, some bone marrow, and a few handfuls of wild cherries. It was then packed in rawhide sacks and sealed with tallow.

Over the course of millennia, throughout the rise and ebb of many cultures, the peoples of the Americas developed a rich larder of fruits and vegetables, spices and condiments; and they perfected cooking methods and preservation techniques to best use this culinary array. This aggregation was the bounty of the Americas, the legacy of those pre-Columbian farmers which has now been dispersed throughout the world.

THE AMERICAN CORNUCOPIA

So what culinary treasures did the Europeans bring back to The Old World? An inventory of the plant foods introduced to Europe, Asia, and Africa from the Americas includes the following:

achiote	cashew	jícama	quinoa
allspice	cassava	Jerusalem artichoke	squash
avocado	chayote	papaya	sunflower
beans (including lima, pinto, pink, red, black, navy, great northern, green beans, etc.)	cherimoya	passionfruit	sweet potato
	chile	peanut	tomatillo
	chocolate	pecan	tomato
Brazil nut	corn	pineapple	vanilla
cactus pear	guava	potato	wild rice

These Native American plant foods have been incorporated into ethnic cuisines all over the world, and have become staples or cash crops important to the economy and wellbeing of many of the earth's peoples.

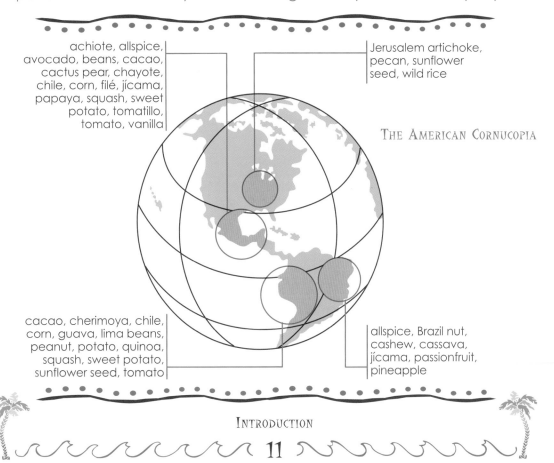

achiote, allspice, avocado, beans, cacao, cactus pear, chayote, chile, corn, filé, jícama, papaya, squash, sweet potato, tomatillo, tomato, vanilla

Jerusalem artichoke, pecan, sunflower seed, wild rice

THE AMERICAN CORNUCOPIA

cacao, cherimoya, chile, corn, guava, lima beans, peanut, potato, quinoa, squash, sweet potato, sunflower seed, tomato

allspice, Brazil nut, cashew, cassava, jícama, passionfruit, pineapple

ACHIOTE

Achiote is made from the small brick-red seeds of the annatto tree. The powder form of the seeds, annatto, is used by the food industry to give a yellow or orange color to butter, margarine, cheddar cheese and smoked fish. Many people are surprised to learn that butter is not yellow—annatto is! Achiote paste, which is prepared from crushed achiote seeds and spices, imparts an earthy, smoky flavor to meat, fish, and poultry when it is rubbed on as a marinade coating before cooking. Besides being an important seasoning used in Mayan cuisine, achiote is used as a body paint even today by tribal peoples. Red symbolizes courage and virility, so achiote paste is often used to paint faces, or as in the case of the Colorado of the Amazon, to sculpt hair styles for the men. Tribal weavers throughout the Americas use achiote to dye wool and other natural fibers a warm saffron-yellow color.

Note

Achiote can be found in Latin grocery stores. Achiote seeds are sold in small cellophane bags; they need to be ground before they can be used as a condiment. Achiote is also available as a paste: ground, mixed with spices and vinegar, and ready to use. Packaged in the shape of a small brick, achiote paste is sometimes called *recado colorado*. The paste is rubbed on chicken, pork, and fish before roasting or grilling and adds a spicy, smoky flavor to the dish. For a substitute, see page 227.

ALLSPICE

Allspice is the one true aromatic spice of the New World. The spice is produced from the small pearl-sized berries of the evergreen pimento tree, a member of the myrtle family that grows wild in the Caribbean and the Amazon. When the Spanish explorers came across the berries, they named the spice *pimento* because the dried berries looked like large peppercorns. Though the Spaniards never found the wealth of spices they were seeking in the West Indies—the true cinnamon, cloves, black pepper, and nutmeg of the East—they did find in "allspice" a combination of the flavors of those prized spices. Today allspice is widely used in Caribbean cooking; in Jamaica, where it is still known as *pimento*, allspice forms the basis of the flavorful jerk seasoning.

AVOCADO

The avocado originated in Mexico and Guatemala and has been grown there for thousands of years. Later, its cultivation spread to South America where it was grown by pre-Inca peoples. In Peru, archaeologists have found avocado seeds and leaves, sometimes buried with mummies, dating back to 750 B.C. The Aztecs called the avocado *ahuacatl*, which means "testicle" (presumably because of the shape of the fruit), and believed—not surprisingly—that it was an aphrodisiac.

In pre-Columbian diets, which contained little meat, avocados provided an excellent dietary source of protein. Today, avocados are referred to as "poor man's butter" in the tropics because their creamy flesh contains 20 times as much fat as other fruits. Because avocados are members of the vegetable kingdom, this "butter" is cholesterol-free. Ranging in size from a few ounces to 4 pounds, avocados are rich in protein, minerals, and vitamins A and B. The leaves can be used to flavor stews, much as bay leaves are.

Note

Also known as alligator pears, perhaps because of the rough texture of the green skin, avocados can be ripened by placing them in a paper bag and then storing them in a warm place. When preparing avocados for a dish such as guacamole, you can keep them from turning brown by sprinkling the exposed flesh with fresh lemon or lime juice. If you have a choice, buy the dark, almost black, rough-skinned Haas avocados (which have a buttery, rich flavor and creamy texture) instead of the shiny, green, smooth-skinned avocados (which have little flavor and a more watery texture).

BEANS

Beans are one of the oldest cultivated foods known to man, and for many peoples of the world today, they remain one of the main staffs of life. Lima beans were being grown in Peru nearly eight thousand years ago, and pre-Maya peoples were growing kidney beans seven thousand years ago in the Yucatán area of Mexico. Most varieties of beans known throughout the world today originated in the Americas or are varieties developed from American stock. The common green bean (also known as the snap or string bean), the lima bean, the wax bean, and all of the familiar dried beans—kidney, pinto, navy, great northern, red, black, and pink—each trace their heritage to the Western Hemisphere. Dried beans are a great source of protein, and they have no cholesterol and comparatively little fat.

Easily grown and stored, beans provided a major component of the ancient American diet. When the Spanish arrived in Mexico, they found that the Aztecs had a rainbow of colored beans available. The remains of beans found preserved in ancient ruins leave clues as to their role in the lives of early peoples. Ancient Americans must have considered them to be a very important food because beans have been found as sacrificial food offerings. For example, the mummy of a young boy, sacrificed to the gods by the Incas, was found high on the slopes of the Andean volcano Aconcagua. Carefully wrapped and dressed, the child had been provided with a pair of sandals and two bags: one was empty, but the other contained cooked beans—a meal for the dead child's journey into the next life.

Note

If you add salt to the cooking liquid before you cook the beans, their skins will be tough—wait until the beans are soft, then add salt to taste.

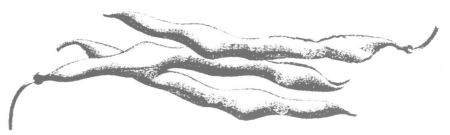

BRAZIL NUT

Brazil nuts are gathered by tribal peoples and peasant collectors from trees that are scattered throughout the rain forest of the Amazon Basin. During the annual harvest, the round pods fall to the ground from the giant Brazil nut trees. These extremely hard capsules are about the size of softballs and contain the seeds of the Brazil nut tree. A falling Brazil nut pod can easily kill a man. These woody pods are so hard, in fact, that they have to be hacked open with a machete before the nuts can be removed. The nuts are dried in wooden shacks before they are sold to middlemen and shipped down river. The income gained from the sale of Brazil nuts provides many forest dwellers with their biggest source of income.

The sale of Brazil nuts brings millions of dollars a year into the international market. Attempts to grow the nuts on plantations have failed—for while the tree grows well and flowers, it produces no nuts. It took scientists a while to figure out the problem. It seems that while no one knows for sure how Brazil nut trees are pollinated, those that produce nuts are visited regularly by euglossine bees. These bees require the pheromones from certain species of epiphytic orchids in order to mate and reproduce. (Pheromones are fragrance chemicals used by animals to communicate with others of the same species.) These particular orchids in turn rely exclusively on the euglossine bees for pollination. So, without the euglossine

orchids, there can be no euglossine bees; and without the euglossine bees, the flowers of the Brazil nut trees remain unpollinated and so, of course, the trees are barren.

Another forest animal, the agouti, has a role in the propagation of Brazil nuts in the wild. After the ripe seed capsule falls to the forest floor, the trees depend on the agouti, a rabbit-sized rodent, to crack open the hard casing so that the seeds can germinate.

Like all biospheres, the rain forest is a complex network of interdependent plants, insects, and animals woven together to support an ecosystem which has evolved over the millennia. If one factor is removed—say the bee or the agouti—the balance of nature will be upset and the overall well-being and regeneration of the rain forest will be affected.

Note

Brazil nuts gathered in the wild have given rise to cooperatives that are owned and operated by forest peoples. This provides the native harvesters with three to ten times the normal income for their labor. Because Brazil nuts have not been successfully domesticated, the income from wild nut harvesting provides an incentive to preserve and protect the rain forest. Hopefully, as demand for Brazil nuts grows, people will realize that it is more profitable to harvest the rain forest's renewable wealth than to cut it down for short-term profits.

CACTUS PEAR

Cactus pears, or prickly pears, are the fruit of the nopal cactus—the one with the paddle-shaped "leaves". About the size of a large egg, the pears are, in fact, big spine-covered berries, as confirmed by the number of seeds inside. Originally native to northwest Mexico and the southwest United States, cactus pears provided prehistoric peoples with fruits in the desert. With the arrival of the Europeans, the nopal cactus was exported and planted abroad. People now enjoy its fruit all over the Mediterranean area, southern Africa, Australia, southwestern Asia, and Central and South America. Cactus pears, in fact, are more popular and appreciated abroad than they are here in their native United States.

Cactus pears have a sweet, soft, grainy pulp that tastes something like watermelon. In Latin America, where many varieties of the fruit are available, cactus pears come in an incredible array of colors. Cut them open and you'll find red, violet, pink, yellow, chartreuse, and ocher flesh. Since the prickly pears are covered with often invisible hair-like stickers (hence the name), be careful when peeling the rind.

Cactus pears are seasonal; they can be found in Mexican markets and some specialty produce stores from fall through spring. The fruit sold in the United States is most commonly a medium green to dark magenta on the outside; the seedy interior flesh varies in color from a yellow gold to a deep magenta red. Choose fruit with a full, deep, even color. It should be tender and yielding, but not mushy. Cactus pears will ripen at room temperature and, when ripe, can be stored in the refrigerator for about a week.

Note

Because of their vivid magenta-colored flesh, cactus pears make wonderful, tropical-looking drinks. Mix the fruit with lemon juice and sugar and then purée; sieve the seeds and chill the liquid. Use this liquid as a base for rum, gin, or vodka. Cactus pear purée can be used to make sorbets, jams, or added to fruit smoothies.

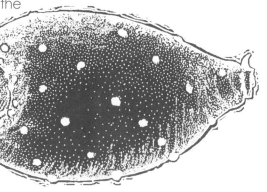

CASHEW

The cashew is an evergreen shrub native to the West Indies and Brazil. It produces a fruit that resembles a pear-shaped apple: the red- or yellow-skinned marañón. Out of the end of this bitter, acidic fruit grows the kidney-shaped cashew nut. It's hard to believe that the shell of this nut is so full of toxin that it has to be removed by a roasting process before the buttery nut within can be eaten.

For many peoples in the Amazon, cashews are a source of income as well as an essential part of their diet. For some, like the Tupí, cashews are actually the principal staple of their diet. Because cashew trees are so highly valued among tribal members, disputes over the trees can sometimes lead to tribal warfare. Some Amazon peoples believe that the regular chewing of cashews prevents tooth decay, and the juice of the fruit is thought to stimulate the brain, improve memory, and relieve fatigue. Cashews are also used to treat dysentery. Some Amazonian tribal people believe that an exclusive diet of cashews will cure illnesses such as leprosy and diabetes.

The Portuguese in Brazil recognized the value of the cashew early on and exported trees to colonies in Goa, Madagascar, Mozambique, and Angola. In Africa and India, the fruits and nuts became an important part of local diets where marañón and cashews are now used in sauces, drinks, and sweets.

Today, there is a worldwide market not only for the delicious nuts of the cashew tree, but also for the by-products, which include oil and a lacquer that offers protection to wood against insects and fungus. Cashew oil, in fact, is used in at least one hundred industrial patents.

CASSAVA

Cassava (*cas-sa'-vah*) is the edible tuber of a plant native to the Brazilian Amazon; it's a relative of the poinsettia. Many North Americans are unfamiliar with cassava, though they are well acquainted with one of its products: tapioca. The long, narrow cassava tubers are covered with thick, rough, dark-brown skin. When the skin is removed, the flesh inside is dense, white, and fibrous. Called *yuca* in Central America and *manioc* in parts of South America, cassava is a staple of many of the ethnic cuisines throughout tropical America and the Caribbean Islands. The sweet, starchy tubers are used in soups and stews just as potatoes would be. They're also made into fritters, chips, flat bread, dumplings, and breads. Cassava can be fried, grilled, and steamed.

In the Amazon, the traditional cyanide-laden wild cassava was used as poison for arrowheads and blowgun darts. After the cyanide was leached out, the cassava was used as a basis for beer. In many traditional cultures today, cassava still remains the popular base for beer. After being grated, boiled, and leached of any poisons, the cassava is chewed by tribal members (enzymes in saliva convert starch to sugar), then put into a large pot with water, where it ferments. Beer from cassava contributes a significant amount of vitamin B to the diets of Amazonian tribal peoples.

During the sixteenth century, Europeans sailing in the Caribbean noted that Native Caribbean peoples made cassava into bread. After leaching the tubers of cyanide, the pulp was sieved and shaped into cakes. These cassava cakes were cooked on griddles. The Portuguese brought the root to Africa where it also became a staple—and no wonder. It's resistant to locusts and drought, and can be left in the ground for up to two years past maturity as a hedge against hunger. The high-calorie tuber today supplies over half the energy requirements of more than 200 million people in Africa. Crop breeders in Nigeria have recently developed an improved variety of "super" cassava which could double the output of the crop and help fight famine in Africa. Because the cassava is an inexpensive staple and because these are difficult economic times, a growing number of middle-class homes in central and western Africa are beginning to switch from the more costly rice and yams to the cassava, which can be eaten whole, grated, or fermented, and used to make various traditional dishes.

CHAYOTE

Also known as a "vegetable pear," the chayote (*cha-yo'-tee*) is the size and shape of a large pear—a furrowed pear that appears to have been gently flattened in a vice. The *chayotli* was cultivated by the ancient Mayans and Aztecs, and was one of their principal foods. Chayotes grow prolifically on vines: one vine can produce more than a hundred chayotes and a myriad of nectar-rich, honey-producing blossoms. Green and squash-like in taste and texture, though not in the squash family, botanists refer to the chayote as a "one-seeded cucumber." Known as *chocho* in Jamaica, *mirlton* in Louisiana, and *christophene* in France, the chayote can be prepared much like zucchini. It can be grated raw into salads, stuffed and baked, sautéed, or stir-fried. The large central seed of a young chayote can also be cooked along with the chayote, then enjoyed separately. It's edible and tasty.

Note

Chayotes are found in large supermarkets and in Latin and Asian markets, especially during wintertime. Choose firm, unblemished, small fruits, as they are the most tender. They can be stored for up to a month, lightly wrapped, in the refrigerator. If you buy the large chayotes, you will need to peel the skin—either before cooking by using a potato peeler, or after cooking by pulling off the skin.

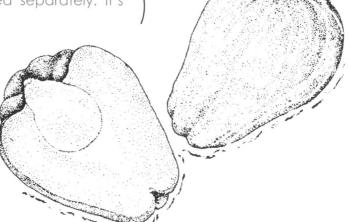

CHILE

The first chiles were tiny berries that grew on vines beneath the canopy of the Amazon rain forest thousands of years ago. One of the first plants cultivated in the New World, chiles, wild and domesticated, have been used by American peoples for at least eight thousand years. Evidence shows that by 5,500 B.C. the Tehuacanos in Mexico were growing their own. Early chile cultivation in Peru dates back to about 2,000 B.C. By the time Columbus traveled to the New World, chiles were being used by the Inca, Olmec, Toltec, Maya, Aztec, and other nations to add spice and flavor to their cooking. Chiles, high in vitamin C, were used in sauces, cooked with meat or fish dishes, used in soups and stews, mixed with salt and tomatoes, or sprinkled on foods as a condiment.

Chiles also played an important medicinal role in the healing arts of the Maya. Chiles were taken internally to treat asthma and stubborn coughs, used externally as a paste to treat aching bones and muscles, and applied as a poultice for sore throats. Interestingly, chiles play a role in modern medicine, too. The principal active ingredient listed in many over-the-counter remedies sold in the United States today—such as liniments for aching muscles and throat disks for sore throats—is *capsaicin*, the chemical in chiles that is responsible for that hot sensation that peppers produce.

Though chiles are now associated with many international ethnic cuisines— Szechwan, Indian, Thai, Korean, Hungarian, to name a few—it was Columbus who introduced this New World spice to the Old World. Anyone familiar with the Columbus saga knows that Ferdinand and Isabella had financed his voyage in hopes of finding a shorter route to the Indies. They were expecting Columbus to bring back gold and spices from the East to fill their kingdom's coffers. Columbus knew that the one spice the royals really wanted was pepper, the black gold of the fifteenth century. On January 2, 1493, Columbus first made a note of chiles in his diary. Since Columbus did not find any black pepper in the New World, he was eager to promote the commercial possibilities of the chile peppers he did find. He wrote of the abundance of chile being grown in the Caribbean and its superiority to black pepper. He envisioned fifty caravels a year sailing for Europe with cargo holds full of chiles and profits.

While Columbus died penniless, his vision of the chile pepper's welcome reception by cooks in the Old World would prove to be accurate. Within fifty years after Columbus introduced chile to the Old World, the use of chiles was widespread. Shops carried a variety of peppers; they were grown in gardens and used both as food and as medicine. The Portuguese introduced them to Asia, where as early as 1542, three varieties were reported growing in Goa on the coast of India. By the seventeenth century, hot peppers were common in the most remote parts of the world. By the eighteenth century, the use of chile in Asian cuisine was so commonplace that it was assumed that chiles were native to Asia.

Ethnobotanists reason that chiles were welcomed by so many different cultures because their flavor spiced up the frequently bland food in limited native diets, masked the off-flavor of foods kept too long without refrigeration, or, as the Chinese found, even added a lift to already highly seasoned food. Chiles were also easy to grow in most warm climates and the seeds saved from one or two chile pods could provide a year's crop for a whole family. And while those eating chiles were unaware of the nutritional benefits, chiles provided vitamins A and C to diets lacking these essential nutrients. Chile eaters probably just felt better than their neighbors did. It is from this kind of observation

and awareness over generations—without knowledge of the scientific basis—that nutritional folk wisdom develops and certain food items become promoted within a culture.

Today, there are at least two hundred varieties of chiles—one hundred of them indigenous to Mexico. They range in heat from the sweet bell pepper to the lethally hot *habanero*; in shape from the skinny *aji* to the plump *manzana*; and in length from the tiny one-quarter-inch *macho* to the nine-inch *chilaca*. Chiles cover the spectrum of colors from green through yellow, orange, red, purple, and brown to almost black.

Note

Chiles are great for diets: they're high in vitamins A and C, and have next to no calories or fat; they increase salivation, improve digestion, and make food taste better. And, according to recent claims by scientists in Japan and Great Britain, eating chiles causes the body to burn up to 25% more calories during the day than it normally would. To top this, researchers are now claiming that *capsaicin* may act as an antibiotic, speed healing in wounds, stop pain when applied as an ointment to wounds, and have anti-cancer effects by preventing the liver from turning some elements into carcinogens.

CHERIMOYA

The cherimoya originated in the Andes; prized by the Pre-Columbian farmers of Ecuador and Peru, it means "fruit of the cold country" in Quechua. Pottery representations of cherimoya have been found in archeological sites dating back to pre-Inca times. From South America, cultivation of the fruit spread north to Central America and the Caribbean. Sometimes called custard apples— because you can eat them with a spoon—cherimoyas have the flavor of a creamy, tropical, strawberry-banana mousse. The fruit contains a full cargo of inedible seeds: shiny, hard, black stones that feel nice to the tongue—like polished river rocks. The cherimoya has been described as looking like a "Stone Age artichoke" because its leathery green skin is covered with scale-like impressions.

Because the female blossom of the cherimoya is so narrow, the wind cannot pollinate the plant—nor can the usual pollinating agents such as bees, butterflies, and hummingbirds. Only a very tiny, night-flying insect exclusive to South America can pollinate this blossom. Cherimoya trees now being cultivated in lands where this insect does not exist must be pollinated by hand. This entails collecting the pollen from a male blossom with very fine-tipped watercolor brushes and then introducing the pollen to the female blossoms. To complicate matters, the female blossoms are only receptive during a twenty-four-hour period, and not all blossoms on the same tree are ready on the same day.

Note

Available winter through spring, cherimoyas weigh between one-half and two pounds. Look for a fruit that is firm and green and devoid of any dark or splotchy marks. Cherimoyas bruise easily in spite of their leathery skins, so be careful. The fruit will ripen at room temperature; when ripe, its skin will turn a darker green and yield to slight pressure. Don't let the cherimoya get overly ripe; refrigerate it when it's ready, or it will be mushy. Cherimoyas are best served halved and eaten with a spoon (discard the seeds as you go). The fruit can also be seeded and puréed and made into sauces for desserts, tropical drinks, and smoothies.

CHOCOLATE

Cocoa beans are native to South America; they were brought into Mexico by the Maya before A.D. 600. The beans grow in seedpods on wide-branched evergreen trees; each pod contains up to forty beans. The pre-Aztecs considered cocoa of divine origin and an important part of the diet of their god, Quetzalcoatl. The Aztecs, Toltecs, Totonacs, as well as the Maya, toasted the cocoa beans and then ground them into a paste on a grinding stone. The cocoa paste was then blended with allspice, cinnamon, or vanilla; sometimes it was spiced with chiles or colored with achiote to give it a reddish tint. The cocoa mixture was then added to hot water, beaten, and served hot and frothy. The word chocolate comes from the Aztec *xocolatl*, which means "bitter water." To the Aztecs, cocoa was considered a special drink, an expensive luxury reserved only for nobles. Their emperor Montezuma, who believed that chocolate was an aphrodisiac, regularly drank his foaming *xocolatl* from cups of pure gold.

Cocoa beans themselves were used as currency in the Aztec Empire. The cocoa beans were bagged in standard quantities, and the price of goods was quoted in the number of beans required to make the purchase. In fact, until 1887, cocoa beans remained an accepted means of paying one's taxes in Mexico.

A craze for chocolate hit Europe when the drink was introduced on the continent in the sixteenth century; there, it was drunk hot with milk and sugar. Later, a whole new school of confectionery art and expertise developed around chocolate making, and chocolate became one of the Western world's sweetest addictions.

CORN

Corn made the ancient American civilizations of the Inca, Maya, and Aztec—and those of North America—possible. Corn was the basis of life and civilization for these cultures; it played a profound role in their art, architecture, religion, and family relationships. Corn was sacred. It became the metaphor for all the basic processes of life; it was central to ceremonies, the cycles of life and death, fertility, growth, and renewal. Each culture had corn gods, and the arrival of corn into each culture was celebrated with myths and legends of gods, goddesses, or sacred animals bringing it to man. For many native Americans today, corn still remains the most sacred food.

Sometime around 2500 B.C., the ancient peoples of America domesticated corn from wild grasses by deliberate cultivation of the seeds. These early agriculturists not only domesticated corn but actually created the plant as we know it today. Ancient remnants of corn have been found in archeological sites in both Central and South America dating back to between 3000 and 4000 B.C. Originally a giant grass, cultivated forms of corn spread from tribe to tribe through South, Central, and North America. Since corn must be hand planted, its cultivation meant the end of nomadic life and the beginning of stable societies which, in turn, produced several major civilizations. Through breeding, corn has, in fact, become the only food plant that requires human help to reproduce. The impenetrable husk must be removed, or the sprouting kernels, crowded together on the cob, will choke to death.

Corn contains incomplete protein and lacks certain vitamins, but Native Americans combined it with beans and occasionally fish, which rounded out their protein requirements, and they processed it with lime or wood ash, which released the niacin stored in the kernel. Chiles and tomatoes added other missing vitamins to the early American diets. Early Mexicans (and many traditional Mexicans today) began their day with a hot bowl of *atole*, or corn mush, sweetened with honey or spiced with chile. The main meal of the day, eaten in the early afternoon, consisted of corn tortillas, beans, and a sauce of tomatoes or peppers. Occasionally the dishes might contain grubs, insect eggs, or pond algae. *Tamales* combined corn meal dough with beans, chiles, green tomato shavings, and shreds of meat or fish, all wrapped in a dried corn husk and steamed.

In South America, the Incas grew corn, which they stored in granaries, and they collected tribute in corn from conquered peoples. They used corn to brew *chicha,* a cloudy beer used to induce ritual intoxication. Today traditional farmers in the Andes still offer *chicha,* the symbolic daughter of the sun, to Mother Earth and the gods of the elements. Pouring the drink into freshly turned soil, the farmers pray for a bountiful harvest of corn. Apart from ritual use, *chicha* still remains the principal beverage consumed in the Andean highlands today.

During Columbus's first voyage to the New World, corn fields stretching up to 18 miles were recorded in Cuba. Native Americans were observed smoking tobacco wrapped in corn husks. After having tasted corn, Columbus declared it "most tasty boiled, roasted, or ground into flour." He brought corn seeds back to Europe with him in 1493, and within a few years of his voyage, the Spanish had introduced corn around the Mediterranean. By the mid-sixteenth century, corn had become familiar enough to Europeans to become the basis of such national dishes as the Italian *polenta* and the Romanian *mamaliga.* Corn was also adopted by the Philippine Islanders and some Asian peoples. In Africa, it was found that corn grew more rapidly than other grains and needed very little cultivation. Because corn weathered drought and the harsh African sun

better than other staple foods, it was often the only food consumed by some poor families.

While there are many varieties of corn, the most common are popcorn, dent corn (which is used to feed animals), sweet corn (for roasting on the ear and eating), and flint corn. Flint corn is the type of corn seen in Mexican and Central American marketplaces sold in bulk. Flint corn dries easily and, when soaked with lime or wood ash and water, it can be ground into *masa,* the flour used to make tortillas and tamales. Large-kerneled flint corn is called hominy in the United States—this is the corn Southerners use to make grits.

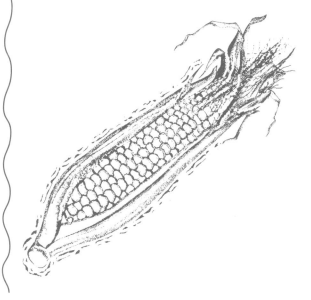

FILÉ

The Choctaws originally gathered the young leaves of the sassafras trees growing wild in the bayous along the Gulf of Mexico. They dried the leaves and ground them into a powder to make a seasoning for their cooking. After the arrival of the European settlers, they sold this seasoning, called filé, in the marketplaces in New Orleans. Filé became an important ingredient in Louisiana cooking and was used as a flavoring and thickener for Creole soups such as gumbo. Filé powder, which has the earthy taste of sassafras, a combination of thyme and savory, is available in supermarkets and gourmet specialty stores. It is often labeled "gumbo filé."

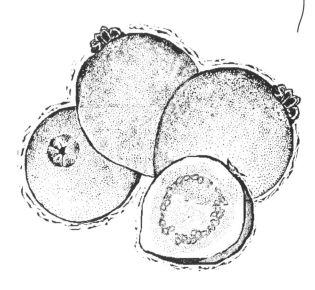

GUAVA

Native to South America, guavas have been domesticated for thousands of years—archaeologists have reported evidence of preserved guavas dating back to 2500 B.C. in coastal Peru.

Guavas are members of the myrtle family of aromatics, which includes eucalyptus, clove, and allspice. There are many varieties of guavas. About two inches in diameter, guavas are actually juicy berries—round or pear shaped—that grow on thirty-foot trees. Their seedy, reddish-pink flesh has a rather gritty texture, which is probably why the Aztec called the guava *xalxocotl*, or "sand plum." Available during summer months, guavas will ripen at room temperature, and as they ripen they will begin to exude a rich tropical fragrance. While varieties of guavas vary in flavor, some tart, some sweet, all of them are intensely aromatic and high in vitamins A and C. When they're ready to eat, they will yield to light fingertip pressure. They can be peeled and eaten (the seeds are said to be good for digestion), or used in fruit salads, or for making sauces, preserves, or pie fillings.

Guavas are prized in Central and South America for making a sweet, dark red paste called *guayabate*—a popular dessert which is eaten like candy or served with a slice of cheese—and for making fragrant, refreshing fruit drinks.

JERK

Jerk is a popular method of barbecuing well-seasoned pork, chicken, or fish. It has given rise to a thriving roadside industry in Jamaica where the jerked meat is cooked over coals in mobile steel-drum furnaces. Originally developed by the Arawaks in the Caribbean, the seasoning and smoking of meats was later perfected by runaway Jamaican slaves and their descendants, called Maroons. Fiercely independent, the Maroons persisted for more than two hundred years in the harsh, remote mountain areas in the center of the island, repelling all efforts to dislodge them. Having learned the art of preserving meat in the wild from the remaining Arawaks on Jamaica, the Maroons then improved on this Native American technique. The result was jerk—a highly spiced and aromatic seasoning combination that included a goodly amount of salt. Jerk was slathered on meats that were then cooked very slowly over a green-wood fire or in a stone-lined pit. Today, jerk is a signature flavor in Jamaican cooking, and it is used to give a highly flavorful "zing" to chicken as well as meats.

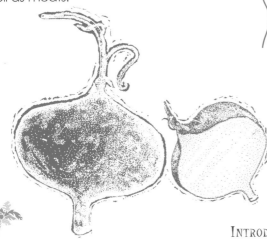

JÍCAMA

A jícama (hee'-kah-mah) resembles a fat turnip with sandy brown skin. This tropical American root vegetable has a crisp, white flesh; its taste and texture are much like a cross between an apple and a water chestnut. Jícamas are native both to Mexico and the headwaters of the Amazon River. The Spanish introduced the jícama to the Philippines in the seventeenth century, and from there its cultivation spread throughout Asia and the Pacific. The tuber became a particular favorite of Chinese gardeners. Today, jícamas are a popular snack food in Mexico; sold by street vendors, crunchy slices of jícama are eaten with a sprinkle of chile powder and a squeeze of lime juice.

Note

Jícamas are becoming more common in supermarkets; they are also available in Latin and Asian markets. The smooth, thin-skinned tubers with juicy—not woody—flesh underneath are the freshest. (To check for freshness, make a tiny scrape in the skin with your fingernail.) Jícamas, uncut and unwrapped, will keep for weeks in the refrigerator. Used in salsas, salads, and stir-fries, low-fat jícamas stay crunchy even when cooked—so they add few calories to a dish but a lot of bite.

PAPAYA

The papaya is native to the tropical lowlands of Central America. The tree itself is a tall, smooth, unbranched trunk with a parasol of leaves stemming out of the top. Amazingly, this tree can grow from a seed to a twenty-foot fruit-bearing tree in little over a year. Often called tree melons, the soft, fragrant, melonlike fruits of the papaya, which can reach twenty pounds each, grow directly out of the leafless trunk of the tree. The latex of the green fruit contains *papain*, a protein digestive enzyme that is used as a meat tenderizer. The pungent seeds of the papaya are edible and said to be a digestive aid; they make a great garnish or addition to salad dressing. Rich in vitamins A and C, the rosy, pumpkin-yellow flesh of the ripe papaya is sweet and fragrant with an earthy aftertaste.

Note

In the United States, papayas are usually harvested when they are green; they will ripen, but never have the wonderful full flavor of the tropical tree-ripened varieties. Most of the papayas available in the supermarkets come from Hawaii. These small, yellow, pear-shaped papayas weigh about one pound. Papayas ripen from the blossom end; as the fruit ripens, the skin turns to a mixture of green, yellow, and orange. A ripe Hawaiian papaya will be bright yellow. When ripe, the papaya gives off a fruity aroma and will yield to light pressure.

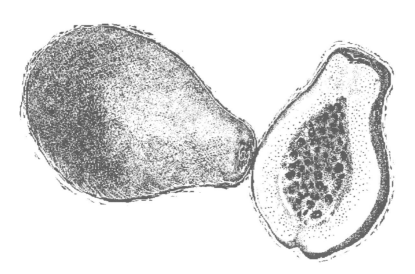

PASSIONFRUIT

Native to Brazil, the passionfruit vine was so named by early Spanish explorers because its large, red flower seemed to contain various symbols of Christ's crucifixion, or Passion. To these men, the five petals and five sepals represented the ten apostles present at the crucifixion; the corona of fine filaments resembled the crown of thorns; the five stamens represented the five wounds in Christ's body; and the three stigmas stood for the nails used in the crucifixion. The explorers interpreted the flower as symbolic of Christ's approval of their missionary work in the New World.

A passionfruit is an oval berry, about the size of a large hen's egg; the variety known as purple passionfruit comes with leathery, purple-brown skin. On the inside, the flesh is slippery and jelly-like, and is contained in transparent little sacks attached around a multitude of dark seeds. This juicy golden flesh is sweet and tangy at the same time, with a rich, floral fragrance. The juice of the passionfruit, popular in tropical America, is just beginning to be introduced to the market in the United States as an ingredient in commercial fruit juice blends. Ornamental varieties of this fragrant vine can be seen growing in warmer areas of the United States such as Florida and California.

Note

The rind of a ripe passionfruit has the dimpled surface texture of a golf ball; it's dark, wrinkled, and dented. Passionfruits ripen at room temperature. If the fruit is firm and smooth, the passionfruit is not yet ripe; when the rind yields to slight fingertip pressure and the liquid can be heard moving inside, then it's ready to be eaten. Refrigerate ripe passionfruits for up to a week (or freeze them in plastic bags). Passionfruits can be eaten as they are—seeds and all—or you can sieve the seeds and use the fragrant pulp as flavoring for sorbets, mousses, ice creams, tropical drinks, fruit sauces, or meat marinades.

PEANUT

Peanuts were domesticated in their native South America. They have been found sealed in vases in ancient Peruvian tombs dating back to 1500 B.C. Later, the Incas used peanuts in religious ceremonies and in burial rites. Pots of peanuts were buried with their mummified dead—sometimes cradled in their arms—to nourish their spirits on their way to the afterlife.

The Spanish introduced the peanut to the Malay Archipelago after first encountering them in Haiti and Peru. In the early 1600s, traders carried peanuts from the Malay Archipelago to mainland Asia, where peanuts soon became a component part of several ethnic cuisines. Portuguese sailors coming from Brazil introduced peanuts to Africa. When Africans were brought to the New World as slaves, they brought peanuts with them and "reintroduced" them to this hemisphere. And though Native Americans had cultivated peanuts in Virginia before the arrival of the European colonists, it was the Africans who were mainly responsible for the widespread cultivation of peanuts in North America, calling them by their Bantu name *nguba* (ground nut) which the colonists rendered as "goober".

Peanuts are not really nuts, but a member of the legume (pea) family. They grow underground and are actually seeds encased in a nut-like shell. After the plant's flowers have been fertilized, the flower stalk elongates and forces the growing seedpod underground, where it grows to maturity (hence the name ground nut). Peanuts are high in niacin, zinc, protein, fat, and fiber, but, like all members of the vegetable kingdom, they contain no cholesterol.

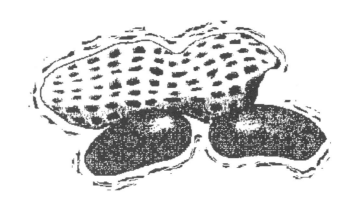

PECAN

The pecan, meaning "bone shell," gets its name from the combination of several Native American languages: the Algonquin *paccan*, the Cree *pakan*, and the Abinaki *pagan*. A species of hickory tree native to Oklahoma and the Mississippi River Valley, the pecan was prized by indigenous American peoples; it may have been the only pre-Columbian tree cultivated in North America. During his trek to the west of Mexico in 1528, explorer Cabeza de Vaca noted that tribes along the Gulf of Mexico gathered together along river bottoms to eat the nuts. They also extracted a milky fluid from pecans and hickories that they used in making corn cakes.

Many tribes used pecans extensively, either mixed with beans, cooked with fruits, pressed into oils, ground into a meal to thicken stews, or roasted to take on treks. Pecans have the highest fat content of all nuts, 70 per cent, and they also have a high caloric content.

Pecan pralines are traditionally associated with old New Orleans. Originally, pralines were a French creation made with almonds. They were Americanized in Louisiana by substituting the New World pecans for the Old World nuts. In the evenings, Creole women would walk along the streets of New Orleans selling these sweet pralines from straw baskets.

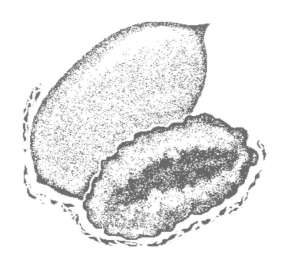

POTATO

By 3000 B.C., potatoes were being grown by primitive farmers in the Andes of Peru. Over the centuries, several hundred varieties of potatoes—including an array of colors, sizes, and shapes—were eventually developed by Native American farmers. Potatoes became an especially important crop to people living at altitudes above 11,000 feet, where corn would not grow. Even today, the potato plays a vital role in the daily lives of Andean peoples; its importance is reflected in the fact that there are about 200 words in the Amayra language to distinguish between the sizes, colors, and textures of this sustaining tuber.

Since ancient times, Andean farmers have made *chuño*, a freeze-dried form of potatoes that will keep for months—or indefinitely if ground into meal. *Chuño* is made in June when, at elevations above twelve thousand feet, the days are warm and sunny but the night temperatures drop below freezing. Small potatoes are spread on the ground to freeze overnight, then they are thawed in the morning sun. After thawing, the potatoes are gathered into little piles, and men and women tread on them with bare feet, squeezing out the moisture that has been released from the potato cells by the freezing process. The potatoes are then spread out to dry in the hot sun and eventually stored. When needed, the freeze-dried potatoes are reconstituted by adding them to soups or stews.

Potatoes, carried in the hulls of ships returning from the New World, were introduced to Europe through various port cities in the sixteenth century. There they were met by varying degrees of acceptance. At first, the tubers were considered poisonous; since potatoes were a member of the nightshade family, most people wouldn't eat them. Then, for a time, the European elite thought that potatoes were a cure for impotence; scarcity and this increase in perceived value subsequently caused the price of potatoes to rise sharply. In Burgundy, potatoes were banned in 1619 because it was thought that eating too many of them would cause leprosy. While Spain, the Lowland countries, and Switzerland were all growing potatoes by the mid-sixteenth century, two hundred years later there was still resistance to the tuber in other parts of Europe. In 1774, starving peasants in Kolberg refused to eat the potatoes sent to the city by Frederick the Great to help relieve famine, and in 1795, the poor of Munich refused to eat the potatoes added to the soup in the city's soup kitchen.

War and political upheaval as well as the military requisitioning of grain crops caused peasants to take a second look at potatoes. No other food crop could produce as many calories per acre; and when left in the ground, the vegetable couldn't be taken by soldiers or trampled or burned during times of war. Peasants learned how to cultivate the tuber and how to cook it. With time, the potato became recognized and accepted throughout Europe as a good subsistence crop. By growing and eating potatoes, peasants could sustain themselves and their families on only a small plot of land. In the eighteenth century, potatoes planted in England and Ireland became the staple of poor farmers. Ireland became particularly dependent on the potato; the peasant diet there often consisted of potatoes and little else. Catherine the Great promoted the potato in Russia as an antidote to famine and succeeded so well that the national drink became vodka. By 1806, recipes for potatoes appeared for the first time in a French cookbook.

Because so many peasant populations depended on potato crops for subsistence, when the potato blight hit Europe in 1845, it was a human disaster. The blight completely destroyed crops and seed plants for the coming year. There was no way for a family to sustain itself or its livestock. Ireland was especially hard hit; those who could not pay rent to their landlords were evicted; disease racked the population and over 1,000,000 people died. Spurred by the famine, another 1,000,000 managed to migrate to the United States, adding a significant new component to the social and economic makeup of the developing nation.

Potatoes are a great nutritional bargain. They are high in potassium, and they are a good source of complex carbohydrates. They also contain goodly amounts of vitamins C and B_6 and assorted minerals—and they are low in calories. (Unless you slather on the butter, there's only 120 calories in an average 6-ounce potato).

Note

Potatoes that are exposed to light for long periods of time will develop a greenish tinge on their skins that extends into the flesh; this is caused by the toxin *solanin*. *Solanin* can cause digestive disturbances if eaten. Always store potatoes in a cool, dark place where light cannot reach them. If you notice a green tinge on the skin, cut or scrape that part off of the potato before using it.

PINEAPPLE

A member of the bromeliad family, pineapples have been cultivated for at least eight hundred years in South America. Symbolic representations of its form were found in pre-Inca ruins. When the Tupí-Guaraní people spread outward from the Paraná-Paraguay Basin, they brought the pineapple with them for food, medicine, and drink (pineapple is fermentable). Through trade, they introduced the fruit to other tribes.

When Columbus landed at Guadeloupe in the Lesser Antilles, he found the local inhabitants cultivating pineapples. The Caribs called the plant *anana*, which meant "fragrance" or "fragrant fruit" in Tupí-Guaraní. The Spaniards thought that the fruit, growing out of a rosette of leathery, spiked leaves, looked like a large pine cone—so they called it a *piña de los Indias* (Indian pine cone), or *piña*. (The English later added the word "apple," a generic term for fruit, and the result was "pineapple.") The Caribs used pineapples as symbols of hospitality, fastening them over doorways as a welcoming sign for visitors. The Europeans adopted this symbolic use of the fruit and it became a feature on shields and crests, doorknockers and bedposts, gates and corners of buildings. The pineapple was also adopted as a sign of friendship in colonial North America. As a food item, the fruit was used fresh; as a garnish; or to soften tough, smoked meat.

When introduced to the European continent, pineapples set off a mini-rage among the upper classes. Royalty were taken by the fruit; gardeners in the France of Louis XIV spent fortunes developing strains that would flourish in the Old World (unfortunately, the climate proved uncooperative). In England, hothouse gardeners who were successful in growing the fruit would rent it out for display on special occasions. Because of its popularity with royalty and because of its regal appearance, with its crown of leaves on a large golden head, the pineapple became known as the "king of fruits."

Picking Out a Pineapple

Because pineapples contain no starch, they must be picked ripe, since they will not sweeten once they are off the plant. Choose a pineapple with deep green leaves in a solid crown and yellow "eyes" along the bottom rows at the base of the plant (the pineapple ripens from the base up). Tug on the leaves—if a leaf comes out, it is a sign that the pineapple is ripe. Avoid overripe pineapples with soft dark areas on their skins. When you get the fruit home, twist the crown of leaves as you would a jar lid—it will come off. Invert the pineapple and wait a day for the sweetest juices to disperse throughout the fruit. Then chill and eat.

QUINOA

Quinoa *(keen'-wa)* is a high-protein grain that has been cultivated high in the Andes for centuries. Ancient farmers found that quinoa could be grown above the tree line where more temperate crops such as corn could not grow. Quinoa, in fact, grows in altitudes over two miles high, right up to the snow line. This nutritious grain was a staple of the ancient Inca, who called it the "Mother Grain;" it provided fuel for their powerful, conquering armies. Quinoa remains an important element in South American cooking. Andean people today use quinoa in making flour and for thickening stews and soups. The tiny golden seeds of this grain—they look like sesame seeds—cook up shiny and translucent, and offer complete protein: they contain all eight essential amino acids. Many people today consider quinoa the super grain of the future because of its highly nutritional content.

Note

Pineapples contain *bromelain*, an enzyme that breaks down protein. This means that meats marinated in fresh pineapple will become more tender—but gelatin dishes will not set. Avoid mixing fresh pineapple with dairy products until the last minute.

SQUASH

Squashes are fruits of various members of the gourd family; they come in a variety of colors, shapes, and sizes. Early Americans domesticated summer squash between five and seven thousand years ago, and many of the varieties we are familiar with today have been cultivated here in the Americas since that time. Rich in folic acid, potassium, and vitamin C, squash was an important ingredient in the diet of Native Americans.

Originally, the earliest squashes contained inedible flesh; they were grown for their large seeds, which contained highly nutritious oils and could be stored in baskets for an extended period of time. The squash seeds could be eaten or ground and used as thickeners in cooking, a technique that is still utilized today in Mexican cuisine. (For example, ground pumpkinseeds form the basis of those popular Mexican sauces called *moles*.) Eventually, the Native American plant breeders developed squashes with edible flesh. These squash, such as zucchini, yellow crookneck, and pumpkins, became major food sources for early Americans. And, as an important plus, the winter squash varieties—acorn, buttercup, pumpkin, butternut, and hubbard—protected by their hard skins, could be stored for several months, providing the people with a hedge against hunger.

Relatives of the squash, gourds also proved very serviceable to early Americans. For thousands of years dried gourds served as handy and useful containers for water; they also provided a vehicle for artistic expression. Even today, gourd carving is an art. In rural areas, dried gourds are intricately carved with animal and village motifs or made into ceremonial masks.

Today, the calabasa, a bright orange squash, is part of the daily fare of many in Central and South America, and in the Caribbean. This huge squash is sold by the piece in open-air market places and used in soups and stews.

SUNFLOWER

The Incas of Peru used to worship the sunflower, believing that it symbolized the sun. When the Spanish invaded Peru, they took home with them gold medallions shaped like sunflowers—and they also took home sunflower seeds. Soon Europeans fell in love with the bright yellow flower, and by the eighteenth century, it had become the centerpiece of many gardens.

The sunflower, a ring of bright yellow petals resembling the sun's corona encircling a dark center of seeds, can reach twelve inches in diameter. Growing on stems up to fifteen feet high, these blooms, almost mystically, always turn their faces towards the sun and slowly follow its path as it traces its arc across the sky.

Sunflowers were perhaps the first crop cultivated by dwellers of the North American plains, and archeologists have found seed caches in Tennessee dating back almost five thousand years. The flowers proved to be very nutritious: sunflower seeds are very rich in iron and are 24 per cent protein by weight; sunflower-seed oil is high in polyunsaturated fat and low in saturated fat. Besides being a nutritious food source, sunflowers were also used by Native American tribes to treat rattlesnake bites, relieve chest pains, and heal cuts. The Hopi made a purple dye from the seeds.

In 1605, French explorer Champlain found Native Americans on the East Coast of North America cultivating the tubers of one species of sunflowers. The natives called them "sunroots." These tubers, now called "Jerusalem artichokes" or "sun chokes," made a hit in seventeenth-century Europe when they were introduced. Fresh and crisp like water chestnuts, with a nutty potato-like flavor, Jerusalem artichokes are a versatile, iron-rich vegetable. They can be eaten raw in snacks or in salads, or they can be baked, steamed, boiled, sautéed, or stir-fried.

SWEET POTATO

The sweet potato originated in Central America, then was carried to South America, where it was cultivated as early as 1,000 B.C. A member of the morning glory family, the sweet potato plant produces long, edible tubers which are extremely rich in vitamin A and contain a fair amount of protein and vitamin C. Commonly mistaken for the sweeter yams, sweet potatoes are fluffier and more delicately flavored. There are many varieties of sweet potatoes, but two are widely grown commercially. One is pale with a thin, light-yellow skin and pale-yellow flesh; it cooks up dry and crumbly, much like a baking potato, and is not considered "sweet." The other sweet potato is a darker-skinned variety with dark-orange skin and vivid orange, sweet flesh. Many people confuse this latter dark-skinned variety with yams.

Columbus first came across sweet potatoes on his first voyage to the New World. Columbus, too, thought sweet potatoes were yams because he called them *niames*, from the West African name for yams. In a letter from a later voyage, Columbus described how sweet potatoes tasted like parsnips when

eaten raw in salads, and how they tasted like squash when cooked with pork, and he raved about how delicious sweet potatoes were when soaked in the milk of almonds. Today, sweet potatoes are eaten throughout Central and South America and the Caribbean in the form of breads, soups, candy, puffs, rolls, pies, potato chips, and tarts. On the world scene, sweet potatoes are grown in more developing countries than any other root crop.

Its high concentration of carbohydrates and vitamin A and its relatively low water content make the sweet potato an excellent food source. It grows well under a wide range of farming conditions including drought, pest infestation, and poor or waterlogged soils. The nutritious sweet potato is inexpensive to produce and easy to cultivate; it has a short growing season and gives generally high yields.

Dr. Dean Edell reports that the Center for Science in the Public Interest set out to identify the most nutritious vegetable. Each vegetable received a score based on its percentage of U.S. Recommended Daily Dietary Allowances (RDAs) for six nutrients plus its fiber content. The winner, with 582 points, was the sweet potato. The sweet potato contains a high content of beta carotene, which is the precursor of vitamin A (essential for maintaining night vision and resistance to infection.) The sweet potato is also high in vitamin C, which builds connective tissue fiber; folate, which allows normal growth and maintenance of the body's cells; calcium, which maintains healthy bones and teeth; iron, which prevents anemia and strengthens the immune system; and copper, which keeps the cardiovascular system running. After sweet potatoes, raw carrots scored next, then collard greens, red peppers, kale, dandelion greens, spinach, and broccoli.

TOMATILLO

Tomatillos look just like little green tomatoes wearing paper wrappers. These little fruits, relatives of tomatoes, have been cultivated since the time of the Aztecs. They have a tart and tangy flavor and are usually used in salsas, sauces, and stews. Unlike red tomatoes, tomatillos are usually never eaten raw. While they can ripen to yellow, tomatillos are generally used while they are green and firm—and always "unwrapped."

TOMATO

Tomatoes were being grown in the river valleys of coastal Peru from the dawn of human settlement. It is thought that tomatoes were originally weeds in cornfields before they were brought under cultivation. The wild tomatoes grew no larger than berries—and they were green—but with careful cultivation, the yields were increased and new varieties developed. Tomato cultivation spread up through Central America into Mexico, and thrived in pre-Maya gardens, where they were thought to have been a staple thousands of years ago. Over the years, farmers bred for factors including color, developing varieties such as the highly prized yellow tomato. Tomatoes were used to season dishes and to make sauces; they provided a valuable addition of vitamins A and C to an essentially corn-based diet. By the sixteenth century, pre-Columbian farmers had developed large red tomatoes and yellow tomatoes, both of which were available in the Aztec marketplaces.

Tomatoes were introduced to Europe in 1523, but they were only eaten in Italy for the following two hundred years. In England, tomatoes were grown purely as ornamentals during that time. The French thought tomatoes were aphrodisiacs; other Europeans thought them poisonous and refused to eat them at all. Sixteenth century cooks in Florence, however, served fried green tomatoes and green tomato *frittatas*. Ripe tomatoes were avoided at first because of their reputed passion-provoking properties; the soft, yielding skin of the ripe red tomato, along with the fruit's sensual red color and its succulent round form, surely meant that the tomato was too sinful for any moral-minded person to eat. The first recipe for ripe red tomatoes reportedly appeared in the nineteenth century—this was a recipe for tomato sauce published in an Italian cookbook.

Today, of course, the tomato is the basis of many sauces and condiments and it is perhaps the most popular produce item in the Western world.

VANILLA

Vanilla, called the "queen of flavorings," is a native of Mexico. A member of the orchid family, vanilla is an epiphyte, a plant that obtains its food and water from the air while it grows anchored to another plant. The vanilla plant produces beautiful, luminous, lime-yellow orchid blossoms that only last a day. These blossoms give way to a cluster of long, green pods: the prized vanilla. Of the over 20,000 varieties of orchids in the world, the vanilla orchid is the only one that produces an edible fruit.

The Aztecs called vanilla *tlilxochitl*—"the black flower"—and used it to flavor their cocoa-based drinks. They, and earlier peoples who lived on the Gulf of Mexico, cultivated and cured vanilla—an incredibly complex feat even by today's standards.

In nature, the vanilla flower can only be pollinated by one species of bee and one species of hummingbird. Without these pollinators, no fruit develops on the plant. Today, plants are cultivated and pollinated by hand using a wooden needle. (This process is complicated by the fact that vanilla orchids bloom only once a year—and then only for a few hours.) After pollination, it takes nine to ten months for the bean to mature. The mature beans, however, do not have the flavor or fragrance associated with vanilla. The green beans must first be cured—another lengthy process. The beans are boiled for twenty seconds to stop them from ripening. Then, for the next three to six months, they are alternately heated in the sun during the day and wrapped in blankets to "sweat" during the night—a process that causes the vanilla beans to ferment. The beans shrink down, turn dark brown, and finally develop that wonderful aromatic vanilla flavor gourmets so highly prize.

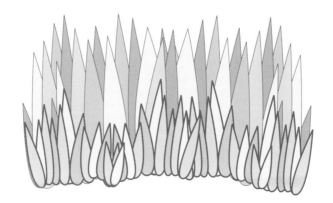

WILD RICE

Wild rice is known for its full-bodied nutty flavor, its chewy texture, and its hefty price tag. Highly prized by gourmets, especially in Europe, wild rice is really not a rice, but rather a long-grain marsh grass native to the Great Lakes area. When the grain is ready in late summer, members of the Sioux and Chippewa nations harvest the wild rice in the traditional way in two-man canoes.

Only Native Americans may harvest the wild rice grown on their reservations. Usually a husband and wife team will paddle out onto the lakes and streams to harvest the rice together. The husband, standing in the back of the canoe, will pole through the tall grass while his wife, sitting in front, bends the heads of the grass over the sides of the canoe using a wooden flail. As she pulls the grass into the canoe, the woman taps the heads lightly with a second flail, releasing the rice seeds into the canoe. After returning to shore, the wild rice is first dried in huge kettles over open fires, then it is thrashed and winnowed to remove the hulls and chaff. The harvest is then stored in birch-bark baskets.

Until recently, wild rice was a scarce commodity in the world marketplace, but a new variety, developed in 1968, has made it possible to grow wild rice on a larger commercial scale and to harvest, dry, and clean it more economically using machinery. This nutritious grain, high in protein, fiber, B vitamins, and minerals, is still only grown in North America, with 80% of the total crop of wild rice coming from Minnesota.

Note

Wild rice is available in supermarkets and gourmet specialty stores. Because it's relatively scarce, it's expensive. But wild rice goes further than regular rice: one cup raw will yield about three and one-half cups cooked. It should be washed well before cooking. The earthy flavor of wild rice combines well with mushrooms, onions, and chopped nuts. Serve wild rice with chicken or fish dishes, or—as the Chippewa do—with wild game.

TOUCANS

Dwelling in the rain forest canopy, toucans are boldly colored birds with patterns of red, yellow, black, orange, green, blue, or white plumage. Their most distinctive feature, however, is their large beak. Toucan bills are huge—often exceeding the length of the bird's body—and are colored bright yellow, orange, or red. Besides being important for courtship display and mate recognition, toucans use their outsized beaks to reach fruit that is far out on fragile twigs. Toucans also use their beaks to intimidate other birds who try to rob their nests, but the beaks are actually very light for their size and are of little use in defense against the toucan's chief enemies: weasels and hawks.

To eat, the toucan will hold a piece of fruit in the very tip of its beak, then deftly snap its head back, open its beak, and toss the morsel down its throat. After feeding on large fruits, the birds fly off, carrying the seeds away from the shadow of the parent trees. After digesting the fruit, the birds often drop the seeds in places where there is enough sunlight for them to germinate and grow; thus the toucan plays a major role in seed dispersal in the rain forest.

Gregarious and noisy, toucans move about in groups of twelve to fifty birds. In early morning and late afternoon their call—a sound resembling a squeaky wheel—can be heard throughout the forest. The birds nest in natural tree holes, which they expand by removing rotten wood. They usually have two to four eggs, and both the male and female toucan share incubating duties. The baby toucans emerge from their eggs with no feathers and develop very slowly. The babies are fed by both parents. After the young toucans learn to fly, they return to roost with their parents—often staying for months before they go off on their own. Toucans are weak fliers; they glide short distances between trees. Unlike other birds, they move their tails up and down during flight. At night when they roost, their tails stand directly up, and the birds sleep with their huge beaks resting on their backs, covered by their raised tails.

While toucans are often hunted for sport or to collect their colorful beaks, they also have a spiritual significance for tribal peoples. To the Yanomamo, the giant toucan was the very first *hekura*—a beautiful, ageless spirit that can be attracted by the beauty of the paint, feathers, fragrance, and melodious songs used in tribal ceremonies.

RAMPHASTOS SULFURATUS

Chapter 2

Cooking Basics

FUNDAMENTALS

Before discussing cooking methods and getting into specific recipes, we need to review the basic elements of really good, creative cooking: stocks and sauces. Often people complain, "I got this recipe from the chef himself, and I followed it exactly, but it doesn't taste the same!" The reason probably lies in one of the key ingredients: the stock. Stock from a can or, worse, from a bouillon cube, does not give the same results as stock produced from boiling bones in your own kitchen. Canned stock will be watery and give only a slight meat or fish flavor to your dish; the bouillon cube will add only a salty flavor—but a thick, homemade stock will give a rich, wonderful aroma and taste to your dishes that will elevate them way above ordinary. Now, it's true that you can use canned stock or bouillon cubes for "stock" in recipes, but your dishes will never taste like the ones you are trying to recreate. Here's a hint: a good restaurant always has a stock pot simmering on the stove.

Roux is another basic component used in restaurant kitchens for making wonderfully flavorful soups and sauces. Roux is simply flour that has been cooked with oil or fat to a varying degree of brownness. It's used as a thickener. Although roux is made of flour, please don't think that using flour as a thickener will give you the same results. The magic of roux lies in the fact that the flour has been cooked with the fat before being added to the recipe; this pre-cooking will add a nutty, rich flavor to your soups and sauces.

A third basic element that requires do-ahead preparation is crème fraîche—or *crema Mexicana*. Crème fraîche is an essential ingredient in Central and South American cooking. Commercial sour cream is a very acceptable substitute, but to give a true Latin American taste to your recipes, nothing will compare to a homemade crème fraîche.

Refer back to the following basic procedures when preparing the recipes in this cookbook. If you lay in a cache of stock and roux in your freezer and container of crème fraîche in your refrigerator, cooking will be a breeze; much of the work involved in cooking is in the making of these three basics—and here, too, is the source of a lot of the flavor and quality!

RICH CHICKEN STOCK

Makes one quart (concentrated)

While it does require a day on your stove to fully cook, this stock is easy to make. The resulting thick, gelatinous stock can be refrigerated for weeks or frozen indefinitely—so you can make it ahead. In fact, you can make enough to supply your cooking needs for several months in just one day. Stock is low in calories, high in protein. You can use it to make soups and casseroles, and to create sauces for meat and seafood dishes. There are many versions and varieties of stocks, this one, Rich Chicken Stock, will allow you to work magic in your kitchen. Just 1 heaping tablespoon of this rich stock concentrate is equivalent to one cup of liquid stock.

- ½ pound carrots
- ½ stalk celery
- 2 medium onions
- 2 heads garlic sliced in half (don't peel)
- ¾ cup chopped fresh parsley
- 3 bay leaves
- Pinch of dried thyme
- 10 peppercorns
- 5 pounds chicken bones and trimmings

Place all of the ingredients, in the order given, in a large stockpot; don't bother to chop the vegetables. Add cold water to cover. Simmer gently, covered, over low heat, for 8 hours. Never boil the stock or it will become cloudy.

Place a large sieve over another large stockpot; carefully strain the liquid. Reserve the liquid; discard the solids. Strain the liquid a second time through a cheesecloth-lined sieve; reserve the liquid and discard the solids. At this stage, there will be about 3 gallons of stock.

Let the stock stand in the refrigerator until the fat accumulates on top, 1 to 2 hours; carefully skim off the fat. The stock should have the consistency of a soft gelatin. Place the stock in a clean pot; cover, and bring to a boil over high heat (it's okay to let the stock boil now because there's no fat). When the stock boils, remove the lid, reduce the heat to medium and simmer until the liquid is reduced to 1 quart, about 2 hours.

Remove the pot from the stove. Let the stock cool completely before storing. Pour the stock into small freezer containers; freeze indefinitely or refrigerate up to two weeks. The stock can be used in any recipe for chicken, beef, pork, or seafood that calls for stock: one heaping tablespoon of this concentrated stock equals one cup of liquid stock; dissolve it in 1 cup of warm water if desired.

Simmering Stockpots

When reducing large quantities of liquid, such as 3 gallons of stock, it is important to ventilate your kitchen. Either use your stove fan or open the windows, otherwise you will create a mini-steambath in your house; the steam will condense on your walls and windows, and the aroma of whatever you are reducing will permeate the air as well as your furnishings. This caveat extends to long-term simmering of beans, soups, stews, and sauces.

ROUX

Makes about 1½ cups

Roux, used as a thickener for sauces and soups, is basically just flour cooked with oil; but because the Roux is cooked before being added to the recipe, the combination of heat and oil gives the flour a wonderfully nutty, full flavor that carries over into your soups and sauces.

To make Roux, you use equal parts of oil and flour, so it's easy to adjust this recipe for any desired quantity. We prefer to use peanut oil in our Roux, but any good vegetable oil would be fine in this recipe. Roux can be made ahead and stored; it will keep for several weeks in a covered jar in your refrigerator, or you can freeze it.

1 cup peanut oil
1 cup all-purpose flour

Heat the oil in a heavy pot or cast-iron skillet. When the oil is hot, remove the pot from the heat. Add the flour; using a whisk, mix the flour and oil thoroughly. Return the pot to the heat; cook over low heat, stirring often, until the flour is brown and gives off a nutty aroma, about 6 to 8 minutes; do not let the mixture burn. Remove the mixture from the heat and store in an airtight container. Bring to room temperature before using.

Using Roux as a Thickener

When using Roux to thicken sauces or soups, always add the liquid to the Roux, not the Roux to the liquid. Both ingredients should be at room temperature. Slowly add the liquid to the Roux, whisking constantly until thoroughly combined. Place the mixture over medium heat and cook, stirring constantly, until thick.

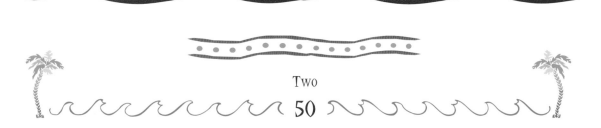

CRÈME FRAÎCHE

Makes about 1 cup

Crème Fraîche is a culture of heavy cream with buttermilk. Variations of this basic French recipe are produced throughout Latin America. Because you are working with a live culture, it's very important that you use sanitized utensils and containers. If you don't want to make your own, you can substitute sour cream in recipes calling for Crème Fraîche, but you won't create the same taste.

1 cup heavy cream
1 tablespoon buttermilk

Mix the cream and buttermilk in a medium-size bowl; place the mixture into a sanitized plastic container. Cover with a cheesecloth or napkin (do not use a plastic lid because the mixture must be able to breathe) and leave it for 2 days at room temperature. Mix well; refrigerate, covered with a plastic lid, to stabilize.

Crème Fraîche will keep well in the refrigerator for ½ to 2 weeks. Use it to top beans, rice, tacos, enchiladas; or to finish sauces; or, with a little sweetening, to top desserts or fresh fruits.

Clean Versus Sanitary

Clean generally means neat and dirt free (for example, clean shoes and a clean floor), whereas *sanitary* specifically means sterile or disinfected (that is, germ and bacteria free). Just because something is clean does not mean that it is also sanitary. Since Crème Fraîche contains a live culture, it is very important that there be no competing bacteria in unseen residue on the container. Uninvited bacteria can cause off-flavors and food-borne illnesses. Before making Crème Fraîche, it is wise to pour boiling water over the containers and utensils that you will use to make sure that they are sanitary.

Review of Cooking Methods

FRYING

When frying, always remember to start with clean oil; don't reuse oil. Peanut oil and polyunsaturated oils, such as sunflower oil, are good for frying. If you are using a frying pan instead of a deep fryer, don't fill the pan higher than halfway up the side with oil. The secret of non-greasy frying is to always maintain the proper temperature in the pan: between 350° and 375°F. Heat the oil to the proper temperature before you start cooking—never put food to fry in the oil before it is sufficiently hot, or the food will be greasy and soggy. The oil should be hot enough to form a seal around the food the minute it hits the pan; this will lock in the moisture and seal out the grease.

Thermometers

If you don't already have a deep-frying thermometer, you should consider buying one; it's an excellent, and often necessary, kitchen tool. Or, better yet, buy a candy thermometer—it's even more versatile, and you'll find that it comes in handy for many different types of cooking.

TIPS FOR FRYING

- Make sure the oil has reached the proper frying temperature before adding food to the pan. Then allow the temperature to rise again to the proper temperature before adding more food.

- Don't crowd the frying pan; cook your food in two or more batches if necessary.

- Never let the oil smoke or burn. If the oil gets too hot and begins to smoke, immediately reduce the heat or remove the pan from the heat to cool down the oil. If allowed to become too hot, the oil will turn brown and develop an off-flavor.

- When frying chicken in a pan, make sure you have enough oil to cover at least half the thickness of the pieces.

- When frying fish, it's best to use a breading or batter. This prevents the fish fillet or steak from falling apart while cooking.

- Placing a screen or grate over your frying pan will keep the grease from splattering over your stove (and you) while allowing the steam to escape.

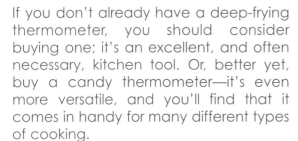

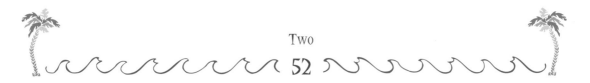

SAUTÉING

Sautéing means to cook small portions of food rapidly over high heat, using a minimum amount of oil. As a general guide, use 1 tablespoon for a 10-inch skillet or 2 tablespoons for a large pot or pan (you can always add oil if necessary as you cook). When sautéing, not all of the food being cooked is touched by the hot oil, so it is important that the pieces of food be flat and of uniform thickness or else they will not cook evenly. When you have finished sautéing, deglaze the pan. Pour about ½ cup of wine or fruit juice (such as apple or mango) into the pan and loosen up the browned bits and the concentrated flavors left in the bottom of the pan. Pour the juices over the cooked food before serving.

BROILING

When broiling, make sure the meat is not too close to the heating element; 2½ to 3 inches is close enough. Put the meat on a perforated double pan with some water in the bottom so that the fat and the meat juices will drip down to the water bath below (this will prevent smoking and burning). Instead of water, you can use wine or fruit juice (such as apple or mango). Try adding fresh herbs and spices to the liquid. The heat will cause the spiced liquid to rise up and infuse the meat with extra flavor.

TIPS FOR SAUTÉING:

- Heat the oil to 350°F before adding the food.

- When heating the oil, never allow it to smoke or burn. If the oil gets too hot and begins to smoke, immediately reduce the heat or remove the pan from the heat to cool down the oil. If allowed to become too hot, the oil will turn brown and develop an off-flavor.

- After adding food to the pan, make sure the oil has returned to the proper temperature before adding more.

- Don't crowd the frying pan; cook your food in two or more batches if you have to.

- Always keep the oil clean; wipe the pan out and add fresh oil before starting another batch.

- When sautéing, sear both sides of the food. When sautéing meat, it's time to turn it over when the top side begins to sweat.

ROASTING

Meats and poultry come out better when roasted in an oven cooking bag. The bag holds the juices and works like a smoker, allowing the steam to penetrate the meat so that it retains its moisture as it cooks. (And because the bags are disposable, there's little cleanup!) Always start with a preheated 400°F oven. Put the meat and any seasoning or condiments into the bag, tie the bag, and place the contents into a roasting pan with at least 2-inch sides. Prick five or six little vents in the bag with a knife tip. Insert a meat thermometer through the bag and into the meat so its tip is in the center of the thickest part of the meat and does not touch fat or bone. Place the prepared meat into the oven. When the outside begins to brown, in 15 or 20 minutes, turn the oven down to 350°F for meat and 280°F for poultry. Roast the meat slowly until the thermometer reaches 180°F. If you aren't using a cooking bag, roast the chicken and turkey in an oven set at no lower than 325°F.

Another great—but entirely different—method of roasting is just "for the birds." It produces a chicken with crisp, nutty-flavored skin and moist flavorful meat. Wash, rinse, dry, and then salt the bird. Rub garlic or herbs, if desired, in the pocket between the skin and the breast. Place the chicken in a shallow roasting pan (this time without the roasting bag). For a 3½-pound bird, cook the chicken, breast side down, in a preheated 475°F oven for 15 minutes, then turn the chicken breast side up, and continue to roast until done, about 40 minutes.

BARBECUING

Never put the barbecue sauce on the meat before you start cooking it. Most barbecue sauces have a high concentration of sugar, which will burn and turn black before your meat is cooked. Marinate the meat first; then while barbecuing, baste the meat with the marinade. If the marinade has no oil in it, put it in a squirt bottle for a more creative approach to basting. When the meat is almost done, that's the time to brush on the barbecue sauce. Your meat will be flavorful and moist—and the sauce will have a great color and taste. Fish such as tuna and salmon, whose natural flavors are enhanced by the smoky flavor of the barbecue, should be basted often with an oil-based marinade to prevent sticking, since the fish have little fat of their own.

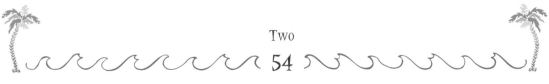

TIPS FOR GRILLING:

- Even cooking temperature is the key to successful grilling.

- When barbecuing, don't be impatient. Before you start to grill, let the coals burn down to an ashy gray color, so that they'll give off a nice, white-hot, even heat. Coals should not be red hot. It usually takes 30 minutes for coals to reach this stage, so plan accordingly and don't rush.

- Gas grills have gauges: set the gauge to medium (350°F to 375°F) and allow the grill to reach that temperature before cooking. Placing food on a grill that has not been adequately preheated will cause the meats to stick, cook unevenly, and have all-around unpleasant results.

COOKING VEGETABLES

The best way to cook green vegetables is to blanch them first. To blanch vegetables, bring water to a boil (use a ratio of two parts water to one part vegetable), add 2 tablespoons of fresh lemon juice or white vinegar (to hold the vegetable's color), and toss in the vegetables. Bring the water back to a boil; then immediately remove the vegetables and plunge them into cold water to stop the cooking process. Store the blanched vegetables in the refrigerator until you are ready to use them. Serve the vegetables cold, as finger foods or in salads. Or warm them in the microwave, sauté them, or add them to soups, stews, or casseroles. Blanching removes little of the vitamins and minerals, and leaves the vegetables with a nice crunch.

GUIDE TO COOKING TIMES FOR FISH

Because the density, texture, fat content, and moisture content varies from fish to fish, each species has a different ideal cooking time. Unlike meat, fish is naturally tender and free from fibers that need to be broken down or softened by cooking—so overcooking fish is particularly counterproductive. You want the cooked fish to be firm, but still juicy. You never want to cook the fish until it flakes (the old standard of doneness) because by then the fish will be tough and dry.

To determine the perfect cooking time, lay the fish (whether it's a steak, fillet, or whole fish) flat on a cutting board, and measure it at its thickest part. For each inch, use the following cooking times as a rough guide; divide the total time in half to get the cooking time per side.

For Example

You have a tilapia fillet that is ½ inch thick. According to the chart, the perfect cooking time for tilapia is 6 minutes for each inch of thickness. Using this guideline, you would cook your ½-inch fillet for 3 minutes (1½ minutes on each side).

MINUTES OF COOKING TIME PER INCH OF THICKNESS

6 MINUTES
- **Sanddabs**
- **Sole**
- **Tilapia**
- **Tuna**

8 MINUTES
- **Halibut**
- **Swordfish**

9 MINUTES
- **Salmon**
- **Shark**
- **Trout**

10 MINUTES
- **Catfish**
- **Mahi Mahi**
- **Rockfish (Pacific Snapper)**

12 MINUTES
- **Monkfish**
- **White Sea Bass**

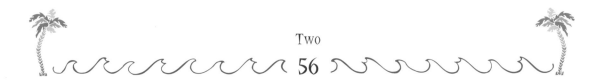

These cooking guidelines are based on those developed by the National Fish and Seafood Promotional Council. The council stresses that the important thing when cooking your fish is that you cook it just until it is firm but still juicy, and has just turned from translucent to opaque. Remember, undercooked fish is preferable to overcooked fish.

Seafood Watch

Many species of fish and shellfish are being overfished; some aquaculture practices cause environmental damage. California's Monterey Bay Aquarium has published The Seafood Watch, a guide to help consumers make wise choices when purchasing seafood. The Seafood Watch recommends which seafood to eat and which to avoid. Since information on fish populations changes daily, the aquarium's web site at www.montereybayaquarium.com provides a current update of the watch list. We are concerned about the environment and the health of our oceans, and we encourage you to support sustainable fisheries as much as possible. When preparing a recipe calling for seafood, try to avoid endangered species; if necessary substitute a fish from the "Best Choices" list—it will taste just as good!

THE "PERFECT" MEAL

At our restaurants, we complement our dishes with servings of fresh vegetables; rice or potatoes or other grains; black beans; and fresh salsas. By utilizing fresh seasonal varieties available at the peak of their ripeness, we are able to meet our goal of creating visual pleasure, gustatory satisfaction, and nutritional balance on each plate. These are factors that you, too, should consider when planning your meals.

VISUAL PLEASURE:

You want to present an appetizing composition on the plate that includes a pleasing contrast of colors and textures.

GUSTATORY SATISFACTION:

You want to present a dish with contrasting and complimentary aromas and tastes (such as hot, spicy, mild, and sweet) that stimulate and please the palate.

NUTRITIONAL BALANCE:

You want your meal to include green and yellow vegetables, complex carbohydrates (for example, rice or whole grains), fresh fruits, and protein.

The art of cooking is to coordinate these factors to produce a meal that is satisfying on all three levels. In other words, it should look good, taste good, and be good for you!

COOKING NOTES

PORTION SIZES, COOKING METHODS, AND UNCOMMON INGREDIENTS

- Most of the recipes serve four, which makes it easy for you to divide them in half to serve two, or to double them to serve eight. The recipes for salsas, sauces, compound butters, and spice mixtures will often make more than you will need for one meal or one recipe. Because these mixtures store so well, once made, you'll have them on hand to create many other great dishes with little further effort on your part.

- When buying fish steaks or fillets, allow 6 ounces per person. So, for recipes calling for $1\frac{1}{2}$ pounds of fish to serve four, buy four 6-ounce fillets or steaks.

- When preparing recipes for fish, refer back to "Review of Cooking Methods" (page 52) and "Guide to Cooking Times for Fish" (page 56). This will simplify the directions and save repetition in the recipes.

- When cooking a whole chicken, allow 1 pound per person. If the chicken is boneless, allow 8 ounces per person. When cooking beef, lamb, or pork, allow 8 to 10 ounces per person. When preparing recipes with chicken or meat, please refer to "Review of Cooking Methods" (pages 52-56) for tips on improving or varying your cooking techniques.

- The recipes in this book generally call for the meat/fish to be sautéed. That is because sautéing is the easiest, tastiest method for cooking all types of fish, and for cooking meat and poultry in general, and the results are predictably wonderful. However, don't be afraid to try a recipe using a different cooking method—say roasting the chicken instead of sautéing it. The salsas and sauces from one dish can be often used in another dish to create new and delicious flavor combinations. Experiment!

- A few of the ingredients used in this book may seem exotic; however, they are becoming increasingly common on supermarket shelves, especially in cities or areas that have a mixture of ethnic populations. Sidebars, notes, and footnotes referred to throughout this book offer suggestions for substitutions for some uncommon ingredients. If you have trouble finding an ingredient in your local supermarket, try looking in natural food stores, gourmet food shops, and Latin American or Asian specialty markets. Mail Order (page 223) lists establishments that can supply you with the specialty foods, chiles, or fresh produce needed for recipes in this book. If you're on the net—just use your search engine to locate one of the many sites that now sell Latin American and Caribbean specialty foods on the World Wide Web.

A Feast of Flavors: • Calypso Salsa • Jerk Spices, • Pico de Gallo
• Chimichurri Sauce • Tomatillo and Avocado Salsa • Fire-Roasted Red
Tomato Sauce • Sun-Dried Cranberry Salsa • Achiote Paste • Papaya Curry Sauce

Fresh Corn Tamales,
with Roasted Red Pepper Sauce and Crème Fraîche

Quesadillas and Guacamole

Shrimp Flautas and **Armadillo Eggs,**
served with *Sweet Jalapeno Dipping Sauce*

Sopa de Lima
(Chicken and Lime Tortilla Soup)

- **Butternut Squash Soup,**
  with Sun-Dried Cranberry Salsa

- Bayou Gumbo

Seafood Ceviche

Caldo de Camarones
(Shrimp Soup)

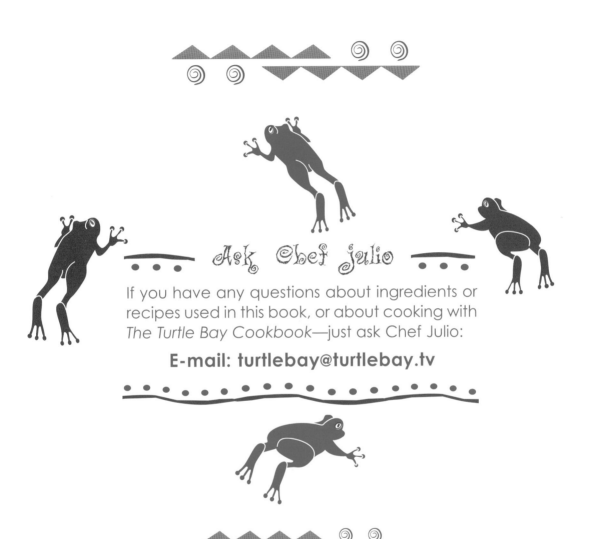

Ask Chef Julio

If you have any questions about ingredients or recipes used in this book, or about cooking with *The Turtle Bay Cookbook*—just ask Chef Julio:

E-mail: turtlebay@turtlebay.tv

TREE FROGS

Tree frogs are the jewels of the rain forest: vivid reds, blues, greens, and yellows contrast with black to form striking patterns on their skins. These frogs are small—some are so tiny that they only measure 1/2 inch in total length. Sticky adhesive pads at the ends of their fingers and toes help the frogs move about—and even cling vertically to—the leaves and branches of the forest as the frogs hunt for insects. Strong hind leg muscles rocket the frogs into the air at the first hint of danger or at the first sight of an insect meal, and they propel swimming frogs quickly through the water. Sticky tongues enable tree frogs to quickly snatch insects from the air.

In the evening, tree frogs provide the night music for the rain forest. Groups of males compete in a loud chorus to attract mates. The female tree frogs make a good audience; lacking vocal sacs, they are usually silent.

The parenting behavior of tree frogs varies greatly among the species. After mating, some tree frogs carry their eggs around in "backpacks." Skinfolds on the backs of these frogs form completely enclosed pouches in which the eggs develop. Other species build mud nests and stand guard over their clutches, catching any insects that threaten their eggs. Other species of tree frogs deposit their eggs on leaves that overhang rivers, lakes, or ponds; then when the tadpoles hatch, they simply fall into the water below. Some species of ground-dwelling tree frogs lay their eggs in the damp forest floor. When these tadpoles hatch, either the mother or father frog returns, and the tadpoles squirm onto this parent's back for a piggyback ride. The adult frog will then carry these little hitchhikers about until they are ready to fend for themselves.

The *kokoe'-pa'*, one species of dart-poison frogs, provides the most extreme example of parental devotion in tree frogs. The *kokoe'-pa'* are ground-dwelling tree frogs, but after their eggs have hatched, the female frogs climb high into the trees, carrying their tadpoles on their backs. They then deposit their young, one by one, into the protective pools of individual bromeliads.

Native only to the American tropics, bromeliads are funnel-shaped plants growing on trees high above the forest floor, festooning them by the thousands. A rosette of leaves forms a basin in the center of the bromeliad where rainwater collects. While bromeliads vary in size, the reservoirs of some of the larger bromeliads can hold over a gallon of water.

The *kokoe'-pa'* females do not abandon their offspring in the bromeliads. Having deposited their tadpoles, each in its own bromeliad pool, these parents will later climb back up the same trees and revisit each plant. On this second trip, the female frogs will lay non-fertile eggs in each of the bromeliad pools so that the developing froglets will be sure to have something nutritious to eat.

Some tree frogs spend their whole lives in bromeliads. Besides rainwater, organic material also collects in their central pools. This provides fertilizer for the plants and food for other tiny animals. Some species of tree frogs lay their eggs directly in these pools. There, the tiny tadpoles hatch and feed on the bacteria and algae in the water. The water in the pool keeps the frog's skin moist, and it also attracts insects for the adult frog's dinner. Some frogs hatch, grow up, and die in one single bromeliad plant, sharing this home with spiders, crabs, and lizards—a tiny world in a plant.

The dart-poison (or arrow-poison) frogs are probably the most famous tree frogs. These brilliantly colored frogs often match the bright-colored tropical foliage around them; and while insects may be attracted to the edible leaves, predators such as bats, rats, snakes, hawks, and large fish will steer clear of these frogs—their neon coloration warns that they are deadly. Glands in the skins of these dart-poison frogs produce a bitter-tasting poison strong enough to paralyze a small animal.

The dart-poison frog family contains over 120 species that live mainly in rain forests from Nicaragua to southeastern Brazil and Bolivia. Tribal peoples hunt the exceptionally poisonous species of frogs, then roast them to excrete their poisons. Hunters coat the tips of their blowgun darts with the collected frog poison; they can coat fifteen darts with the poison from just one frog—and one dart can paralyze a bird or small monkey, which the tribe hunts for food.

The poison that the frog produces is actually an anesthetic that is 160,000 times more powerful than cocaine. Known as *tetrodotoxin*, this substance is used in western medicine as a painkiller, anesthetic, and muscle relaxant. *Tetrodotoxin* is also used by voodoo doctors in Haiti to induce trances and create zombies.

Frogs have been around for more than 200 million years. They are an important link in the global food chain. Scientists are finding that, like many forest plants, tree frogs are a rich source of potentially beneficial chemicals. Because frogs eat low on the food chain, they also serve as early warning indicators of problems in the environment. In several areas of the planet, whole species of frogs have disappeared; in Costa Rica the golden toad has not been seen for years. Serious attention must be paid to the alterations that are being made in the habitats of these creatures, because what affects them, ultimately, will affect us.

DENDROBATES AURATUS

Chapter 3

Fresh Salsas,
Condiments, and Spices

FEAST OF FLAVORS

Using a variety of herbs, spices, seeds, and nuts in these recipes adds another dimension of flavor to the dishes. Combining seasonal fruits and vegetables into the fresh salsas not only stimulates the taste buds but adds complexity, color, and nutritional value to any meal.

CHILE PEPPERS

Chile peppers are one of our favorite seasoning ingredients. Chiles come in dozens of varieties, each one with its own particular taste and degree of hotness. We often use serranos, jalapeños, pequins, habaneros, arboles, or pasillas in our recipes. Please don't be afraid to season with peppers: when used in proper proportions, chiles will contribute a lot of flavor and zest to your dishes (as well as a good amount of Vitamin C) without overwhelming the other ingredients.

Caution

NEVER touch your eyes after chopping a chile without washing your hands first!

ROASTING PEPPERS

GAS RANGE METHOD: If you have a gas stove, you can easily roast a small quantity of peppers by holding them over the flame using either a fork or tongs, or by placing them on a wire screen directly over the burner. Roast each pepper, turning frequently, until the skin is charred on all sides, 3 to 4 minutes. When the pepper skins have turned black, transfer the peppers to a bowl; let them cool. Peel, seed, and devein the peppers under cold running water.

OVEN METHOD: If you have an electric stove, or if you want to roast a large number of peppers, use your oven. Preheat the oven to 450°F. Spray the peppers with nonstick cooking spray, and place them on a baking sheet. Bake the peppers until their skins begin to blister, about 45 minutes. Remove the peppers from the oven, place them in a plastic bag, and seal it. Set the bag aside for 10 minutes to allow the chiles to "sweat"—they will now peel easily. Peel, seed, and devein the peppers under cold running water.

SALSA BRAVA

Makes about 6 cups

Salsa Brava is a sort of Caribbean cole slaw. It's a wonderful accompaniment to any spicy meal—it's low calorie, flavorful, and nutritious too! It will keep for a week in the refrigerator, so it's a great make-ahead dish. Adjust the number of chiles to your taste, giving it just the right amount of kick.

- **2 medium carrots, julienned**
- **½ small head white cabbage, shredded**
- **½ medium onion, diced**
- **½ green bell pepper, diced**
- **½ red bell pepper, diced**
- **4 serrano or jalapeño chiles, finely chopped**
- **1½ teaspoons salt**
- **½ teaspoon freshly ground black pepper**
- **1 cup white vinegar**
- **½ tablespoon sugar**

Combine the carrots, cabbage, onion, green and red bell peppers, chiles, salt, and black pepper in a large bowl. Stir in the vinegar and sugar. Pack the salsa in an airtight nonreactive container and refrigerate for at least 8 hours before serving to allow the cabbage to pickle.

CALYPSO SALSA

Makes about 3½ cups

This salsa is tangy and fruity, with the flavor of pineapple and ginger. It's great with fish, chicken, and pasta dishes—or spoon it on grilled pork chops.

- **1 cup diced fresh pineapple**
- **1 cup diced orange sections**
- **½ cup diced jícama**
- **¼ cup diced red onion**
- **½ cup diced red bell pepper**
- **1 serrano or jalapeño chile, minced**
- **1 tablespoon freshly squeezed lime juice**
- **½ teaspoon minced fresh ginger root**
- **1 tablespoon minced fresh mint**
- **1 tablespoon passionfruit glaze (page 229) or honey**

Combine all of the ingredients in a medium-size nonreactive bowl. Cover and refrigerate, allowing the flavors to marry for a few hours before serving.

Putting Out The Flames

The *capsaicin* in chile will not stop burning if you drink water; this will only spread the *capsaicin*—and the pain—around in your mouth. Instead, drink something basic like milk to neutralize the chile's bite, or eat dairy products or starches such as rice, bread, or potatoes. Alcohol, such as beer or wine, is also effective, as it dissolves the *capsaicin*.

SALSA FRESCA

Makes about 6 cups

Use this flavorful, colorful salsa to garnish meat, egg, and seafood dishes. It's also great as a dip for tortilla chips.

- **1½ cups diced jícama**
- **1 cup diced red onion**
- **3 cups diced tomatoes**
- **3 serrano or jalapeño chiles, minced**
- **5 tablespoons chopped fresh cilantro**
- **¼ cup freshly squeezed lemon juice**
- **1 teaspoon salt**
- **½ teaspoon freshly ground black pepper**

Combine all of the ingredients in a nonreactive medium-size bowl; mix well. Adjust the salt and pepper to taste. Serve immediately or cover and refrigerate until ready to use.

Note

Use only fresh chiles in the salsa recipes. Do not use canned or pickled chiles such as jalapeños; you will be very disappointed with the results. Only fresh chiles will do—except for when the recipe calls specifically for chipotles in adobo, which are smoked chiles canned in adobo sauce.

MANGO SALSA

Makes about 3 cups

This salsa is one of everyone's favorites. It goes especially well with chicken.

- **1½ cup diced fresh mangos (ripe but firm)**
- **½ cup diced jícama**
- **½ cup diced red bell pepper**
- **1½ to 2 serrano or jalapeño chiles, finely diced**
- **½ cup diced, seeded, and drained tomatoes**
  (slice the tomatoes in half first, squeeze out the seeds and excess juice, and then dice)
- **2 tablespoons chopped fresh cilantro**
- **2 tablespoons freshly squeezed orange juice**
- **1 tablespoon freshly squeezed lime juice**
- **Salt and freshly ground black pepper to taste**

Combine all ingredients in a nonreactive, medium-size bowl; mix well. Add salt and pepper to taste. Cover and refrigerate for 4 hours before serving to allow the flavors to marry.

SUN-DRIED CRANBERRY SALSA

Makes about 3 cups

This salsa is a tasty accompaniment to chicken, duck, turkey, pork—and it's dynamite on salmon. For a change of pace, try it on enchiladas.

- 1½ cups diced tomatoes
- ¾ cup diced jícama
- ¼ cup diced red bell pepper
- ¼ cup diced red onion
- ¼ habanero chile or ½ fresh jalapeño chile, minced
- 4 tablespoons sun-dried cranberries
- 2 tablespoons chopped fresh cilantro
- 2½ tablespoons freshly squeezed lime juice
- ¼ teaspoon freshly ground black pepper
- 1 teaspoon salt

Combine all of the ingredients in a medium-size nonreactive bowl. Let the salsa stand 30 minutes at room temperature to allow the flavors to marry before serving. Serve at room temperature. Cover and refrigerate any remaining salsa.

Freshly Squeezed Citrus Juices

There is no substitute for the freshly squeezed lemon and lime juices called for in the recipes in this book. Bottled lemon and lime preparations, especially, will not give the desired results.

CRANBERRY CITRUS SALSA

Makes about 4 cups

This salsa is great on duck, pork, chicken, and fish. It can be served either hot or cold. Try it mixed with rice. It's especially good on turkey: try it next Thanksgiving to add a little "kick" to your holiday bird.

- 2 cups fresh or frozen cranberries
- 1 cup chopped yellow or red onions
- ½ cup freshly squeezed orange juice
- Zest from 1 orange, grated*
- 1 jalapeño chile, seeded and chopped
- ½ teaspoon minced fresh ginger
- 2 tablespoons + 2 teaspoons firmly packed light brown sugar
- 1 teaspoon honey
- 1½ tablespoons rice vinegar
- ½ to 1 tablespoon hot red pepper sauce
- 2 tablespoons chopped fresh cilantro

Combine all of the ingredients in a medium saucepan; cook over high heat until the liquid comes to a boil. Remove from the heat; cool, stirring occasionally, making sure not to split the cranberries! Refrigerate covered in an airtight container until ready to use.

*The zest of the orange is the outermost, colored peel of the fruit. To remove the zest, use a zester or the fine side of a vegetable grater.

POSOLE SALSA

Makes about 3 cups

Posole Salsa is excellent on salads and on fish, chicken, or meat dishes.

- ½ cup canned yellow hominy, rinsed in cold water and well drained
- ½ cup canned white hominy, rinsed in cold water and well drained
- ⅓ cup diced red bell pepper
- 1 cup Salsa Fresca (page 67)
- 2 tablespoons chopped fresh cilantro
- ½ large chipotle chile (canned smoked jalapeño chile), minced
- ⅓ cup freshly squeezed lime juice
- 2 tablespoons olive oil
- 1 tablespoon sugar
- ⅛ teaspoon salt

Combine all of the ingredients in a clean medium-size plastic container with a tight-fitting lid; mix well. Refrigerate for 8 hours before serving to allow all of the flavors to marry.

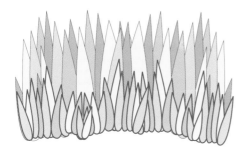

SUN-DRIED TOMATO AND SERRANO CHILE PESTO

Makes about 4 cups

Sun-dried Tomato and Serrano Chile Pesto is excellent on steamed artichokes, fish, lamb, and steaks—and it tastes great spread on French bread. Add more serrano chiles if you like it "hot"!

- ½ pound sun-dried tomatoes
- 1 tablespoon rice vinegar
- 1 cup warm water
- 1 cup slivered or sliced almonds
- 5 tablespoons chopped fresh basil
- 2 tablespoons balsamic vinegar (do not substitute)
- 1 tablespoon minced serrano or jalapeño chiles
- ½ cup freshly grated Parmesan cheese
- ½ cup fresh corn kernels (or use frozen, thawed)
- ½ cup olive oil
- 1½ tablespoons bottled hot red pepper sauce

Combine the tomatoes, rice vinegar, and water in a small nonreactive bowl. Let the ingredients soak for 1 hour; drain.

Add the almonds, basil, and tomato mixture to a food processor or blender; coarsely chop. Transfer the mixture to a large bowl; mix in the remaining ingredients; combine thoroughly. Refrigerate covered in an airtight container for up to one week.

TOMATILLO AND AVOCADO SALSA

Makes about 3 cups

This salsa is one of our most popular—a nice tangy, creamy salsa with a beautiful green color that complements chicken, pork, beef, seafood, and even eggs. Serve it as a dip for Tostones (page 111) or chips; use it to top enchiladas or omelets, or as the basis for a seafood cocktail. Serve it with Fajitas (page194), Quesadillas (page 116), or tacos, or as an accompaniment to grilled steaks or chops.

> 1 pound tomatillos, husked, washed, and quartered
> 3 tablespoons minced onion
> 1/3 teaspoon minced garlic
> 3 tablespoons chopped cilantro
> 1 serrano chile, minced
> 2 teaspoons salt
> 2 large ripe Haas avocados, peeled and pitted
> 1 cup cold water

Place the quartered tomatillos, onion, garlic, cilantro and salt into a blender or food processor. Blend well for 2 minutes. Add the avocados, blend for 30 seconds more. Add the water and blend until salsa has a smooth, sauce-like consistency (about 30 seconds). Keep refrigerated in an airtight nonreactive container. Serve chilled.

WILD RICE SALSA

Makes about 4½ cups

Try this salsa on salads, or serve it with chicken, fish, or meat dishes. It's delicious. The wild rice gives the salsa a nice body with a nutty flavor, while the chipotle chile adds a smoky bite.

> 1 cup uncooked wild rice
> 1/4 cup diced red bell pepper
> 1 1/2 cups Salsa Fresca (page 67)
> 2 tablespoons chopped fresh cilantro
> 1 large chipotle chile (canned smoked jalapeño chile), minced
> 1 cup diced jícama
> 1/2 cup freshly squeezed lime juice
> 2 tablespoons olive oil
> 1 1/2 tablespoons sugar
> 1/4 teaspoon salt

Combine the wild rice and 4 cups of water in a medium saucepan; heat the mixture over medium heat just until it comes to a boil. Reduce the heat to low; simmer, covered, until the grains begin to open (about 1 hour). Remove from the heat and drain. Spread the rice in a shallow pan and cool it in the refrigerator for 1 hour.

Combine the remaining ingredients in a nonreactive medium-size bowl, add the cooled rice, and mix well. Refrigerate covered in an airtight container for at least 8 hours to allow the flavors to marry. Store refrigerated for up to 4 days.

PICO DE GALLO

Makes about 4 cups

This salsa is a pickled mixture of fresh minced onions, chiles, and other vegetables. It will keep for weeks in your refrigerator. It's a great condiment for rice, omelets, salads, seafood, and chicken dishes as well as for traditional Latin dishes such as tamales, tacos, and enchiladas. Watch out, though, Pico de Gallo is habit forming!

> **1 pound onions, minced and rinsed in cold water**
> **¾ cup minced carrots, rinsed in cold water**
> **¾ cup minced red bell pepper, rinsed in cold water**
> **5 habanero chiles,* minced**
> **1 cup rice vinegar**
> **1 cup white wine vinegar**
> **5 teaspoons sugar**
> **2½ teaspoons salt**

Combine all of the ingredients in a large glass or plastic container with a lid; mix well. Cover and chill ingredients for 4 hours before using. Store covered and refrigerated in an airtight container.

SPICY PICKLED ONIONS

Makes about 1 cup

This tangy condiment really has a bite. It complements rice and beans and other starchy dishes, and it adds a distinctive flavor contrast to chicken and pork dishes.

> **1 red onion, diced then rinsed with cold water**
> **1 habanero chile, minced**
> **2½ tablespoons freshly squeezed lime juice**
> **½ teaspoon salt**

Place the diced and rinsed onion and the minced habanero in a small nonreactive bowl. Add the lemon juice; stir. Add the salt; mix well. Allow 30 minutes for the onion to pickle before serving. Refrigerate, covered, in an airtight container until ready to use; the onions will keep for up to 2 weeks. Serve chilled.

*If necessary, substitute 2 fresh jalapeños for each habanero.

AVOCADO SALSA

Makes about 3 cups

This salsa is wonderful with Grilled Chicken Breast Criollo (page 191) or any blackened fish that is sautéed with Cajun Blackening Spices (page 76).

- 2 medium-size Haas avocados, ripe but not "mushy," peeled and diced
- 1 tablespoon freshly squeezed lemon juice
- 1½ cups peeled, seeded, and diced tomatoes (see note this page)
- 2 serrano chiles, minced
- 3 tablespoons chopped green onions
- 3 tablespoons red wine vinegar
- 2 tablespoons olive oil
- 3 tablespoons chopped fresh cilantro
- Salt and freshly ground black pepper to taste.

Place the avocados in a medium-size bowl; sprinkle the lemon juice over the avocados; mix very gently. Add the tomatoes and the remaining ingredients to the bowl and mix together very gently. Adjust the seasoning to taste. Cover and refrigerate the salsa for at least 30 minutes before serving to allow the flavors to marry. Serve chilled.

CACTUS PEAR SALSA

Makes about 4 cups

Serve chilled on roasted duck, pork, swordfish, shark, or salmon.

- 10 ripe, very red cactus pears, peeled
- Juice of 2 freshly squeezed lemons
- ½ cup freshly squeezed orange juice
- 2 serrano or jalapeño chiles, minced
- 1 medium red onion, diced
- 1 green apple (or pear), unpeeled, diced
- 1 tablespoon fresh thyme, chopped
- ⅛ teaspoon ground cumin
- ⅛ teaspoon ground allspice
- 1 teaspoon sugar or honey
- Pinch of salt

Place 7 of the cactus pears, the lemon juice, and the orange juice in a medium saucepan; bring the liquid to a boil. Reduce the heat to low; simmer, covered, until the fruit is soft, about 10 minutes. Remove the saucepan from the heat and set it aside.

Skinning A Tomato

Bring a small pot of water to boil. Place the tomato in the boiling water for 45 seconds; remove it using a slotted spoon, then quickly place it in a bowl of iced water. The skin will now slip off easily.

CACTUS PEAR SALSA, cont.

Place a medium-size sieve or food mill over a medium-size bowl. Push the cooked fruit (along with the juice) through the sieve with the back of a wooden spoon, or process through the food mill, until only the seeds remain. Reserve the liquid; discard the solids.

Dice the remaining 3 cactus pears and add them to the strained cactus pear juice. Add the remaining ingredients to the cactus pear mixture; mix well. Refrigerate covered in an airtight container for up to 1 week.

Peeling a Cactus Pear

Peeling a cactus pear seems a little tricky, but it's actually easy. Even though the cactus pears sold commercially have been deprickled, tiny little hairs remain, which can be really annoying. To avoid pricking yourself, take a fork and push it into the side of the pear.

While holding the pear firmly with the fork, slice about ½ inch off the top and bottom ends with a sharp knife. Then make a slit in the skin that runs the length of the fruit; cut through the skin to the flesh, but don't cut through the flesh. Push the skin away from the fruit with the knife as you roll the fruit away from you with the fork. The skin will peel away, and you can then pick-up the fruit with your hands.

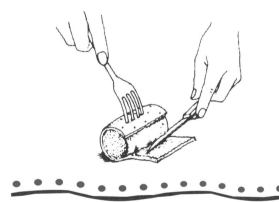

JAMAICAN JERK SPICES

Jerk refers to the Caribbean method of preserving meats, fish, and poultry by using a dry or wet rub of herbs and spices. Most of the recipes in this book use the dry rub since the ingredients are easier to assemble, the recipe is easier to mix in large quantities, and dry rub will keep for an indefinite period of time. However, you can easily substitute the wet rub in any of the recipes calling for jerk spices.

JAMAICAN JERK SPICES—DRY

Makes about ½ cup

Use this very spicy, aromatic, and addictive mixture on barbecue, rub it on roasts, use it to make fajitas or sautéed vegetables. Experiment with it in different dishes—the sky's the limit!

- **2 teaspoons ground red pepper (Cayenne pepper) or 1 teaspoon ground dried habanero chile**
- **2 tablespoons allspice**
- **1 tablespoon nutmeg**
- **4 teaspoons salt**
- **4 teaspoons sugar**
- **1 teaspoon freshly ground black pepper**
- **2 tablespoons chopped dried onion**
- **1 ½ teaspoons dried onion powder**
- **2 tablespoons garlic powder**
- **1½ teaspoons dried thyme**
- **1½ teaspoons mustard seed**
- **⅛ teaspoon ground cloves**
- **1½ teaspoons dried orange peel**

Using a spice grinder or mortar and pestle, finely grind all of the above ingredients. Store in a tightly sealed jar.

Ground Red Pepper

Not to be confused with chili powder (a mixture of chiles and spices used to make chili beans and chile con carne), ground red pepper (also called Cayenne pepper) is ground, dried red chile peppers. It is readily available in the spice section of the supermarket.

JAMAICAN JERK SPICES—WET

Makes about 1 cup

Jerk seasoning imparts the taste of the West Indies to your meal. Rub this wet spice mixture inside the cavities of chicken, turkey, and split pork loins. Rub some more mixture on the outside, then barbecue, roast, or rotisserie the meat for a tasty treat. The chiles add the kick to this dish, so add as much as you like.

2 fresh habanero chiles (4 if you like "hot"), finely chopped —or use 3 to 6 jalapeños
¼ cup ground allspice
1 tablespoon ground cinnamon
1 tablespoon ground nutmeg
2 teaspoons salt

1 tablespoon molasses
1 medium onion, chopped
¼ cup freshly squeezed lime juice
2 tablespoons chopped green onions
2 tablespoons orange zest*
1½ teaspoons tamarind paste, mango chutney, or molasses

Combine all of the ingredients in a food processor or blender; process or blend until well mixed and a paste forms. The mixture will keep in a sealed jar in the refrigerator for about one week.

Be Careful!
While preparing the Jamaican Jerk Spices mixture, be careful not to be breathe in the spices or touch your eyes.

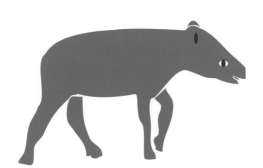

*The zest of the orange is the outermost peel of the fruit without any of the pith (white membrane). To remove the zest, use a zester or the fine side of a vegetable grater.

CAJUN BLACKENING SPICES

Makes about ½ cup

This recipe will make enough spicy coating for about 8 to 10 servings of meat or fish. You can double or triple the recipe if you'd like; this spice mixture stores well. You can adjust the degree of "hotness" by controlling the amount of ground red pepper you use. Remember, however, this seasoning is supposed to be spicy. Use it on pork, chicken, and fish. Grilling gives you a taste of the Louisiana bayous. When cooked over high heat, the Cajun spices caramelize and turn black, creating a unique flavor.

- **4 tablespoons paprika**
- **2 teaspoons ground red pepper (Cayenne pepper)**
- **2 teaspoons salt**
- **1 teaspoon ground white pepper**
- **1 tablespoon onion powder**
- **2 teaspoons garlic powder**
- **2 teaspoons dried thyme**
- **2 teaspoons dried oregano**
- **2 teaspoons dried basil**

Combine all of the ingredients in a small bowl; mix well. Store the spices covered in an airtight container until ready to use.

Coating Note

To coat chicken or fish, just put the desired amount of Cajun Blackening Spices into a paper or plastic bag, add a piece of chicken or fish, seal, and shake. Remove the coated piece, set aside, and shake up the next piece.

Be Careful!

While preparing the Cajun Blackening Spices mixture, be careful not to breathe in the spices or touch your eyes.

TAPIRS

apirs live in the low light and high humidity of the rain forest's understory. The largest land animals in Latin America, these tropical American tapirs can grow to be over six feet long and weigh six hundred pounds. Tapirs have long, moveable snouts—shorter versions of elephant trunks—which they use to pick up fallen fruit, to strip leaves and buds from branches, or to grasp branches and carry the leaves to their mouths. Tapirs have a really well-developed sense of smell; they travel along with their snouts to the grounds waiting to catch a whiff of ripe fruit—and when they catch the scent, they're off to feed. Using their snouts, tapirs stroke leaves until they find the ones that smell just right to eat. Waving these mini-trunks in the air, tapirs sniff for any scent of danger from their enemy, the jaguar. Though they look like giant pigs, when in danger, tapirs are capable of running swiftly from their predators.

Tapirs travel alone or in pairs. Usually nocturnal, they trot along the tunnel-like paths that they have worn through the dense undergrowth of the forest. These paths may extend for miles. Tapirs spend much of their time in water or mud. The water cools them and allows them to get rid of pests—especially ticks. A coat of mud on their hides protects them from insect bites. In the water, tapirs are excellent swimmers; there they dive to the bottom to root for swamp grass and water plants to eat.

Female tapirs have only one baby every two or three years, the birth taking place after a thirteen-month gestation. After mating, tapirs go their separate ways and the female raises her offspring alone. Like deer, baby tapirs are born with camouflage: their little brown bodies are patterned with white stripes and spots that gradually fade as the animals grow into adulthood. The adult tapirs' coats are dark brownish-gray, and the fur is short and thick, like woolen velvet.

While tapirs may look like huge pigs, they are actually related to the horse and the rhinoceros. These peaceful, reclusive creatures have been roaming the earth for the last 13 million years—and they've hardly changed at all. But their range, which once included Europe and North America, has shrunk severely. With their habitat being destroyed and the animals being hunted for meat, their numbers have seriously declined. Despite the fact that the tapir is the national animal of Belize, it is heading for extinction there and throughout Central America.

Though they are shy and seldom seen, tapirs are important to the perpetuation of the rain forest. Unlike most large herbivores, they eat many kinds of fruits—and in large quantities—along with other vegetation. After digesting these fruits, tapirs unknowingly distribute their seeds throughout the forest floor as they travel along, This insures the fruits' dispersal and propagation, and helps to maintain the equilibrium of the rain forest's delicate ecosystem.

TAPIRUS BAIRDI

Chapter 4

Sauces, Marinades, and Butters

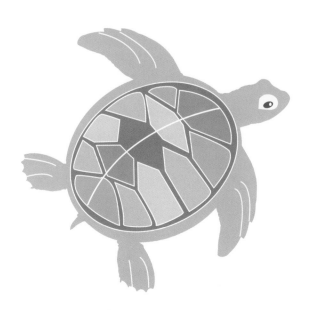

SWEET JALAPEÑO DIPPING SAUCE

Makes about 1½ cups

Try Sweet Jalapeño Dipping Sauce with Armadillo Eggs (page 106) or Sweet Potato Corn Cakes (page 103). Sweet Jalapeño Dipping Sauce makes a tasty glaze for chicken—brush it on as the chicken roasts. It makes a great dipping sauce for whole fish, too.

> 1 cup unsweetened pineapple juice
> 2 jalapeño chiles, seeded and julienned
> 4 teaspoons honey
> ¼ cup sugar
> 2 tablespoons + 2 teaspoons freshly squeezed lime juice
> ¼ cup rice vinegar
> 2 tablespoons + 2 teaspoons red wine vinegar
> 2 tablespoons + 2 teaspoons freshly squeezed orange juice
> 1 heaping tablespoon grated orange zest*

Combine all of the ingredients in a medium saucepan; cook over medium heat until the mixture just comes to a boil. Reduce the heat to low and simmer for 20 minutes. Remove the sauce from the heat; cool. Refrigerate covered in an airtight container for up to 2 weeks.

*The zest of the orange is the outermost peel of the fruit without any of the pith (white membrane). To remove the zest, use a zester or the fine side of a vegetable grater.

GREEN CASHEW SAUCE

Makes about 2 cups

This flavorful mayonnaise gets its green color from the fresh cilantro. Besides adding a tangy twist to sandwiches, this sauce can be tossed with pasta for a "Latino" pesto. Serve Green Cashew Sauce with grilled tilapia or other fish: place a spoonful of the sauce on a plate, spread it out, then place the cooked piece of fish on top. To complete the presentation, garnish the fish with Salsa Fresca (page 67).

> 1 cup roasted, salted cashews
> 2 garlic cloves, peeled
> 1 teaspoon chopped shallot
> 2 serrano chiles, chopped
> ¼ cup peanut oil
> 3 tablespoons rice vinegar
> 1 tablespoon water
> ⅔ cup chopped fresh cilantro
> Salt and freshly ground black pepper to taste

Place the cashews, garlic, shallot, and chiles in a food processor; process until the mixture forms a paste. With the food processor running, slowly add the oil in a thin, steady stream until the mixture is thoroughly combined. Add the vinegar, water, and cilantro, and process until the mixture becomes a smooth green paste. Season with salt and pepper. Serve immediately, or refrigerate covered in an airtight container for up to 2 weeks.

FIRE-ROASTED RED TOMATO SAUCE

Makes about 3 cups

This is a tasty variation of fresh tomato sauce: it's not a stewed sauce and it's served cold. Fire roasting the tomatoes gives the sauce a distinct flavor. Serve it with Empanadas (page 114), chips, tacos, egg dishes, and grilled meats.

1½ **pounds medium tomatoes**
2 **tablespoons minced onions**
1 **teaspoon minced serrano chile**
2 **tablespoons olive oil**
1 **tablespoon freshly squeezed lime juice**
2 **teaspoons salt**
½ **teaspoon black pepper**

Fire roast the skins of the tomatoes evenly on all sides; allow to cool. Do not remove the skins! Chop the tomatoes into pieces and place them in a blender or food processor. Add the onion and chile; blend for 2 minutes. Add the oil, lime juice, salt, and pepper; blend for 30 seconds more. Keep refrigerated in an airtight nonreactive container. Serve chilled.

Fire Roasting Tomatoes

A really quick way to roast a tomato—or a chile—is to use a small blowtorch; it takes 30 seconds to roast a tomato this way. Place the tomato on a grill rack on the stovetop or on another heavy-duty surface. Using the blowtorch, scorch the skin of the tomato evenly on all sides. Allow the tomato to cool, then remove the skin if desired.

Mini or micro torches (about 6 inches tall) are also available at hardware stores. They are easier to hold than the larger ones but they will require a little more time to roast a tomato—about 60 seconds. We have even used them on fresh ears of corn. The results are wonderful.

As always when using flame, be very careful. Blowtorches are not for use by children.

ROASTED RED PEPPER SAUCE

Makes about 2 cups

Serve this sweet, colorful, intensely flavorful sauce on Sweet Corn Tamales (page 120), or on any grilled or sautéed seafood dish.

- 3 roasted* red bell peppers, peeled and seeded
- 2 cups dry white wine
- 2 tablespoons minced shallots
- 1 teaspoon minced garlic
- ½ cup heavy cream
- ¼ teaspoon ground red pepper (Cayenne pepper)
- ¾ cup butter, softened
- ½ teaspoon salt

Place the bell peppers in a food processor; purée. Set aside.

Combine the wine, shallots, and garlic in a 12-inch skillet; cook over medium heat until the liquid reduces to 3 tablespoons, about 10 minutes. Reduce the heat; add the cream, 1 tablespoon at a time, to the wine mixture; stir well. Do not let the mixture boil! Add the ground red pepper, the puréed bell peppers, and the butter to the wine mixture; mix well.

Place a medium-size sieve over a medium-size bowl. Strain the mixture, reserving the liquid; discard the solids. Add the salt, mixing well. Serve immediately, or refrigerate covered in an airtight container; reheat gently.

*See "Roasting Peppers," page 65.

UXMAL PIBIL SAUCE

Makes about 7 cups

This flavorful sauce allows you to recreate the flavor of meats cooked in the classic Mayan style—wrapped in banana leaves and pit-roasted—that are so popular throughout the Yucatán Peninsula, but you won't need the the banana leaves or the pit! Use this rich, red sauce for braising chicken, pot roasts, ribs, and pork butts.

- 1 tablespoon peanut or vegetable oil
- 1¼ cups diced onions
- ¼ cup chopped garlic cloves
- ½ green bell pepper, chopped
- ½ red bell pepper, chopped
- ½ habanero chile, chopped
- 1 very ripe plantain (make sure it's ripe!), peeled and chopped
- 2½ tablespoons chopped cilantro
- 3 sprigs fresh mint, chopped
- 1 cup Fresh Tomato Sauce (see page 88)
- 1 46-ounce can unsweetened pineapple juice
- 2 tablespoons firmly packed dark brown sugar
- 3 ounces achiote paste (for substitute, see "Achiote Paste," page 227)

Heat the oil in a 12-inch skillet. Add the onions, garlic, green and red bell peppers, chile, and plantain. Cook slowly over low heat, stirring occasionally, until the ingredients begin to brown and become soft (it will take about 20 to 30 minutes). Add the cilantro, mint, Fresh Tomato Sauce, pineapple juice, brown sugar, and achiote paste. Stir well; bring the mixture to a simmer and cook for another 10 minutes. Remove from the heat.

Place the mixture in a food processor or a blender; purée until smooth. Place a medium-size sieve over a medium-size bowl. Strain the sauce, reserving the liquid; discard the solids. If the liquid is too watery after you have strained it, return it to the skillet and cook it over medium heat until it has the desired consistency. Use immediately, or refrigerate covered in an airtight container.

Plantains
The Cooking Banana

Plantains are also known as cooking bananas. Though native to Asia, plantains are extremely popular in Latin America and used extensively in everything from soups to desserts. When green, the plantain is used just as a potato would be in soups and stews; like a potato, it can be thinly sliced and pan fried. Tostones (page 111), thinly sliced and deep-fried plantains, are a finger food that can be eaten with a variety of salsas and often appear as a staple in Latin Caribbean meals. When the plantain is yellow with black spots, it is ripening but not yet sweet. A half black, half yellow plantain is ripe, and when it's baked with a little butter, brown sugar, and cinnamon, it makes a wonderful dessert. A black plantain is really ripe, sweet, and full-flavored. It can be used to flavor sauces and curries. In all cases, plantains must be cooked before the are eaten.

ROASTED GARLIC SAUCE

Makes about 1½ cups

Try Roasted Garlic Sauce on pasta, chicken, roast pork, or on any grilled or sautéed fish; it's particularly good on sautéed calamari steaks.

- **12 whole garlic cloves, roasted (see note on this page)**
- **1 tablespoon peanut or vegetable oil**
- **2 tablespoons chopped garlic**
- **1 tablespoon all-purpose flour**
- **1 cup heavy cream**
- **½ cup milk**
- **2 teaspoons chopped fresh parsley**
- **2 teaspoons freshly squeezed lemon juice**
- **½ teaspoon salt**
- **¼ teaspoon freshly ground black pepper**

Crush half of the roasted garlic cloves in a small bowl; set aside.

Heat the oil in a 10-inch skillet. Add the raw chopped garlic, and cook over medium-high heat, stirring frequently, until the garlic begins to brown, 3 to 5 minutes. Add the flour, a little at a time, stirring constantly until a paste forms. Slowly add the cream, milk, and the reserved crushed garlic cloves, stirring constantly. Reduce the heat to low; simmer for 3 minutes. Add the parsley and lemon juice. Season with salt and pepper. Serve immediately over pasta, chicken, or fish; use the remaining whole roasted garlic cloves to garnish the dish.

Roasting Garlic

Preheat the oven to 350°F. Slice the stem end off of a whole head of garlic. Place the garlic, cut side down, in a small greased baking dish; roast until soft, about 30 minutes. Remove from the oven; cool to lukewarm. Squeeze the garlic head from the bottom, releasing the whole cloves from the cut end. Any remaining roasted garlic can be stored in the refrigerator covered in an airtight container for up to two weeks.

VERACRUZ SAUCE

Makes about 5 cups

Veracruz sauce is easy to make and very versatile. Besides being great on fish, such as grilled snapper, mahi mahi, swordfish, halibut, and barracuda, it can be used over pasta to create a tangy vegetarian entrée. Try this colorful sauce over grilled chicken, too.

- 1 tablespoon olive oil
- 3 large garlic cloves, minced
- 4 serrano chiles (add more or fewer to taste), cut lengthwise, leaving the pieces large enough to pick out of the sauce if desired.
- 1 medium onion, sliced
- 1 green bell pepper, sliced
- 1 red bell pepper, sliced
- 1 yellow bell pepper, sliced
- ½ cup Rich Chicken Stock (page 48) or white wine
- 3 tomatoes, peeled, seeded, and diced (see note below)
- 3 tablespoons coarsely chopped cilantro

Heat the olive oil in a 12-inch skillet over medium heat. When the pan is hot, add the garlic and chile; cook until they begin to sweat (about 1 minute). Add the onions and toss the ingredients in the pan; cook for 2 minutes. Add the bell peppers and cook for 2 minutes more. Add the chicken stock (or the white wine) to deglaze the pan. Cover and cook until the liquid boils and the vegetables are soft, about 1 minute. Add ⅔ of the tomatoes, cover, and cook until soft, about 2 minutes. Add the salt, stir, and remove from the heat. Add the remaining tomatoes and the cilantro, stirring gently so that the tomato pieces retain their "body." Taste the sauce; add additional salt if necessary. Serve immediately or refrigerate covered in an airtight container; reheat gently.

Skinning a Tomato

Bring a small pot of water to boil. Place the tomato in the boiling water for 45 seconds; remove it using a slotted spoon; then quickly place it in a bowl of iced water. The skin will now slip off easily.

CAYMAN CURRY SAUCE

Makes about 5 cups

This aromatic, fruity, full-flavored sauce is great on catfish, snapper, and soft-shell crab.

¼ cup peanut oil
¼ cup diced onion
1 teaspoon minced garlic
Pinch of crushed red pepper flakes
¼ cup all-purpose flour
3 cups water
4 cups unsweetened pineapple juice
2 tablespoons curry powder
½ cup raisins
½ cup shredded sweetened coconut
1 small ripe banana, chopped
½ cup chopped raw almonds
½ teaspoon salt
4 teaspoons sugar

Heat the oil in a large saucepan; add the onion, garlic, and red pepper flakes. Cook over medium heat, stirring frequently, until the onion has softened, 3 to 5 minutes. Add the flour, a little at a time, stirring constantly until a paste forms. Slowly add the water and then the pineapple juice, stirring constantly to prevent lumps. When the mixture begins to simmer, reduce the heat to low; add the curry powder, raisins, coconut, bananas, almonds, salt, and sugar. Simmer until the mixture has been reduced by one-fourth, 10 to 12 minutes.

Transfer the mixture to a blender or food processor; purée. Place a medium size sieve over a medium size bowl. Strain the mixture, reserving the liquid; discard the solids. Serve immediately or refrigerate covered in an airtight container; reheat gently.

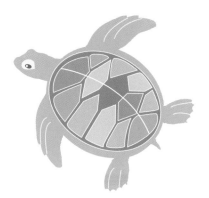

TOMATILLO SAUCE

Makes about 4 cups

This tart and tangy sauce is a wonderful sauce to use when preparing braised pork chops, a typical dish in the Yucatán area, see Pork Chops Braised in Tomatillo Sauce (page 183).

- 1½ pounds tomatillos, husks removed, rinsed in cold water
- 1 teaspoon salt
- 2 garlic cloves
- ½ bunch cilantro
- ½ medium white onion
- 1 jalapeño chile
- 1 tablespoon butter

Place the tomatillos, the garlic, cilantro, onion, and jalapeño chile in a blender or food processor; blend well until puréed.

In a 10-inch skillet, brown the butter over medium heat. Add the tomatillo mixture to the pan; bring the mixture to a rapid boil. Reduce the heat to low and simmer for 2 minutes, stirring constantly. Remove from heat. Use immediately or refrigerate covered in an airtight container for up to one week; reheat gently.

Skinning a Tomato

Bring a small pot of water to boil. Place the tomato in the boiling water for 45 seconds; remove it using a slotted spoon, then quickly place it in a bowl of iced water. The skin will now slip off easily.

FRESH TOMATO SAUCE

Makes about 4 cups

Perfect for egg dishes, pasta, and fresh fish! You can adjust the kick of this sauce with the habanero chile; add more if you like it spicy.

- 1 red bell pepper, halved and seeded
- 4 garlic cloves, peeled
- 1 medium yellow onion, chopped
- 12 tomatoes (about 5 to 6 ounces each), peeled, halved, and seeded (see note this page)
- 2 teaspoons freshly ground black pepper
- 4 teaspoons salt
- 6 tablespoons rice vinegar
- 2½ teaspoons sugar
- ¼ habanero chile, minced (use ½ if you like your sauce spicy)

Preheat the oven to 350°F. Place the bell pepper, cut side down, the garlic, and the onion in a small baking dish. Roast until soft, about 30 minutes.

Combine the roasted vegetables, tomatoes, black pepper, salt, vinegar, sugar, and chile in a food processor or a blender; purée until smooth. Cover and refrigerate, up to one week, until ready to use.

PAPAYA CURRY SAUCE

Makes about 6 cups

Even fruitier and smoother tasting than Cayman Curry Sauce, Papaya Curry Sauce is wonderful on fish or on chicken breast fillets. Use it as a dip for fried shrimp or calamari.

> **4 cups Cayman Curry Sauce (page 87)**
> **One 1-pound papaya, pared* and chopped (about 2 cups); seeds reserved**

Combine the Cayman Curry Sauce and the papaya in a food processor or blender; purée until smooth. Set aside.

Place a small sieve over a small bowl. Place the papaya seeds into the sieve; with the back of a spoon or by hand, push the seeds against the sieve to release their liquid. Add the liquid to the curry sauce; mix well. Serve immediately, or refrigerate covered in an airtight container; reheat gently.

*A papaya peels easily with a potato peeler.

CHIMICHURRI SAUCE

Makes about 4 cups

This is our version of a popular sauce served in many parts of Latin America, especially in the cattle-raising regions. Besides being used to accompany grilled meats, it makes a great marinade for steaks. Use it to baste on beef steaks when barbecuing. And for a really tasty fish dish, marinate snapper or mahi mahi fillets in Chimichurri Sauce before charbroiling them—*sabroso!*

> **4 cups coarsely chopped parsley (stems discarded)**
> **1 cup olive oil**
> **1 tablespoon garlic**
> **3 serrano chiles**
> **1½ teaspoons salt**
> **¼ teaspoon freshly ground black pepper**
> **¼ cup lime juice**

Place the parsley, olive oil, garlic, chiles, salt, and pepper in a blender or food processor; purée 3 minutes. Continue to purée while slowly adding the lime juice to the mix; purée 1 minute more. Refrigerate covered in a nonreactive airtight container for up to 2 weeks.

RED HILLS JERK SAUCE

Makes about 1½ cups

Red Hills Jerk Sauce is excellent served over rotisseried or roasted chicken—or brush it on the chicken as it roasts. This sauce is also wonderful on pork.

- ½ cup mango chutney
- ½ cup corn syrup
- 7 tablespoons cider vinegar
- 4 tablespoons Jamaican Jerk Spices, Wet (page 75)
- 8 tablespoons molasses
- ½ cup water
- 1 teaspoon bottled hot red pepper sauce

Combine the chutney, corn syrup, and 3 tablespoons of the vinegar in a food processor or blender; purée until smooth.

Combine the chutney mixture and the remaining ingredients in a small, nonreactive bowl; mix well. Serve at room temperature. Refrigerate covered in an airtight container for up to 2 weeks.

CRIOLLO MARINADE

Makes about 2½ cups

This marinade has the wonderfully smoky flavor of achiote. Use it to marinate meats such as chicken, turkey, ribs, fish, and prawns; then barbecue, sauté, or grill as you wish.

- 1 cup soy sauce
- 1 cup peanut oil
- 1 tablespoon Cajun Blackening Spices (page 76)
- 2 teaspoons freshly ground black pepper
- 4 tablespoons achiote paste (for substitute, see "Achiote Paste," page 227)
- 1 tablespoon finely minced garlic

Combine all of the marinade ingredients in a large bowl; whisk until the oil and soy sauce are well blended. Refrigerate in a clean plastic container with a tight-fitting lid for up to 2 weeks.

YELLOW PEPPER BEURRE BLANC

Makes about 1 cup

This is a quick and lovely sauce to make when yellow bell peppers are in season. Because the sauce must be used when it is ready—it will not keep in the refrigerator—make only the amount you will need for the meal at hand. Double the recipe if you are serving a large number of guests. Try Yellow Pepper Beurre Blanc on everything—fish, pork, chicken, and even rice.

- **1½ yellow bell peppers**
- **¼ cup minced shallots**
- **¼ cup dry white wine**
- **1 cup butter, cut into 16 pieces**
- **¼ teaspoon salt, or to taste**
- **1 teaspoon sugar, or to taste**

Roast and clean the yellow bell peppers (see "Roasting Peppers," page 65). Place the roasted bell peppers in a food processor or blender; purée. Set aside. (This step can be done ahead; keep the pepper purée covered and refrigerated).

Combine the shallots and white wine in a 10-inch skillet; cook over medium heat until the liquid reduces down to one-fourth of the original amount. Reduce the heat to low; add the bell pepper purée to the reduction and mix well.

Using a whisk, add the butter to the mixture, a piece at a time, as you continue to whip the ingredients. Do not let the mixture come to a boil or the sauce will break. When the butter has been incorporated into the sauce, add the salt and sugar. (Taste the sauce first; adjust the amount of sugar to your taste, depending on the sweetness of this year's pepper crop.) When the ingredients are well blended, remove the sauce from the heat. Serve immediately.

Hold The Sauce!

If you must make Yellow Pepper Beurre Blanc in advance, you can hold the sauce over a warm water bath for up to 2 hours.

MANGO BUTTER

Makes about 4 cups

If 4 cups of Mango Butter seems like an excessive amount, you can easily halve this recipe to make about 2 cups; but once you try this recipe, you'll never go back to plain butter. Mango Butter is excellent served on fish, calamari steaks, pasta, and vegetables. If you can't find passionfruit glaze, you can easily substitute your own Apricot-Lime Glaze (page 212).

> **1 pound butter, at room temperature**
> **2 ripe mangos, peeled, pits removed, and chopped (about 2 cups of fruit)**
> **4 tablespoons passionfruit glaze or Apricot-Lime Glaze**
> **2 tablespoons freshly squeezed lime juice**
> **1½ cups Japanese* or other unseasoned dried bread crumbs**
> **2 tablespoons minced fresh parsley**

Place the butter in a large bowl; using an electric mixer, whip it until it is stiff and white. Set aside.

Place the mangos in a food processor or blender; purée. Add the mango purée, passionfruit glaze, lime juice, bread crumbs, and parsley to the butter. Mix well. Cover and refrigerate in an airtight container until ready to use, or freeze it.

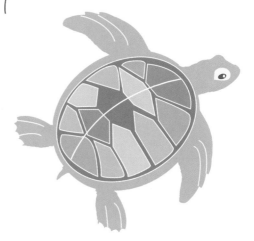

*Japanese bread crumbs (*panko*) can be found with other bread crumbs and batter mixes in most supermarkets and are available through mail order.

CHIPOTLE CHILE BUTTER

Makes about 2 cups

Use this lightly smoky, rich-flavored butter with its hint of chile to top grilled steaks or fish just before serving. Or use it for sautéing fresh vegetables, shrimp, or mushrooms—try it with portobello mushrooms for a really "meaty" vegetarian dish.

- **1 tablespoon minced shallots**
- **1 teaspoon minced garlic**
- **3 chipotle chiles (canned, smoked jalapeño chiles)**
- **¼ cup chopped fresh cilantro**
- **½ pound butter, at room temperature**

Combine the shallots, garlic, chiles, and cilantro in a food processor. Process until smooth. Place the butter in a large bowl; using an electric mixer, whip the butter until it is stiff and white. Add the shallot mixture to the butter; mix until well combined. Cover and refrigerate in an airtight container until ready to use.

Roll Up The Butter!

You can roll any compound butter in plastic wrap and shape it into a tube. After it has been refrigerated, the butter will be hard, and you can easily slice off the exact amount you need. Better yet, freeze the butter and it will keep for months.

HABANERO-PEACH BUTTER

Makes about 3 cups

This condiment is very low in sodium—but high in flavor. The recipe makes enough butter to accompany several batches of Caribbean Spiced Mahi Mahi (page 195). The butter will keep well refrigerated—just slice off the appropriate amount as you need it. Try it on other dishes; it adds a lightly spicy and fruity flavor to chicken, pork, and seafood dishes.

- **2 tablespoons olive oil**
- **2 habanero chiles, minced (4 minced jalapeño chiles may be substituted)**
- **½ medium red bell pepper, minced**
- **½ medium shallot, minced**
- **6 tablespoons balsamic vinegar***
- **1 tablespoon honey**
- **3 large ripe peaches, pitted and sliced (leave skins on for texture and color)**
- **¾ pound unsalted butter, softened**

Heat the oil over high heat in a medium saucepan. Add the chiles, bell pepper, and shallot; cook over high heat for 2 minutes. Add the vinegar and the honey to the chile mixture, reduce the heat to low and simmer until almost all the liquid has evaporated, about 3 minutes. Remove the mixture from the heat; cool.

Place 2 of the peaches and the butter in a food processor or blender. Process until well mixed. Add the cooled chile mixture to the peach and butter purée, and process until well blended. Transfer the butter mixture to a small bowl.

Mince the remaining peach by hand, add it to the butter mixture, and blend well. Cover and refrigerate in an airtight container until ready to use, or freeze it.

Roll Up The Butter!

You can roll any compound butter in plastic wrap and shape it into a tube. After it has been refrigerated, the butter will be hard, and you can easily slice off the exact amount you need. Better yet, freeze the butter and it will keep for months.

*For this recipe, do not substitute another type of vinegar for the balsamic vinegar.

ROASTED HABANERO BUTTER

Makes about 4 cups

This recipe can easily be halved to yield about 2 cups, but you'll enjoy it so much you'll just have to make more—sooner than you expect. Since it stores well and can be used for so many dishes, it's smart to make a good-sized batch. Use this flavorful compound butter to sauté vegetables; to toss with simple pastas; or to top baked potatoes, fish, and grilled steaks. Try simply buttering your bread with it; it's delicious!

- 1 teaspoon peanut oil
- 2 habanero chiles, roasted* and minced
- 1/4 cup diced onion
- 2 tablespoons minced garlic
- 1 pound butter, at room temperature
- 2 tablespoons tomato paste
- 2 tablespoons rice vinegar
- 2 tablespoons freshly squeezed lime juice
- 1 teaspoon salt
- 1 teaspoon sugar
- 6 green onions, finely chopped
- 2 tablespoons chopped fresh parsley
- 1/2 cup finely chopped Brazil nuts
- 1/2 cup Japanese** or other unseasoned dried bread crumbs

Heat the oil in an 8-inch skillet. Cook the roasted chiles, diced onion, and garlic over medium-high heat until golden brown, about 5 minutes. Remove from the heat; cool.

Place the butter in a large bowl; using an electric mixer, whip it until it is stiff and white. Add the cooled vegetable mixture to the whipped butter; mix, using the electric mixer, to combine. Add the tomato paste, vinegar, lime juice, salt, and sugar; continue to mix until all the ingredients are well combined. Add the green onions, parsley, Brazil nuts, and bread crumbs; mix well. Remove the compound butter from the mixer, cover and refrigerate in an airtight plastic container until ready to use, or freeze it.

*See "Roasting Peppers," page 65.

**Japanese bread crumbs (*panko*) can be found with other bread crumbs and batter mixes in most supermarkets and are available through mail order.

SEA TURTLES

G reen sea turtles have been navigating the open oceans since the time of the dinosaurs, more than 150 million years ago. These ancient reptiles are well adapted for their water world. Over the eons, the sea turtles' limbs have evolved into powerful flippers that can propel them through the water at speeds up to 35MPH. Their shells are lighter and more streamlined than those of land-bound tortoises. And while sea turtles cannot retract their heads into their shells as most land turtles can, their shells have been called "the most highly developed protective armor" of any vertebrates that have ever lived. Salt glands located behind their eyes allow sea turtles to rid their bodies of excess salt absorbed from seawater—they do this by shedding "salt tears." And even though turtles are air breathing and must come to the surface for air every few minutes, when they are resting or asleep, adult sea turtles can remain on the bottom for several hours. This is because sea turtles can tolerate higher concentrations of carbon dioxide in their blood than other air-breathing animals can, and they can store up large quantities of oxygen in their muscles and blood that their bodies can utilize when they are sleeping.

The green sea turtle is one of seven species of sea turtle. An adult green can reach up to five feet in length and weigh up to four hundred pounds. The life span of this turtle is thought to be forty to fifty years—some even say up to eighty years—but no one really knows for sure. It wasn't until the 1950s that scientists even began studying sea turtles seriously, and this study has been complicated by the fact that these generally solitary turtles swim over vast distances and across international boundaries, usually under water and, therefore, out of sight.

Green sea turtles can be found grazing in lagoons and bays throughout the warmer oceans and the Mediterranean Sea, but their most important nesting beaches are Tortuguero in Costa Rica, Aves Island in the Caribbean, and Ascención Island in the middle of the Atlantic Ocean. Every two or three years, when it's time to nest, the female returns to lay her eggs on the same beach where she herself was hatched. It is often a long voyage and, in some cases, an incredible one: turtles that usually graze in the sea grass pastures off of Brazil swim twenty-eight hundred miles round trip to nest on the shores of tiny Ascención Island. This island is only seven miles wide—it can't be seen from more than a few miles away. The migrating turtles, swimming against the current, must navigate through miles and miles of empty ocean—with no visible reference points to guide them—to arrive at this specific island. How the sea turtles locate Ascención Island, or any of their nesting beaches, is still a mystery to scientists. They theorize that the turtles must be using the earth's magnetic fields to navigate, or that, in conjunction with the magnetic fields, the turtles are also orienting themselves to the sun and using it as a compass.

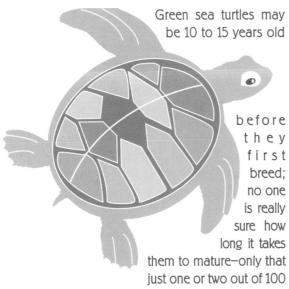

Green sea turtles may be 10 to 15 years old before they first breed; no one is really sure how long it takes them to mature—only that just one or two out of 100 hatchlings will ever make it to adulthood. Breeding takes place on the water's surface. The male has a longer tail than the female and he uses it to grasp the female during mating. With the male clasped onto the female's back, his slightly concave bottom shell fitting over her top shell, the two ride the waves in a nuptial embrace that can last for hours. Many weeks later, when the breeding season is over, the male turtle will return to his sea grass pastures, while the female, with hundreds of eggs fertilized by multiple males developing within her, prepares to nest on her natal beach.

The female waits for nightfall before crawling up onto the beach where she will seek a spot above the high tide mark for her nest. Since she is built for swimming, this land journey is difficult for her—she must drag herself (and she can weigh several hundred pounds) over the sand with her front flippers. She digs her nest patiently, using her rear flippers to scoop out the sand and fling it away, until she has dug a U-shaped hole as deep as her flippers can reach. When the hole is deep enough, she begins releasing her eggs—up to 100 eggs that look and feel like soft ping-pong balls. All the while the turtle seems like she's in a trance; curious people, loud noises, and even menacing dogs surrounding her will not distract the turtle once this process of egg laying has begun. Tears leak from her eyes—but this is from the gland that washes excess salt water from her system. When the eggs have been deposited in the hole, she begins the laborious process of covering up the nest before she again negotiates the beach. She drags herself, now exhausted, towards the water, leaving in her wake tracks that look like a small tractor has passed over the sand.

But she is not finished. Over the next several weeks, the female will return to the beach to build a new nest and lay more eggs every two weeks, until she has made up to seven nests. And all through this breeding season she has gone without eating. After the nesting season ends, she will make the long journey back to her feeding grounds and begin to regain the weight she has lost. It may take her four years to get into breeding shape again.

Meanwhile back on the beach, warmed by the sun, the turtle embryos develop in their eggs. Like crocodiles, the sex of the developing turtle embryo is determined by the incubation temperature. Days with sand temperatures of less than 84°F produce more males, while warmer days with temperatures above 85°F will produce more females. More extreme temperatures will produce turtles of all one sex.

After a period of 2 to 3 months, the baby turtles are ready to hatch from their eggs. Using an egg tooth—a temporary spine on the tip of their nose—the turtles scratch an opening in the leathery eggshell. For a day or two after they have "pipped," the tiny turtles wait quietly, until all of a sudden the entire nest comes alive in a surge of energy, and all the little turtles work together to dig out from the nest. The hatchlings emerge from their nest at night—daylight would make them easy targets for gulls and pelicans—and immediately make their way down the beach and out to the sea.

There are dangers awaiting them at night, too: crabs and raccoons patrolling the beach, hungry sharks, bluefish, and mackerel waiting in the water. Lights from new developments along the beaches can confuse the baby turtles because the hatchlings orient to the sea by light. Until recent times, the sea was illuminated by the moon and stars, while the dunes and sand were relatively dark. Now with electric lights shining at night, the baby turtles can head the wrong way, get caught by the rising sun, and dehydrate, or be drawn to the highways and run over by cars.

Baby turtles are poor swimmers, so those who do make it to sea tend to float along on beds of sargassum weed. Drifting on currents away from their natal beaches, the young turtles feed on tiny crabs and shrimp. As they develop and mature, their diets change to a vegetarian one based on sea grasses. Eventually, they arrive at their adult sea pastures off the continental coasts where they will stay until they are ready to breed. Though years have passed, when it's time to breed, the newly mature turtles will unerringly return to their ancestral breeding grounds—making the same amazing journey that countless generations of sea turtles have made before them.

Green sea turtles used to be so plentiful that Columbus, sailing the Caribbean, named three islands *Las Tortugas* because of the prevalence of green sea turtles he saw there. One of his crew, noting the abundance of the turtles, said that the waters off of the Cayman Islands seemed to be full of little rocks. Sadly, this is not the case today. Green sea turtles have long been hunted for their meat and for their eggs. Green turtle meat is the prized ingredient in turtle soup. While some species of sea turtles feed on shellfish and fish, adult greens graze only on algae and sea grasses. This vegetarian diet may explain why their meat is so tasty. (In fact, the green sea turtle's name comes from the color of its body fat, which is green from its vegetarian diet—not from the color of its shell, which is actually olive green or dark brown.) The green sea turtle's eggs have long been regarded as aphrodisiacs, as well as good eating. And while countries have passed laws against the slaughter of nesting turtles and against the taking of their eggs, poaching is still a lucrative side line, especially when third world countries have little money for patrols and enforcement of these laws.

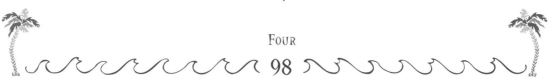

In recent times, green sea turtles have also had to contend with a series of environmental problems caused by man. As Anne and Jack Rudloe chronicle, besides being killed for meat, jewelry, cosmetics and leather, and having their nesting grounds taken by land developers for hotels, beach houses, and strip malls, the turtles are disoriented by bright lights on beaches, drowned in fishing nets meant for shrimp, ground up by dredges used to maintain open shipping channels, run over by pleasure boats, poisoned by pollution, entangled by marine debris and fishing line, and starved by ingesting plastic trash, mistaken for food, that will not pass through their digestive systems.

Traditionally, the turtle has held an important role in the mythology of many cultures. Some ancients believed that the world was carried on the back of a giant turtle, others believed that the turtle saved mankind from the Big Flood by ferrying humans on its back. The Mayas carved turtles into their temples as symbols of fertility and as gods of rain. The Iroquois, the Seneca, and the Maidu, as well as other Native American tribes, have honored Turtle as central to their creation myths. Ironically, it seems that the fate of the turtle, which legend credits with saving, supporting, and providing for mankind, is now in the hands of man. The future of the sea turtle population depends on the creation and application of wise and judicious laws of commerce and environmental development.

CHELONIA MYDAS

Chapter 5

Appetizers

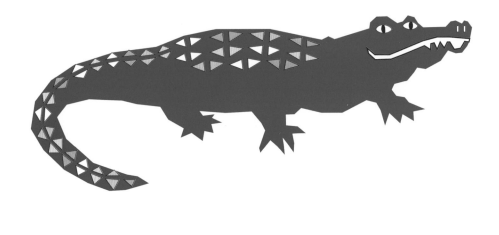

SWEET POTATO CORN CAKES

Makes 18 patties

Besides being a spicy-sweet appetizer that really wakes up your taste buds, these little cakes make a great side dish or accompaniment to a vegetarian meal. Serve them hot, topped with a compound butter such as Mango Butter (page 92), Chipotle Chile Butter (page 93), or Roasted Habanero Butter (page 95), or with a spicy sauce such as Roasted Red Pepper Sauce (page 83).

> 4 cups baked or canned sweet potatoes (or yams)
> 1 cup corn
> 2 tablespoons minced jalapeño or serrano chiles
> 2 tablespoons chopped red bell pepper
> 4 green onions, minced (optional)
> $\frac{1}{2}$ cup shredded Monterey Jack cheese (optional)
> 2 cups Japanese* or other unseasoned dried bread crumbs
> $\frac{1}{4}$ cup honey
> $\frac{1}{2}$ teaspoon ground cinnamon
> $\frac{1}{2}$ teaspoon freshly ground nutmeg
> 2 eggs

Mash the sweet potatoes in a large bowl, using a potato masher or a fork. Add the remaining ingredients to the sweet potatoes; mix well.

Using your hands, form the mixture into 18 patties, each about $\frac{1}{2}$ inch thick and $2\frac{1}{2}$ inches in diameter. If the mixture won't hold together, add more bread crumbs, 1 tablespoon at a time.

Spray a 12-inch skillet with nonstick cooking oil spray (or use just enough peanut oil to cover the bottom of the pan). Heat the pan; cook the patties over medium heat, turning once, until golden brown, about 6 minutes. Do not overcrowd the pan; cook in batches. Serve hot topped with a compound butter or a tangy sauce.

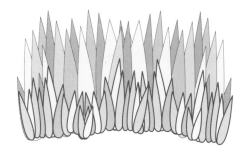

*Japanese bread crumbs (*panko*) can be found with other bread crumbs and batter mixes in most supermarkets and are available through mail order.

GUACAMOLE

Makes about 3 cups

Serve in a bowl garnished with 2 or 3 thin slices of lime or a sprig of cilantro. Guacamole tastes great with tortilla chips, Flautas (page 113), or Tostones (page111). It also makes a great garnish for tacos, tostadas, fajitas, enchiladas, and other Mexican entrées.

- **2 large Haas avocados, ripe but not mushy, peeled and pitted**
- **¼ cup freshly squeezed lemon juice**
- **⅓ cup diced onions**
- **2 teaspoons minced serrano or jalapeño chiles**
- **½ cup diced tomato**
- **⅓ cup diced red bell pepper**
- **1 tablespoon chopped fresh cilantro**
- **1 teaspoon salt**
- **½ teaspoon freshly ground black pepper**

Using a fork, coarsely mash the avocados in a medium-size bowl; add the lemon juice; mix well. Add the remaining ingredients to the avocado mixture; stir until uniformly mixed. Refrigerate, covered, in an airtight nonreactive container until ready to use.

Note

HOW TO KEEP GUACAMOLE FROM TURNING BROWN:

- Reserve the avocado pit and place it in the bowl with the guacamole.

- Sprinkle lemon juice over the exposed surface of the guacamole; mix well before serving.

- Keep the guacamole tightly covered and refrigerated.

SPICY PECANS

Makes about 2 cups

Use these nuts as beer or cocktail accompaniments or as a garnish on green salads or pastas. Before storing the nuts, be sure they have cooled completely, or they'll loose their crunchiness.

- **2 tablespoons butter**
- **1 teaspoon olive oil**
- **1 pound whole pecans**
- **1 tablespoon crushed red pepper flakes**

Combine the butter and oil in a 10-inch skillet; cook over medium heat until the butter melts. Add the pecans to the butter mixture; cook, stirring frequently, 10 minutes. Add the red pepper flakes; cook, stirring frequently, 5 minutes more. Remove from the heat; place in a colander, and drain the excess oil. Cool. When the nuts are completely cool, store them, covered, in an airtight container.

SPICY ROASTED PEANUTS

Makes about 2 cups

Whip up a batch of Spicy Roasted Peanuts to use as a garnish and to add crunch and zing to casseroles. Serve them as a finger food with soft drinks, beer, or cocktails. It is important to use a thick habanero hot sauce or another thick hot pepper sauce in this recipe; Tabasco sauce or similarly watery hot sauces will make the nuts soggy.

- **One 1-pound can of honey roasted peanuts**
- **2 tablespoons habanero hot sauce**

Preheat the oven to 300°F.

Combine the peanuts and the habanero sauce in a small bowl; toss until all of the peanuts are well coated. Spread the nuts onto a cookie sheet; bake until the nuts are dry and crunchy, 6 to 10 minutes.

Cool uncovered. Store cooled nuts, covered, in an airtight container. (Don't place them in the storage container until they are completely cooled or they will get soft!)

ARMADILLO EGGS
STUFFED JALAPEÑO PEPPER

Serves 4 to 6

These stuffed chiles make great adult finger food at barbecues, parties, and informal gatherings. Serve them with Sweet Jalapeño Dipping Sauce (page 81).

16 large jalapeños, roasted
16 strips (¼ x 1 inch) Monterey Jack or cheddar cheese
½ cup yellow cornmeal
½ cup Japanese* or other unseasoned dried bread crumbs
½ cup all-purpose flour
¼ teaspoon salt
3 eggs
Peanut or vegetable oil, for deep frying

Preheat the oven to 350°F. Spray the peppers with non-stick cooking spray (or rub lightly with oil). Place the chiles on a baking sheet; bake until the skins begin to blister, about 20 minutes. Remove them from the oven and place them, hot, into a plastic bag; seal the bag. Set aside for 10 minutes to allow the chiles to sweat. Remove the chiles from the bag; under cold, running water, carefully peel off their skins—be careful not to split the chiles open. Leave the stems on.

Place chiles onto a work surface; with a thin-bladed, sharp knife, cut a small slit in each chile to remove the seeds. Using your fingertips, open the slit just enough to stuff in one strip of cheese. Set aside.

Mix the cornmeal, bread crumbs, flour, and salt in a medium-size bowl; stir well. Place the eggs in a small bowl; beat.

Dip one stuffed chile into the egg mixture, then into the cornmeal mixture, and coat completely; transfer to a plate. Repeat for the remaining chiles. Set aside for 10 minutes to allow the coating to set.

Heat 6 inches of oil in a deep fryer, or in a deep, heavy skillet, to 325°F. Carefully lower the chiles into the hot oil; fry until golden brown, 2 to 3 minutes. Drain the chiles on paper towels. Serve with dipping sauce or salsas.

*Japanese bread crumbs (*panko*) can be found with other bread crumbs and batter mixes in most supermarkets and are available through mail order.

CHICHA DE PIÑA

Serves 4

This tropical American beverage is a great non-alcoholic accompaniment to barbecue, seafood, and spicy Mexican entrées—as well as an excellent choice for luncheons. It can be served either hot or cold. Since it utilizes the skin and the core of a fresh pineapple—the parts usually discarded—it's the perfect way to get the maximum yield from the "king of fruits." So, the next time you buy a pineapple to make a salsa or a dessert, save the core and skin and enjoy a refreshing Chicha de Piña.

1 fresh, ripe pineapple, fruit removed (reserve for another use), skin and core chopped

2 tablespoons coarsely chopped fresh ginger root

6 cups water

¾ cup sugar

2 tablespoons freshly squeezed lime juice

Mint sprigs, optional

Cinnamon sticks, optional

Combine the pineapple skin and core, ginger, and water in a medium saucepan; bring to a boil. Add ½ cup of the sugar, reduce the heat to low, and simmer until the flavors are released, about 15 minutes. Remove from the heat.

Place the pineapple mixture in a food processor or blender; coarsely chop. Place a medium-size sieve over a medium-size bowl; add the chopped pineapple mixture and strain. Reserve the liquid; discard the solids. Cool.

When the liquid has cooled, add the lime juice. Sweeten to taste with the remaining sugar; the drink should be slightly tart. Serve chilled, garnished with sprigs of mint, if desired. Or, heat gently before serving and garnish with cinnamon sticks, if desired.

Note

COOKING WITH THE KING OF FRUITS

Pineapples contain *bromelain*, an enzyme that breaks down protein. This means that meats marinated in fresh pineapple will be tender, but gelatin dishes will not set. Don't mix fresh pineapple with dairy products until the last minute.

FLAMINGO BAY SHRIMP CAKES WITH BRAZIL NUTS AND HABANERO BUTTER

Serves 4 or 8

This dish, which always gets rave reviews, will serve 4 as a luncheon entrée and 8 as an appetizer course.

½ pound calamari steak
3 eggs
1½ teaspoons salt
¾ teaspoon hot red pepper sauce
¼ teaspoon curry powder
1 cube (4 ounces) butter, melted
3 green onions, finely chopped
½ cup chopped Brazil nuts
1 pound rock shrimp, chopped
2½ cups Japanese* or other
    unseasoned dried bread crumbs
Peanut oil, for cooking
4 tablespoons Roasted Habanero
    Butter (page 95)
½ cup heavy cream
6 tablespoons Salsa Fresca (page 67)

Place the calamari steak in a food processor or blender; purée until it forms a paste.

Combine the eggs, salt, red pepper sauce, curry powder, and melted butter in a large bowl. Mix in the calamari purée. Add the green onions, Brazil nuts, and shrimp; stir well. Add the bread crumbs, a little at a time, mixing well after each addition.

Form the mixture into 16 patties. Heat about 1 tablespoon of oil in a 12-inch skillet. Cook the patties over medium heat, turning once, until brown and crispy, 8 to 9 minutes. Be careful not to overcrowd the pan; fry in batches if necessary.

While the patties are cooking, combine the Roasted Habanero Butter and the cream in a small saucepan; cook over low heat just until the butter melts and mixes with the cream. To serve, spoon the warm Habanero Butter sauce over the cooked cakes, and top each cake with a teaspoon of Salsa Fresca. Serve immediately.

*Japanese bread crumbs (panko) can be found with other bread crumbs and batter mixes in most supermarkets and are available through mail order.

TOSTADITAS

Makes 30 appetizers

If you don't have Chicken Criollo on hand, any leftover shredded beef, pork, lamb, shrimp, or seafood will do as tasty substitutions. Or, try crumbled, cooked chorizo or linguiça sausage.

> **2 cups mashed potatoes**
> **2 cups prepared masa harina***
> **Peanut oil, for frying**
> **¾ cup Green Cashew Sauce (page 81)**
> **½ pound shredded Chicken Breast Criollo (page 191)**
> **1¼ cups Salsa Brava (page 66)**

Flatten each ball with your fingertips to form a circle about 2½ inches in diameter.

Mix the mashed potatoes and masa harina together in a large bowl. Shape the mixture into 30 balls, about 1 ounce each. Flatten each ball with the fingers of your hand to form flat disks about 2½ inches in diameter. Press the edges of each disk with your fingertips to form a smooth, uniform rim.

Heat 2 inches of oil in a deep fryer or deep, heavy skillet, to 370°F. Fry 5 to 6 tostaditas at a time (do not overcrowd the pan) until golden brown on the outside, 3 to 5 minutes. As the tostaditas are done, remove them from the pan; drain on paper towels. Repeat until all the tostaditas are fried.

Spread about 1 teaspoon of the Green Cashew Sauce on each tostadita, top with 1 tablespoon of the shredded chicken. Garnish each Tostadita with 2 teaspoons of Salsa Brava. Serve warm.

*Prepared according to the package to make the *masa*—or dough—for tortillas. The mixture should have the consistency of pie dough. Add more water if needed. For more on masa harina, see page 228.

CASUELITAS

Makes 20 appetizers

These golden-fried "little pans" (or casseroles) are the perfect containers for any savory filling. This recipe calls for zucchini, but be creative! Try crabmeat, sautéed shrimp, Avocado Salsa (page 72), chili, or Black Beans Otomí (page147) topped with Crème Fraîche (page 51).

6 tablespoons Chipotle Chile Butter (page 93)
2 pounds zucchini, diced
4 tablespoons freshly grated Parmesan cheese
2 cups mashed potatoes
2 cups prepared masa harina*
Peanut or vegetable oil, for deep frying

Melt the butter in a 12-inch skillet. Add the zucchini; cook, over medium heat, stirring often, until slightly soft, 3 to 4 minutes. Add the cheese; stir and remove from the heat immediately. Set aside.

Mix the mashed potatoes and masa harina in a large bowl. Shape the mixture into 20 balls, about 1½ ounces each. Press your thumb deeply into the center of each ball; continue shaping the dough, pinching and rotating it, to form a little "pan" that is 2½ inches in diameter and ½ inch deep.

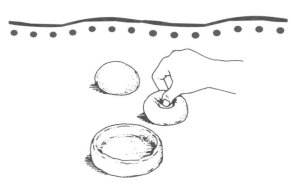

Press your thumb into the center of each ball; continue pinching and rotating the dough until you form a little "pan" 2½ inches in diameter, with ½-inch sides.

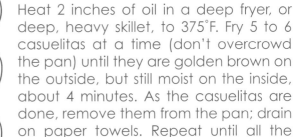

Heat 2 inches of oil in a deep fryer, or deep, heavy skillet, to 375°F. Fry 5 to 6 casuelitas at a time (don't overcrowd the pan) until they are golden brown on the outside, but still moist on the inside, about 4 minutes. As the casuelitas are done, remove them from the pan; drain on paper towels. Repeat until all the casuelitas are fried.

Fill the casuelitas evenly with the zucchini mixture. Serve immediately.

*Prepared according to the package to make the *masa*—or dough—for tortillas. The mixture should have the consistency of pie dough. Add more water if needed. For more on masa harina, see page 228.

TOSTONES

Serves 4

These firm, golden-fried plantain patties are easy to make and very versatile. They make great appetizers, or you can serve them as accompaniments to an entrée. Place them along side Seafood Ceviche (page 149) for a knockout taste combination, or with Black Beans Otomí (page 147) and Crème Fraîche (page 51). Tostones are the perfect utensils for any of the fresh salsas—they make great scoops.

2 medium-sized green plantains (they must be green), sliced in 1-inch-thick segments (about 6 slices per plantain)
Peanut oil, for deep frying
Salt, to taste

Heat 2 inches of oil in a deep fryer or deep, heavy skillet to 350°F. Carefully add the plantain sections to the hot oil. Fry until they are golden brown and begin to float, about 5 minutes.

Remove the plantains from the oil; drain on paper towels. Salt to taste while they are still hot. Place each plantain section between two pieces of waxed paper or two cloth napkins; press the plantain with the heel of your hand, forming a little golden patty about ¼ inch thick.

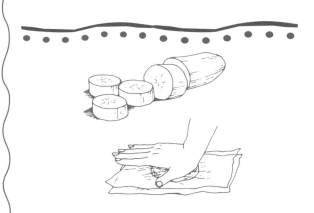

Place each fried plantain between two pieces of waxed paper. Press plantain with the heel of your hand to form a little golden patty about ¼ inch thick.

Reheat the oil to 350°F. Refry the pressed tostones, turning once, for 3 minutes. Remove from the oil; drain on paper towels. Salt again if necessary.

MUSSELS IN CILANTRO AND SERRANO CREAM SAUCE

Serves 2

This dish looks as good as it tastes. The broth is especially tasty, so be sure to serve it with plenty of bread. Try varying the recipe with small clams such as manilas, cockles, or littlenecks. Garnish with Salsa Fresca (page 67) if you want to add a little more color and tang—and don't forget the warm French bread!

- 1 teaspoon olive oil
- 2 tablespoons butter
- 2 teaspoons minced shallots
- 1 teaspoon minced garlic
- 12 New Zealand green-lipped mussels (or use the local variety), in their shells, scrubbed, cleaned, and debearded
- 1/2 cup dry white wine
- 1/4 cup heavy cream
- 1 tomato, diced
- 1/4 cup diced red onion
- 1 tablespoon chopped fresh cilantro
- 1 serrano or jalapeño chile, minced
- Salsa Fresca optional

Heat the oil and butter in a 12-inch skillet. Add the shallots, garlic, mussels, and wine; cook over medium heat, covered, until the mussels open, about 3 minutes. (Discard any mussels that haven't opened.) Reduce the heat to low, and simmer, uncovered, until the liquid has been reduced by half, about

4 minutes. Add the cream, tomato, onion, cilantro, and chile; cook for 2 minutes more.

To serve, arrange the mussels on a serving plate. Continue cooking the cream sauce in the pan over medium heat until it is reduced by half, about 2 minutes more.

Pour the sauce over the mussels and serve immediately. Garnish with Salsa Fresca if you wish.

Note

Since the shellfish need room to open, only two servings can be made in one pan. For additional servings, just repeat the process. If you're feeling adventurous, double the recipe and cook it in two separate pans simultaneously.

Cilantro

Cilantro is also known as Chinese parsley. It's the fresh green leaves of the coriander plant; the dried seeds of the plant are ground to make the spice known as coriander. Fresh cilantro is available in many supermarkets as well as in Asian and Latin markets.

FLAUTAS DE CAMARONES
SHRIMP FLUTES

Makes about 3 cups

Flauta is the Spanish word for "flute", and these crunchy, golden-brown flutes—each stuffed with a shrimp—make great finger food for parties as well as favorite luncheon or informal dinner entrées. Be sure to cook them in several batches, so the oil remains at 350°F, or else the Flautas will be soggy and greasy. Properly cooked, they'll be crispy on the outside and the shrimp will be juicy and tender within. Serve with Guacamole (page 104) and Green Cashew Sauce (page 81), or with Salsa Brava (page 66) and Crème Fraîche (page 51). Add a side of Black Beans Otomí (page 147), some rice, and a green salad and you've got dinner!

Peanut oil for deep frying
12 (4-inch) corn tortillas
12 extra-large shrimp (16-20 size), butterflied

Heat 2 inches of oil in a deep fryer or deep, heavy skillet, to 350°F. Using tongs, dip the tortillas, three or four at a time, into the hot oil until they have softened, 6 to 10 seconds. Drain on paper towels and cool.

Place 1 shrimp, opened lengthwise near the bottom of one tortilla. Roll the shrimp in the tortilla and secure it with a toothpick. Repeat to make 12 flautas.

Fry the Flautas in the hot oil in several batches until the tortilla is crispy and lightly golden, about 2 minutes. Serve warm.

Selecting Shrimp

Shrimp is named and priced by its size and the number per pound. No two sources seem to agree on the exact definition of these size and weight categories; but here's a list you can use as a guide.

Colossal	Fewer than 10 to a pound
Jumbo	10-15 to a pound
Extra large	16-20 to a pound
Large	21-25 to a pound
Medium	26-30 to a pound
Small	31-35 to a pound
Tiny	36 or more to a pound

1. Butterfly each shrimp.

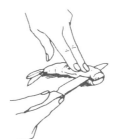

2. Place 1 shrimp along the bottom of a tortilla.

3. Roll the shrimp in the tortilla and secure with a toothpick.

EMPANADAS DE QUESO

Makes 8 empanadas

Empanadas are typical street food found all over the Yucatán, Central America, and the Caribbean. Each country—and each region—has its own "typical" recipe for these tasty cheese- or meat-filled deep-fried pastries. This recipe uses potatoes and corn in its dough, and cheese as its filling—you can experiment with other fillings. For a full-flavored, savory snack, serve Empanadas de Queso as they do in Playa del Carmen, topped with Salsa Brava (page 66) or Tomatillo and Avocado Salsa (page 70).

- **2 medium baking potatoes, peeled and diced**
- **4 cups cool water**
- **2 teaspoons salt**
- **1 cup of masa harina***
- **½ cup + 4 teaspoons warm water**
- **¾ cup shredded Monterey Jack cheese**
- **¾ cup shredded mozzarella cheese**
- **1 cup peanut oil, for cooking**

Place the diced potatoes in a 3-quart saucepan, add the cool water, and bring the liquid to a boil over high heat. Reduce the heat to medium and cook the potatoes, covered, for 8 minutes. Remove from heat and drain through a colander. Place the potatoes in a medium-size bowl and mash with a fork. Add 1 teaspoon of salt and mix well.

Combine 1 cup of masa harina and 1 teaspoon of salt in a medium-size mixing bowl; mix well. Add the warm water and mix using your hands. When the masa has the consistency of the mashed potatoes, combine the masa and the mashed potatoes and mix very well using your hands. There should be about 2 cups of the masa/potato mix. Set aside. In a small bowl, combine the Jack cheese and the mozzarella cheese, mixing loosely with your fingers.

Divide the dough into 8 equal-sized balls. Place a ball onto a plastic bag or a sheet of plastic wrap. Cover with

*Masa harina and cornmeal are not the same thing. Masa harina is made from kernels of corn that have been soaked in lime, dried, and then specially ground. Masa is traditionally used to make tamales and tortillas; it is available in the flour section of many supermarkets and in Latin grocery stores as well as through mail order.

another plastic bag or sheet and, using your hand, press the ball into a disk about 5 inches in diameter. Remove the cover. Place 3 tablespoons of the cheese mix into the center of the disk; using the bottom plastic sheet, fold the disk over and press the ends together with your finger tips, forming a "turnover". Repeat the procedure with the remaining balls of dough.

In a 12-inch skillet or a wok, heat 1 cup of peanut oil over medium heat until the oil is 325°F. Place 3 empanadas into the pan and cook until brown, turning once, about 3 minutes. Remove from the oil and drain on paper towels. Repeat with the remaining empanadas. Serve hot, topped with Salsa Brava or Tomatillo Avocado Salsa. If you want to make these ahead, they can be reheated in a toaster oven.

CROCODILE TEARS

Serves 2

This drink is festive and tropical; it's refreshing on a hot day, and goes well with spicy appetizers. Besides tasting so good—it's unbelievably simple to make! This recipe makes two individual glasses of Tears; for more servings, increase the recipe proportionately and use a pitcher.

> 1/2 cup ice
> 2 slices each: lemon, orange, and grapefruit (peels on)
> 1 cup white wine
> 1 cup lemon-lime soda
>   (e.g. 7-Up, Sprite)
> Maraschino cherries, for garnish

Divide the ice into two large glasses; place a slice of lemon, orange, and grapefruit into each. Using a spoon, smash the fruit against the ice to release the juices. Add 1/2 cup of the white wine and 1/2 cup of the soda to each glass; stir. Garnish with the maraschino cherries and serve immediately.

QUESADILLAS

Serves 4

A quesadilla is a cheese-filled tortilla turnover. This is a real crowd pleaser—and kids love them. The variations on the basic quesadilla are endless. They make a quick lunch or casual dinner entrée—just add a green salad and maybe a side of beans or rice.

- ½ pound Monterey Jack cheese, shredded
- ½ pound sharp cheddar cheese, shredded
- ½ pound mozzarella cheese, shredded
- 4 (12-inch) flour tortillas
- 2 cups Tomatillo and Avocado Salsa (page 70) or Fire-Roasted Red Tomato Sauce (page 82)

In a medium-size bowl, loosely mix the cheeses together using your fingers. Divide the cheese mixture into four equal portions. Heat a flat grill or a 12-inch skillet to 300°F over medium heat; place the tortilla on the grill or in the pan; spread one portion of cheese evenly over the tortilla. When the cheese begins to melt, about 2 minutes, fold the tortilla in half and continue to cook for 4 minutes, turning once. Repeat with the remaining tortillas.

Cut each quesadilla into 4 pieces; serve each portion with ½ cup of salsa.

VARIATIONS ON THE BASIC QUESADILLA:

When the cheese is melting on the tortilla, add 6 tablespoons of additional filling (see possibilities below), spreading evenly over the cheese; fold the tortilla and continue to cook as above.

QUESADILLAS WITH CHORIZO
- 1½ cups of sliced or crumbled, cooked Chorizo (page 148)

CHICKEN QUESADILLAS
- 1½ cups of chopped, cooked chicken

SHRIMP QUESADILLAS
- 1½ cups of chopped, grilled shrimp

JAMAICAN CURRY CRAB CAKES

Serves 4 to 6

These tasty crab cakes make excellent appetizers, welcome at any occasion. They're also great luncheon entrées. The distinctive curry flavor blends well with the taste of the crabmeat. Serve them with Cayman Curry Sauce (page 87), and garnish with Salsa Fresca (page 67).

> **2 cups (about 1 pound) crabmeat (rock or Dungeness crab)**
> **3 eggs**
> **½ teaspoon salt**
> **¼ teaspoon hot red pepper sauce**
> **1 teaspoon curry powder**
> **1 tablespoon chopped fresh parsley**
> **2 tablespoons melted butter**
> **½ cup cashew nuts, finely chopped**
> **1 cup Japanese* or other unseasoned dried bread crumbs**
> **Peanut oil, for cooking**

Place a medium-size colander into a medium-size bowl; add the crabmeat, and set aside to drain.

Beat the eggs in a medium-size bowl; add the salt, red pepper sauce, curry powder, and parsley; mix well. Stir in the melted butter; set aside.

Squeeze the crabmeat to eliminate any excess water, and shred it with your fingers (be on the look out for any shell fragments!). Add the crabmeat to the egg mixture; stir to combine. Add the cashew nuts and the bread crumbs to the bowl; stir well. Cover and refrigerate for 1 hour.

Shape the chilled crab mixture into 12 patties. Heat about 1 tablespoon of the oil in 12-inch skillet. Cook the patties over medium heat, turning once, until golden brown, about 7 minutes. Be careful not to overcrowd the pan; fry in batches if necessary. Serve immediately.

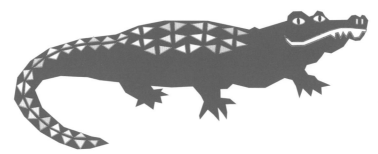

*Japanese bread crumbs (*panko*) can be found with other bread crumbs and batter mixes in most supermarkets and are available through mail order.

CHICKEN PUPUSAS
SALVADORIAN–STYLE STUFFED TORTILLAS

Serves 6

The pupusa is a traditional "fast food" sold by street vendors in El Salvador. It's a thick, handmade tortilla stuffed with a savory filling and cooked to a golden brown. Other versions of pupusas, called by different names, are popular throughout Central America. Some favorite fillings include cheese, chicken, and pork skin cracklings. Serve garnished with Salsa Brava (page 66) or Pico de Gallo (page 71), and a side of Black Beans Otomí (page 147).

- 3 ¾ cups masa harina*
- 2 ½ cups warm water
- ½ teaspoon freshly ground black pepper
- 1 teaspoon cumin
- ½ teaspoon hot red pepper sauce
- 1 green bell pepper, chopped
- 4 tomatoes, chopped
- 1 medium red onion, chopped
- ½ cup shredded mozzarella cheese
- ⅔ cup shredded, cooked chicken
- 2 tablespoons corn oil for cooking

Combine the masa harina and water in a medium-size bowl. Mix thoroughly until the dough just holds together; it will have the consistency of pie dough. Divide the dough into 12 balls: six 2-ounce balls and six 3-ounce balls. (The larger balls will make bottoms for the stuffed pupusas; the smaller balls will serve as the lids.) Set aside.

Place the black pepper, cumin, red pepper sauce, bell pepper, tomatoes, and onion in a food processor or blender; purée until well blended.

Flatten one 3-ounce ball of tortilla dough into a 5½- to 6½-inch disk. In the center of the tortilla, place 1 tablespoon of the puréed vegetable mixture, 1 tablespoon of the mozzarella cheese, and 2 tablespoons of the shredded chicken meat.

Flatten one 2-ounce ball of tortilla dough into a 4- to 5-inch disk and place it over the larger tortilla, covering the filling. Press the edges of both tortillas together so that they form a sealed pocket. Repeat this process five more times.

*Masa harina and cornmeal are not the same thing. Masa harina is made from kernels of corn that have been soaked in lime, dried, and then specially ground. Masa is traditionally used to make tamales and tortillas; it is available in the flour section of many supermarkets and in Latin grocery stores as well as through mail order.

CHICKEN PUPUSAS, cont.
SALVADORIAN-STYLE STUFFED TORTILLAS

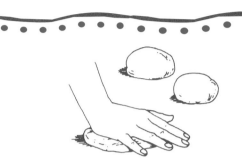

1. Flatten each ball of dough.

2. Place a smaller tortilla over the filing and seal the edges.

Pour 1 teaspoon of oil into a medium-size nonstick skillet and spread it around with a paper towel. Heat the oil; add 1 or 2 pupusas. Cook over medium heat, turning once, until golden brown on both sides, about 8 minutes. Repeat until all the pupusas are cooked.

CHEESE PUPUSAS

Substitute 1¼ cups of shredded Monterey Jack or mozzarella cheese for both the chicken and cheese in the pupusa filling. When filling the tortillas, top the tomato and pepper purée mixture with 3 tablespoons of cheese. Continue as directed.

SWEET CORN TAMALES

Serves 8

These tamales capture the sweet taste of summer in a corn husk. Serve them unwrapped, topped with a tablespoon of Roasted Red Pepper Sauce (page 83) and accompanied by Black Beans Otomí (page 147), Crème Fraîche (page 51), or Salsa Fresca (page 67). Or you can eat them with your fingers just as they come out of the corn husk—they're irresistible!

6 ears of fresh corn, with husks
¾ cup cornmeal
¼ cup masa harina*
1 to 3 teaspoons sugar, to taste
½ cup margarine
1 teaspoon salt

Remove the husks from the corn; set husks aside.

With a knife, cut the corn kernels from the cobs. Put the kernels in a food processor or a blender; purée. Add the corn purée, corn meal, and masa harina to a medium-size bowl; mix well. Add the sugar, margarine, and salt to the corn mixture; mix thoroughly.

Place individual sections of the corn husks onto a work surface; place 2 rounded tablespoons of the corn mixture in the middle of each section. Fold one side of the husk over the filling; then fold the other side on top and bring the bottom up to make a neat, secure "envelope" (the top will be open). Place the folded husk on top of another corn husk, open side down. Repeat the folding pattern. You should have approximately 16 to 20 tamales when finished.

Layer the tamales, on their sides, in a stockpot. Cover the tamales with warm water, leaving the top layer exposed. Cook over low heat 1 hour and 15 minutes.

Note

The cornmeal and masa are used to tighten up the mixture and give the dough its proper consistency—add more or less, depending on the moistness of the corn purée. The corn mixture should be loose but have enough body to hold its shape.

*Masa harina and cornmeal are not the same thing. Masa harina is made from kernels of corn that have been soaked in lime, dried, and then specially ground. Masa is traditionally used to make tamales and tortillas; it is available in the flour section of many supermarkets and in Latin grocery stores as well as through mail order.

SWEET CORN TAMALES, CONT.

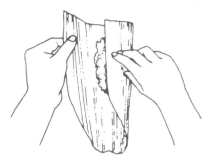

1. Fold one side of the husk over the corn mixture.

2. Fold the other side of the husk on top.

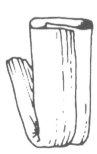

3. Bring the bottom of the husk up to make a neat envelope (the top will be open).

4. Place the folded husk on top of another husk, open end down.

5. Repeat Steps 1 through 3.

6. Layer the tamales, on their sides, in a stockpot.

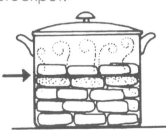

CROCODILES

rocodiles belong to a group of reptiles called crocodilians, which includes alligators and gharials. These animals date back to the Upper Triassic period, some 200 million years ago. Crocodiles saw the arrival of the dinosaurs—they most likely dined on them—and witnessed the extinction of those great lizards. Today, crocodiles are the world's largest reptiles. While most reptiles have very small brains, crocodilians have relatively large brains and may be the most intelligent reptiles of all. These animals exhibit many subtle and complex behaviors on a par with those of birds and mammals. Because crocodilians continue to grow throughout their lives—and some scientists think that may be well over 100 years in the wild—males can grow to be more than 15 feet long and weigh over 500 pounds. (A saltwater crocodile captured off the coast of India was reported to have measured more than 27 feet long and weighed over 1,000 pounds.) All crocodilians have at least 60 strong sharp teeth which they use to capture their prey. They are able to replace lost or worn out teeth by growing new ones. A single croc may go through as many as 3,000 teeth in its lifetime.

The American crocodile, *Crocodylus acutus*, can be found in the waters of northern Peru and Venezuela, north along the coasts of Central America and Mexico to Jamaica, Hispañola, Cuba, and the southern tip of Florida. American crocodiles are not known to be aggressive; in fact, they prefer to stay as far away from man as possible. Attacks by American crocodiles on humans are almost unheard of.

Crocodiles are excellent hunters: they're fast, strong, and very good at stalking their prey without being seen. Because their eyes and nostrils are on top of their heads, they can stay almost totally submerged while they swim up to their prey, surprising their dinner before it has a chance to realize what has happened. Crocodiles usually eat turtles, small mammals, and birds.

Nesting time for the crocodiles begins in late January and continues through March. The females choose their sites carefully, sometimes searching for weeks along sandy beaches before finding the right spot. Having chosen a nesting site, the female croc digs a hole in the sand—12 to 16 inches deep—in which to lay her eggs. Then, in the middle of the night, she lays a clutch of about 23 eggs, covers them, and leaves them to incubate in the warm sand for 85 to 90 days.

The temperature of the nest will determine the sex of the developing crocodiles. Nest temperatures above 91°F or below 88°F will produce males, while mid-range nest temperatures around 89°F will produce females. Therefore, in many nests, unless the temperature differs between the layers of eggs, crocodile siblings will be all the same sex.

Toward the end of the incubation period, the female crocodile makes nightly visits to the nest. When she hears the grunts of her hatching offspring, the mother croc digs open the nest. She may gently crack the eggs with her jaws to help free the emerging young. Then she picks up the hatchlings in her mouth and carries them to the water. Crocodile specialist Dr. John Thorbjarnarson notes that in protected lagoons, the young crocs may stay together in pods near their mothers for as long as a year. The presence of the mother croc keeps hungry predators such as hawks and herons away from the little ones.

One species of New World crocodile, the Orinoco crocodile, is on the 1993 Top Ten Most Endangered Species list issued by the World Wildlife Fund. Because this crocodile, like many others, has been hunted for its hide, has had its habitat invaded, and has been shot as vermin, today its numbers are severely reduced. In order to reestablish this species, the Wildlife Conservation Society (founded in 1895 as the New York Zoological Society) has funded the Orinoco Crocodile Project to breed and rear these crocs in captivity and then release them back into the wild. Santos Lusardo National Park, along with a research station, has been established in Venezuela to protect the Orinoco crocodile population. At last report, two thousand captive-bred crocs have been released into the Capanaparo River.

CROCODYLUS AURATUS

Chapter 6

Soups, Chowders, and Gumbos

GULF PORT SEAFOOD GUMBO

Serves 8 to 10

Filé, which gives this gumbo its distinctive flavor, is available in the seasoning section of most supermarkets. To add more kick to this tasty gumbo, increase the amount of serrano chile. If you're substituting larger shrimp or oysters, be sure to cut them in half. Rich, thick, and hearty, this gumbo makes a great main dish; just add a green salad and some crusty French bread—and dinner is served!

4 rounded tablespoons filé powder
½ teaspoon crushed red pepper flakes
½ teaspoon dried oregano
1 teaspoon freshly ground black pepper
Pinch of dried thyme
2 tablespoons vegetable oil
1½ cups chopped onions
1 serrano or jalapeño chile, diced
2½ teaspoons minced garlic
¾ cup Roux (page 50), at room temperature
10 cups clam juice or shellfish broth
½ cup (¼ pound) bay scallops
10 ounces diced fresh Pacific snapper (rock cod)
1 cup (½ pound) bay shrimp or rock shrimp
1 cup (½ pound) shelled small fresh Pacific oysters
½ red bell pepper, diced
½ green bell pepper, diced

Combine the filé powder, red pepper flakes, oregano, black pepper, and thyme in a small bowl. Mix well; set aside.

Heat the oil in a 10-inch skillet. Add the onions; cook over medium heat, until soft, about 3 to 5 minutes. Add the chile, garlic, and the reserved spice mixture to the onions; continue to cook, stirring often. Add the Roux; mix to coat the onion mixture.

Slowly add the clam juice, stirring continuously with a wire whisk, until the Roux and spices are evenly blended in the liquid. Allow the mixture to come to a slow boil, stirring occasionally; reduce the heat to low; simmer until the liquid thickens, about 15 minutes. Add the scallops, snapper, shrimp, and oysters; cook 1 to 2 minutes. Add the bell peppers; cook for another 5 minutes. Serve immediately, or cover and refrigerate; reheat gently to serve.

HAM AND OYSTER GUMBO

- Use the Gulf Port Seafood Gumbo recipe (this page).
- Substitute ¾ cup Rich Chicken Stock (page 48) dissolved in 2½ quarts of water for the clam juice (or use 2½ quarts chicken broth).
- Substitute 3½ cups (1 pound) diced honey-cured ham for the scallops, snapper, and shrimp.
- Increase the amount of oysters to 2 cups.

BAYOU GUMBO

Serves 8 to 10

This is one of our favorite gumbos. It calls for Cajun (andouille) sausage, which is a spicy, heavily smoked sausage traditionally used in gumbo and jambalaya. Enjoy this rich, full-flavored gumbo served over rice as a main dish, or invite your friends over for a casual dinner and serve a make-ahead meal that will win rave reviews.

- 4 tablespoons peanut oil
- 2 cups chopped onions
- $\frac{1}{2}$ teaspoon crushed red pepper flakes
- 1 tablespoon salt
- $\frac{1}{2}$ teaspoon freshly ground black pepper
- $\frac{1}{2}$ teaspoon dried oregano
- Pinch of dried thyme
- $2\frac{1}{2}$ tablespoons filé powder*
- $\frac{1}{2}$ cup Roux (page50)
- 1 cup Rich Chicken Stock (page 48) dissolved in 3 quarts of water (or use 3 quarts of chicken stock)
- 1 can (16 ounces) chili sauce
- 1 stalk celery, chopped
- 1 green bell pepper, chopped
- 1 red bell pepper, chopped
- $\frac{1}{2}$ tablespoon minced garlic
- 2 carrots, diced
- 2 pounds chicken wings
- 1 pound Cajun sausage (Polish sausage can be substituted), cut into $\frac{1}{4}$-inch pieces
- 1 teaspoon hot red pepper sauce
- $\frac{1}{2}$ pound crab meat

Heat the oil in a large stockpot. Add the onions; cook over medium heat, stirring frequently, until softened, 3 to 5 minutes. Add the red pepper flakes, salt, black pepper, oregano, thyme, filé powder, and Roux; continue to stir. Slowly add the chicken stock, stirring constantly and mixing well. Add the chili sauce and bring the mixture to a boil. Reduce the heat; simmer 10 minutes to allow the Roux to cook. (Taste the broth—if you can taste the flour from the Roux, it isn't cooked yet).

Add the celery, bell peppers, garlic, carrots, chicken wings, sausage, and red pepper sauce to the mixture. Continue to simmer the broth, skimming the fat from the surface every 5 minutes, until the chicken is cooked, about 20 minutes. Just before serving, stir in the crabmeat and adjust the seasoning. Serve immediately.

Note

Cajun cooking, a combination of French and Southern cuisine, was developed in the bayou country of Louisiana by Cajuns, descendants of Acadians who were forced from their Canadian homeland by the British in 1785. Cajun food is a robust, country-style cooking that uses spices, roux, filé powder, garlic, Cayenne, tomatoes, green peppers, onions, and celery as well as pork, crayfish, and a variety of seafood.

*Filé powder can be found in the spice section of most supermarkets or through mail order.

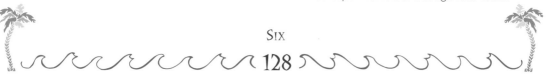

SOPA DE LIMA
CHICKEN AND LIME TORTILLA SOUP

Serves 4

This is a traditional chicken soup from the Yucatán—each village has its own version and they're all wonderful. The sweet tang of lime and the toasted corn taste of the tortilla chips, combined with the flavors of fresh tomatoes and savory chicken stock, make this a soup that's good enough to serve as a main course. This is our version, lean and tasty.

- **2 chicken breasts (about 2½ pounds), halved, rinsed and dried**
- **7 cups cool water**
- **1 garlic clove, smashed**
- **¼ onion, chopped**
- **1 medium carrot, chopped**
- **1 tablespoon + 1½ teaspoons salt**
- **1 medium tomato, diced**
- **2 green onions, chopped**
- **1 tablespoon chopped fresh cilantro**
- **Pinch freshly ground black pepper**
- **5 tablespoons freshly squeezed lime juice**
- **4 very thin slices habanero chile (optional)**
- **2 cups tortilla chips**
- **4 thin slices of lime, for garnish**

Place the chicken breasts in a 3-quart saucepan, add the cool water, and heat until the liquid is almost to a boil. Reduce the heat to medium low; add the garlic, onion, and carrot; continue to cook, uncovered, for 50 minutes. Add 1 tablespoon of the salt, and simmer for 10 minutes more.

Place the tomato, green onions, cilantro, 1½ teaspoons salt, and the pepper in a medium-size nonreactive bowl; add 1 tablespoon of the lime juice and mix well. Add the tomato mixture to the soup; stir well. (Add the habanero chile slices if you'd like.) Serve immediately, apportioning a half chicken breast to each bowl. Add 1 tablespoon of lime juice to each bowl of soup, then top each bowl with ½ cup tortilla chips. Garnish each serving with a lime slice.

SOPA DE CALABACITAS
SPICY PUMPKIN SOUP

Serves 4 generously

This is a great autumn soup that will really take the chill off of a frosty night. When you buy your pumpkins for Halloween, or if you are lucky enough to have your own pumpkin patch, pick out a few for this delicious soup. To cut calories, substitute evaporated nonfat milk for the heavy cream. This soup is delicious garnished with Roasted Red Pepper Sauce (page 83) or Salsa Fresca (page 67). For a different taste treat, try it topped with Mango Salsa (page 67) and chopped fresh pineapple.

- 2 pounds fresh cooked or canned pumpkin (about 4 cups)
- 1 habanero chile, seeded and minced (or use 2 jalapeño or serrano chiles)
- 3 garlic cloves, minced
- 1/4 teaspoon ground cinnamon
- 1/4 teaspoon dried thyme
- 1/4 teaspoon freshly ground nutmeg or allspice
- 1/2 cup freshly squeezed orange juice
- 2 tablespoons peanut oil
- 1 red bell pepper, seeded and chopped
- 1 green bell pepper, seeded and chopped
- 1 red onion, diced
- 1/2 cup Rich Chicken Stock (page 48) dissolved in 4 cups of water (or use 4 cups chicken stock)
- 1 cup heavy cream
- 1 cup fresh or frozen corn kernels
- 2 1/2 teaspoons salt
- Freshly ground black pepper to taste

Combine the pumpkin, chile, garlic, cinnamon, thyme, nutmeg, orange juice, peanut oil, bell peppers, onion, and chicken stock in a large saucepan; cook over high heat, stirring occasionally, bringing the liquid to a boil. Reduce the heat to low; simmer 20 minutes. Remove from the heat.

Pour the soup mixture into a food processor or blender, or use an immersion blender; purée until smooth. Return the puréed mixture to the saucepan. Add the cream and the corn; heat gently until warm. Season with the salt and pepper. Taste; add more salt if necessary. Garnish and serve.

Cooking Fresh Pumpkins

Preheat the oven to 350°F. Select a 4 to 5 pound pumpkin, cut it in half, and remove the seeds. Place the pumpkin halves in a large baking dish, cut side up, with about 1 inch of water in the bottom of the dish to prevent burning. Bake until the flesh is tender and can easily be pricked with a fork, about 1 1/2 hours. Remove the pumpkin halves from the oven and allow to cool. Scoop the pumpkin flesh from the skin, using a large spoon or ice cream scoop. Use immediately or cover and refrigerate for up to 1 week.

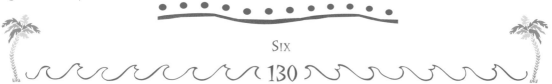

BLACK BEAN SOUP

Serves 4

If you are making a pot of Black Beans Otomí, then this soup will be a snap to make. It's a hearty luncheon entrée or a satisfying first course at dinner. Try serving it Mexican-style, topped with a poached egg and freshly grated cheese. Salsa Fresca (page 67), and Crème Fraîche (page 51) or sour cream also make wonderful garnishes.

- **1 tablespoon olive oil**
- **½ onion, chopped**
- **½ serrano or jalapeño chile, diced**
- **1 teaspoon minced garlic**
- **5 cups liquid strained from Black Beans Otomí (page 147)**
- **½ cup cooked Black Beans Otomí (to add body to soup)**

Optional Accompaniments

- **4 poached eggs**
- **4 rounded tablespoons freshly grated Monterey Jack or Parmesan cheese**
- **4 tablespoons Salsa Fresca**
  Crème Fraîche or sour cream

Heat the oil in a large pot. Add the onion, chile, and garlic; cook over medium heat, stirring frequently, until the onions are soft, 3 to 5 minutes. Add the black bean liquid and the black beans to the onion mixture; continue cooking until the flavors are well blended, 15 to 20 minutes. Carefully check the seasoning. Add salt if necessary. Serve immediately in individual bowls with a poached egg on top (optional); garnish each bowl with a tablespoon of Salsa Fresca and Crème Fraîche or grated cheese.

Note

Two Recipes in One!

This recipe is an accompaniment to the recipe for Black Beans Otomí (page 147). Just at the point when the black beans are almost cooked (they are usually pretty thick at this point, since most of the liquid in the pot has been reduced and absorbed), add 6 cups of water, stir well, and allow the mixture to come to full simmer. (If your beans are cooked and you still have a lot of unabsorbed liquid in the pot, don't add any more.) The liquid should be a rich brown. Strain off 5 cups of the liquid.

ZUCCHINI BISQUE BARBERO

Serves 8 to 10

This bisque has the texture and richness of a cream-based soup—but without all the calories. The soup freezes very well, so this is a great recipe to use when your garden produces an abundance of zucchini. If you like, you can add cooked pasta shells to give the dish a little more body. Top the bisque with Salsa Fresca (page 67) for some added zing.

8 tablespoons Rich Chicken Stock (page 48) dissolved in 6 cups of water (or use 6 cups chicken stock)

¾ **pound lean bacon, cooked, drained of grease, and broken into ½-inch pieces**

2 dashes Worcestershire sauce

3 pounds (about 15 small) zucchini, cut in quarters

4 large carrots, cut in quarters

4 stalks celery, strings removed, cut in quarters

5 garlic cloves, whole

1 onion, cut in half

2 teaspoons salt

1 teaspoon freshly ground black pepper

2 cups peeled* and diced tomatoes

*See "Skinning a Tomato," page 72.

Combine the chicken stock, bacon pieces, Worcestershire sauce, zucchini, carrots, celery, garlic, onion, salt, and pepper in a large pot or Dutch oven; bring the liquid to a boil. Reduce the heat to low; simmer, uncovered, 1 hour.

Place the vegetable mixture in a food processor or blender (or use an immersion blender); purée. Return the mixture to the pot; add the tomatoes. Increase the heat to medium-low; slowly bring the liquid to a simmer. Cook 10 minutes; serve immediately.

CORN ISLAND SEAFOOD CALDO

Serves 4 generously

This tangy seafood soup makes a wonderful luncheon entrée or dinner course. The fresh vegetables complement the variety of seafood and add color and texture to the caldo. This soup is low in fat, but very high in flavor.

- 1 cup bay scallops, rinsed (about ½ pound)
- 1 cup rock shrimps, rinsed (about ½ pound)
- Two 8-ounce snapper (or rock cod) fillets, rinsed and cut into 1-inch cubes
- 8 mussels in their shells, scrubbed and debearded
- 4 cups water
- 1 cup diced tomatoes
- ½ cup fresh corn kernels (or use frozen corn, thawed)
- ¼ cup diced red onion
- ¼ cup diced jícama
- ¼ cup julienned carrots
- 1 serrano or jalapeño chile, finely minced
- 2 tablespoons chopped fresh cilantro
- 4 teaspoons freshly squeezed lime juice
- Salt and pepper to taste

Combine the cleaned seafood and cold water in a medium saucepan. Cook, over medium heat, until the liquid simmers and the mussels open, about 5 minutes (discard any mussels that do not open). Add the tomatoes, corn, onion, jícama, carrots, and chile. Bring the liquid to a boil, reduce the heat, and simmer for 2 minutes. The vegetables will still be fresh and crisp. Gently stir in the cilantro and lime juice; season with salt and pepper. Serve immediately.

Note

Serrano chiles are small tapered chiles with a snappy fresh bite. If necessary, fresh jalapeño chiles can be substituted one for one.

CALDO DE CAMARONES
SHRIMP SOUP

Serves 4

This delicious, low-calorie, heart-smart caldo won First Place for entrées in the 1993 Art for the Heart cooking competition sponsored by the Carmel Mission Trails Chapter of the American Heart Association.

5 cups water
1 pound large shrimp (21-25 size,* about 24 shrimp), peeled, deveined, and quartered
$\frac{1}{4}$ cup julienned carrots
$\frac{1}{4}$ cup diced celery
2 tablespoons diced red onion
2 teaspoons finely sliced garlic
$\frac{1}{4}$ teaspoon freshly ground black pepper
$\frac{1}{2}$ teaspoon crushed red pepper flakes
1 teaspoon salt
$\frac{1}{2}$ sprig of fresh mint, with stem (about 5 to 6 large leaves)
$\frac{1}{3}$ cup fresh corn kernels shaved from the cob (frozen corn kernels can be substituted for fresh)
$\frac{1}{2}$ cup diced tomato
4 heaping tablespoons Sun-Dried Cranberry Salsa (page 68)

Combine the water, shrimp, carrots, celery, onion, garlic, black pepper, red pepper flakes, salt, and mint in a large saucepan; cook over medium heat, stirring occasionally, until the liquid begins to simmer, 7 to 10 minutes.

Remove the mint sprig; set it aside. Add the corn and tomato to the shrimp mixture; continue to simmer for 2 minutes more.

Chop the reserved mint leaves and return them to the shrimp mixture, stir well. Serve immediately, garnishing each bowl with 1 heaping tablespoon of the Sun-Dried Cranberry Salsa.

*For shrimp sizes, see "Selecting Shrimp," page 113.

BUTTERNUT SQUASH SOUP

Serves 8

This recipe is so easy to make—and the results are delicious. Butternut squash has a rich nutty flavor and a beautiful golden color; this soup makes an elegant presentation at a special meal—or a hearty soup course on a cold winter night. If you want to make the soup ahead of time, or if you're planing to serve it over the course of several days, do not add the cream until just before serving. Then add the proportionate amount of cream (2 tablespoons per cup) to the amount you are heating up. Garnish with Sun-Dried Cranberry Salsa, or another fruit salsa, to give the soup a nice complementary tang.

- **8 cups fresh cooked butternut squash (about 2 medium squash)**
- **8 cups of water**
- **1 tablespoon salt**
- **5 tablespoons packed brown sugar**
- **½ teaspoon nutmeg**
- **1 pint heavy cream (or half-and-half)**
- **¾ cup Sun-Dried Cranberry Salsa (page 68), for garnish**

Place the cooked squash and the water into a large saucepan. Bring the liquid to a boil; cover; reduce the heat to low and simmer for 30 minutes. Pour the mixture into a food processor or a blender (or use an immersion blender); purée until smooth. Return the puréed soup to the pot. Add the sugar, salt, and nutmeg; stir. Simmer for five minutes. Add the cream and gently heat until warm. Remove from heat and serve immediately, garnished with a tablespoon of Sun-Dried Cranberry Salsa.

Note

COOKING FRESH BUTTERNUT SQUASH:

Preheat the oven to 350°F. Select 2 medium sized squash, cut them in half lengthwise, and remove the seeds. Place the squash halves face up in a large baking dish (use two dishes if necessary); add 1 inch of water to the bottom of the baking dish. Bake squash until the flesh is tender and can be easily pricked with a fork, about 1½ hours. Remove squash from the oven and allow to cool a bit. Separate the flesh from the skin using a large spoon or ice cream scoop. Use immediately or cover and refrigerate for up to 1 week.

BAHAMIAN SEAFOOD CHOWDER

Serves 10 to 12

This is our tangy version of the traditional Boston-style clam chowder; it includes more seafood and a spicy finish. If you are using canned clams, drain them first, reserving the liquid, and make sure you have 1 pound of clam meat. Add the reserved liquid to the broth. Feel free to substitute littlenecks, count necks, or small cockles for the Manila clams. You can also substitute half-and-half, milk, or evaporated nonfat milk for the heavy cream to cut down on calories and fat.

Note

A NOTE BEFORE YOU START:

Bahamian Seafood Chowder can be made ahead of time or served at more than one meal. Don't add the cream and store the soup, covered, in the refrigerator. When you want to serve the chowder, reheat it gently, and add 2 cups of cream (or half-and-half) for each quart of the chowder base that you are planning to serve.

3 pounds Manila clams, washed and purged*
3 quarts water
1 pound chopped clams—fresh, frozen, or canned (reserve the liquid if using canned)
¼ cup peanut or vegetable oil
4 stalks celery, chopped
1¼ medium onions, chopped
¼ teaspoon dried thyme
2 crushed bay leaves
1 cup Roux (page 50)
4 medium potatoes, peeled and diced into 1-inch cubes
¾ cup (6 ounces) scallops
¾ cup (6 ounces) rock shrimp
Pinch of salt and freshly ground black pepper to taste
2 quarts heavy cream
1 cup Salsa Fresca (page 67)

Combine the Manila clams and the water in a large stockpot; cook over high heat, bringing the liquid to a boil. Remove from the heat.

Place a large sieve over a large pot. Strain the clam mixture, reserving both the liquid and the clams (be careful not to add any sand that may have settled to the bottom of the pot).

Remove the clams from the clamshells. Set the clam meat aside and discard

*To purge clams, place the live clams in cold water for 7 minutes. Change the water and repeat the process two more times. This allows the clams to clean the sand from their systems so it won't end up in your soup.

the shells. In a small bowl, combine the Manila clams and the chopped clams. Set aside.

Heat the oil in a large pot. Add the celery, onions, thyme, and bay leaves; cook over medium heat until the onions are soft, about 5 minutes. Add the clams to the onion mixture; cook, stirring frequently, 2 minutes.

Add the strained broth and the reserved liquid (if you used canned clams) to the clam mixture. (Be careful not to add any sand that may have settled to the bottom of the broth!) Simmer until the clams are tender, about 15 minutes.

Remove 1 cup of clam broth from the pot; allow it to cool to warm. Place the Roux in a small bowl; while whisking, slowly add the warm clam broth; whisk until the Roux has dissolved. Pour the Roux mixture into the pot with the clams; gently stir until well combined.

Add the potatoes; simmer for 10 minutes. Add the scallops and the rock shrimp; continue simmering until the potatoes are cooked, about 15 minutes. Adjust the seasoning by adding salt and pepper to taste.

Add the cream; stir to combine thoroughly. Gently heat until warm; serve immediately. Garnish each bowl with 2 tablespoons of Salsa Fresca.

SOPA DE AGUACATE
CHILLED AVOCADO CREAM SOUP

Serves 4

Served chilled, Sopa de Lima makes an elegant soup course for a summer dinner or luncheon, or enjoy a bowl at a back yard barbecue on a hot summer's day.

- $\frac{1}{2}$ cup Rich Chicken Stock (page 48) dissolved in $3\frac{1}{2}$ cups water (or use 4 cups chicken stock)
- 6 medium Haas avocados
- 1 cup of half-and-half
- 2 tablespoons freshly squeezed lemon juice
- $\frac{1}{2}$ teaspoon Worcestershire sauce
- 2 teaspoons salt
- $\frac{1}{4}$ teaspoon pepper
- 1 medium tomato, diced
- 4 sprigs of cilantro

In a medium saucepan, bring the chicken stock to simmer over medium heat. Remove from the heat and allow to cool. Peel 5 of the avocados; cut them in quarters; discard the seeds. Place the avocado pieces in a blender or food processor; add the chicken stock and the cream; purée, about 1 minute. While processing, add the lemon juice and Worcestershire sauce. Add salt and pepper to taste. Refrigerate before serving; serve chilled. Peel and slice the remaining avocado. Garnish each bowl with a slice of avocado, a tablespoon of diced tomato, and a sprig of cilantro.

SLOTHS

The sloth is a shaggy mammal whose face looks something like the Wooky in the *Star Wars* films. This dog-sized animal has developed some very unique adaptations to life in the rain forest canopy. The sloth has strong, hooked claws that are used to grip the branches of trees. With these powerful claws locked around a branch, the sloth can hang upside down, motionless, for hours at a stretch. This grip is so strong that even after a sloth dies, the animal will remain suspended from the tree branch high above the forest floor. For this reason, native forest peoples usually don't waste their time hunting for sloths—they know that even if they shoot a sloth, they won't be able to get it down, even by shaking the tree. In the constant humidity and regular downpour of the rain forest, the sloth remains relatively dry because its fur grows from its belly towards its backbone (the reverse of other mammals). So when it rains, the water just runs off the shaggy fur of the upside-down animal.

Sloths are famous for their lethargy—they even sneeze in slow motion. In fact, they are the slowest-moving mammals on earth. One female sloth was recorded moving at a speed of five yards a minute (less than 1/5 of a mile per hour) while hurrying to her distressed baby!

Sloths spend their whole lives in trees. There they eat, sleep (a good eighteen hours a day), or just hang motionless. Unlike that of most mammals, a sloth's body temperature varies with the environment—so sloths hang in sunny openings in the forest canopy to "catch some rays" and absorb the heat of the sun.

Sloths seem to be designed for immobility. The three-toed sloth has nine vertebrae in its neck—that's two more than most mammals. These extra neckbones allow the sloth to turn its head in almost every direction (about 270°). So, hanging from a branch, the sloth can twist its head to browse on its favorite cecropia tree without even having to move its body.

BRADYPUS TRIDACTYLUS

Sloths even mate and give birth to their young while suspended from branches. The newborn sloth has tiny claws, which it uses to grip onto its mother's belly soon after birth. Cradled in its mother's arms, wrapped in her limbs and shaggy hair, the newborn sloth is warm and well protected—and scarcely visible. For a month or two the baby sloth will hitch a ride with its mother, but it soon learns to move slowly about by itself. By five months, the little sloth has mastered the art of "hanging around" on its own.

Gentle and peaceful, sloths are relatively defenseless. Their best protection against their enemies is actually their very slowness and their protective coloration. Because they move so slowly, sloths are hard to detect; and because of the camouflage provided by algae—tiny plants—growing in their fur, sloths are hard to see. These algae give the animals a greenish tint in wet conditions, and in times of drought, the algae turn yellow, allowing the sloths to blend in with the scenery around them. With its head down on its chest, a sleeping sloth looks a lot like a bunch of dried leaves. If they are attacked, sloths can defend themselves by biting and by slashing with their hooked claws, but they usually protect themselves against their enemies—jaguars, ocelots, tree snakes, and birds of prey—by curling up into impenetrable balls.

Besides the green algae, sloths also support and provide camouflage for various species of moths, ticks, beetles, fleas, and mites that live in their fur. Several hundred insects may live on one individual sloth. One particular species of moth is only found in the sloth's fur, and is thought to feed on the algae growing there. This moth lays its eggs in the sloth's dung. After the eggs hatch, and the caterpillars have passed through larval and pupal stages, the next generation of moths fly out looking for a new sloth coat to live in—and the cycle begins again.

Sloths rarely come down to the forest floor. On the ground they are almost helpless against their enemies because they cannot run or even walk. They must pull themselves along by their hooked claws, dragging their bellies on the ground. The muscles in their legs—so well adapted to hanging from tree limbs—are too weak for walking, and their curved claws prevent them from standing upright. In spite of the difficulty sloths have maneuvering on land, they make a trip to the forest floor once a week. Three-toed sloths digest their meals slowly and only defecate once a week. Like cats, these sloths bury their droppings. To do so, they climb down to the base of a tree—very slowly—and dig a hole in the ground with augerlike motions of their short, blunt tails. This is the time when the sloths are in the greatest danger because they are exposed to their enemy, the jaguar. But by burying their waste, the sloths are actually performing a service to the rain forest. They are recycling the nutrients they have consumed—less those their bodies need—and planting the seeds of the fruits they have eaten so that a new generation of trees can take root.

Note

One unusual aspect of sloths that may prove particularly beneficial to humans is their vital resistance to infection. Serious wounds heal quickly and rarely become infected. Scientists are studying sloths hoping to understand how this biological mechanism works in the animals' bodies.

Chapter 7

Sides and Salads

WILD RICE AND POSOLE SALAD

Serves 8 to 10

This recipe is actually a combination of Wild Rice Salsa and Posole Salsa, and it makes a great salad dish or a vegetarian entrée. Canned chipotle chiles (smoked jalapeño chiles) are available in Latin groceries or in well-stocked supermarkets. Hominy will be found in the canned vegetable section of the supermarket and in Latin groceries. White and yellow hominy are interchangeable, so don't panic if you can only find one variety; just double the amount and you're good to go.

- 1 cup wild rice
- 4 cups water
- $\frac{1}{2}$ cup canned yellow hominy, rinsed and drained
- $\frac{1}{2}$ cup canned white hominy, rinsed and drained
- 1 cup diced red bell pepper
- $1\frac{1}{2}$ chipotle chiles (canned smoked jalapeños), minced
- $2\frac{1}{2}$ cups Salsa Fresca (see page 67)
- 4 tablespoons chopped fresh cilantro
- 1 cup freshly squeezed lime juice
- 4 tablespoons olive oil
- $2\frac{1}{2}$ tablespoons sugar
- $\frac{1}{4}$ teaspoon salt

Combine the rice and the water in a medium saucepan; cook over medium heat until the grains open, about 1 hour. Remove from the heat and drain. Transfer the rice to a large bowl and place it in the refrigerator to cool.

Combine the remaining ingredients and the cooled rice in a large nonreactive bowl; mix well. Cover and refrigerate for 8 hours, allowing the flavors to marry. Serve chilled.

MIXED GREENS WITH SPICY PECANS AND HONEY MUSTARD VINAIGRETTE

Serves 4

6 cups of mixed baby greens, rinsed, dried, and chilled
8 cherry tomatoes, halved
24 Spicy Pecans (page 105)
¾ cup Honey Mustard Vinaigrette (this page)

Arrange 1½ cups of the mixed greens on each of four salad plates. Top each salad with 6 Spicy Pecans and 4 tomato halves. Spoon 2 tablespoons of the Honey Mustard Vinaigrette over each salad and serve.

HONEY MUSTARD VINAIGRETTE
Makes 2 cups

This tasty little vinaigrette will keep for weeks in the refrigerator, just keep it covered and shake well before using.

10 tablespoons (5 ounces) red wine vinegar
6 tablespoons country-style Dijon mustard
1 tablespoon honey
1 teaspoon salt
½ teaspoon freshly ground black pepper
1¼ cups peanut oil

Combine the vinegar, mustard, honey, salt, and pepper in a container with a tight-fitting lid—a jar or a salad dressing container would be ideal. Cover and shake well. Add the oil and shake until there is no visible separation between the oil and the other ingredients. Chill before serving. Refrigerate any remaining dressing.

COSTA RICAN RICE

Serves 6 to 8

This is an almost foolproof recipe for fluffy rice. Costa Rican rice is a perfect side dish for many of the entrées in this book.

- 1 tablespoon peanut oil
- $\frac{1}{3}$ cup diced red or green bell pepper
- $\frac{1}{2}$ cup diced onion
- 2 cups long grain rice, well rinsed
- $1\frac{1}{3}$ cups water
- 2 teaspoons tomato paste
- $\frac{1}{4}$ teaspoon freshly ground black pepper
- 2 teaspoons salt
- 2 tablespoons freshly squeezed lime juice
- 1 teaspoon olive oil

Heat the peanut oil in a medium-size saucepan. Add the bell pepper and the onion; cook over medium heat, stirring often, until the onion begins to brown. Add the rice, water, tomato paste, black pepper, salt, and lime juice; mix well. Bring the liquid to a boil. Add the olive oil to the rice mixture, put a lid on the saucepan, and immediately turn the heat down to simmer. Allow the rice to simmer without disturbing (don't even peek!), until all the liquid is absorbed, about 20 minutes. Serve hot.

COCONUT LIME RICE

Serves 8 to 10

This is the perfect complement to any seafood dish or chicken entrée—and it's delicious on its own, too! For a different twist, try this recipe using freshly squeezed lemons instead of limes.

- 3 cups water
- 2 cups shredded sweetened coconut
- 1 tablespoon olive oil
- 1 cup Basmati rice
- 1 teaspoon salt
- $\frac{1}{4}$ teaspoon freshly ground pepper
- 2 tablespoons freshly squeezed lime juice

Combine the water and shredded coconut in a small saucepan; simmer over medium heat for 5 minutes. Place a small strainer over a small bowl. Strain the coconut mixture; reserve the liquid; discard the coconut solids. You should have about 2 cups of coconut milk. Set aside.

Heat the oil in an 8-inch skillet; add the rice. Stir and cook over medium heat until the grains of rice begin to change color from clear to solid white on the ends, about 7 minutes.

Add 2 cups of the reserved coconut milk to the rice; bring the mixture to a boil. Add the salt, pepper, and, just before putting on the lid, the lime juice. Cover the rice and immediately reduce the heat to simmer. Allow to cook undisturbed (don't peek while it's cooking!) until the liquid is absorbed, about 20 minutes. Serve hot.

VEGETARIAN BLACK BEANS

Serves 8 to 10

This recipe makes the same great beans as the Otomí recipe—but vegetarian style. Make sure you heed the Bean Tips & Caveats on the next page! Garnish the beans with Salsa Fresca (page 67) and Crème Fraîche (page 51). Vegans, omit the Crème Fraîche.

- **4 to 5 bay leaves**
- **4 carrots**
- **2 cups chopped onions**
- **1 cup chopped red or green bell peppers**
- **2 quarts of water**
- **1 pound dry black beans, sorted, rinsed, and drained**
- **¼ cup peanut oil**
- **2 tablespoons minced garlic**
- **2 serrano or jalapeño chiles, halved**
- **1 teaspoon salt (or more to your taste)**
- **Freshly ground black pepper to taste**

Place the bay leaves, carrots, 1 cup of the chopped onions, bell peppers, and water in a large stockpot. Bring the liquid to a boil; lower the heat to simmer and cook for 30 minutes, until the vegetables are tender. Remove and discard the bay leaves; purée the mixture in a food processor or blender until smooth. Allow the vegetarian stock mixture to cool.

Combine the beans, the remaining cup of chopped onions, the oil, garlic, and chiles with the vegetarian stock in a large, heavy stockpot—or clay pot. Bring the liquid to a slow boil. Reduce the heat to low and simmer, stirring occasionally, until the beans soften and the liquid thickens, about 4 hours. The longer the beans cook, the more they will soften and the thicker and richer the stock will become. (Important: check the pot and add a cup or so of liquid if necessary to prevent the beans from scorching.) Season with salt and pepper; cook 1 more hour, adding more liquid if necessary. Remove chile halves before serving. Serve the beans hot, topped with a tablespoon of Salsa Fresca.

BLACK BEANS OTOMÍ

Serves 6

Crème Fraîche (page 51) and Salsa Fresca (page 67), either together or separately, make great garnishes for this dish.

1 pound dry black beans, sorted, rinsed, and drained
1 cup chopped onions
¼ cup peanut oil
2 tablespoons minced garlic
2 serrano or jalapeño chiles, halved
½ cup Rich Chicken Stock (page 48) and 2 quarts water, room temperature, or use 2 quarts chicken stock
1 teaspoon salt (or more to your taste)
Freshly ground black pepper to taste

Combine the beans, onion, oil, garlic, and chiles with the Rich Chicken Stock and 2 quarts of water in a large, heavy stockpot or clay pot. Bring the liquid to a slow boil. Reduce the heat to low, and simmer, stirring occasionally, until the beans soften and the liquid thickens, about 4 hours. The longer the beans cook, the more they will soften and the thicker and richer the stock will become. (Important: Check the pot occasionally and add a cup or so of liquid if necessary to prevent the beans from scorching.) Season with salt and pepper; cook 1 hour more, adding more liquid if necessary. Remove chile halves before serving. Serve the beans hot, topped with Crème Fraîche or sour cream, and a tablespoon of Salsa Fresca.

Bean Tips and Caveats

- Carefully sort through the dry beans. Often small rocks are inadvertently included in the package and are hard to distinguish from the beans—until you bite into one!

- Use a clay pot, if you have one, and your beans will be even more flavorful. Generations of Latin cooks swear by this.

- Don't add salt to the beans until the last hour of simmering time. Salt will toughen the skins if added too early, and it will increase the cooking time.

- Season carefully! Beans need salt or they will taste very flat. As a rule of thumb, start with a teaspoon of salt for 1 pound of beans and go from there. Just remember to add the salt in the last hour of cooking.

- When cooking beans, slow and easy is the best. Let them simmer on a very low heat, uncovered. There's nothing worse for cooks than a pot of scorched beans! Stir the simmering beans occasionally and add 1 to 2 cups of water when necessary. Don't worry about having runny beans, the beans will absorb the liquid as they cook and the rest will steam out of the pot. If your beans are too watery, just let them continue to cook until you are satisfied with the consistency.

CHORIZO

Serves 8 to 10

This is our favorite chorizo recipe—it carries the full spicy flavor of Mexican chorizo without most of the fat. This is a "skinless" version of the sausage; when cooked, the meat has a nice crumbly texture. We use it in egg dishes, pasta sauces, tacos, enchiladas, etc. This chorizo gets its wonderful spiciness from the achiote paste and the combination of cumin with hints of cinnamon and clove.

- 6 tablespoons apple cider vinegar
- 1 medium onion, chopped
- 2 tablespoons minced garlic
- ½ red bell pepper
- 2 teaspoons black pepper
- 2 teaspoons dried oregano
- ¼ teaspoon ground cloves
- ¼ teaspoon ground cinnamon
- 1 tablespoon ground cumin
- 2 teaspoons salt
- 4 tablespoons achiote paste (for substitute, see "Achiote Paste," page 227)
- 1 pound ground lean pork (have the butcher grind pork shoulder for you)
- 1 pound ground lean beef

Put all of the ingredients except the pork and the beef into a food processor or blender; blend well. Transfer the spice mixture to a large nonreactive bowl; add the pork and beef. Using gloves, mix the spices and the meat by hand until they are well blended. Cover the bowl and refrigerate overnight.

To cook, place the desired amount of chorizo into a preheated skillet, cook over medium heat stirring occasionally, until the chorizo is crumbly and browned, about 5 to 6 minutes. Remove from the heat. Place the chorizo on a large plate covered with paper towels to absorb any excess grease. Transfer to a serving dish; serve immediately. Refrigerate any leftovers in an airtight covered container for up to one week.

SEAFOOD CEVICHE

Serves 2

For variety, instead of using only scallops, you can use any combination of fresh scallops, shrimp, and fish to equal 1 pound of seafood in this recipe. It is very important that the seafood be as fresh as possible, since the ceviche will be "cooked" by citrus juices instead of by heat. Cut all of the seafood into uniform ½-inch cubed pieces so that each piece will "cook" at the same rate. Serve each portion garnished with a slice of avocado and a wedge of lime. Tortilla chips make a nice accompaniment. It is best to serve this dish on the same day that it's made.

1 pound very fresh scallops (or a one-pound combination of fresh scallops, prawns, and fish)
½ cup freshly squeezed lemon juice
¼ cup freshly squeezed Seville orange juice
(or use the freshly squeezed juices of ¼ grapefruit, ½ orange, and 1 lime)
½ cup diced red onions, rinsed in cold water after dicing
½ teaspoon minced garlic
½ cup peeled,* seeded, and diced tomato
2 serrano chiles, finely diced
½ cup diced red bell pepper
¼ teaspoon freshly ground black pepper
Salt to taste

Cut the scallops into ½-inch cubes. Combine the scallops and the citrus juice in a large plastic bag or in a nonreactive bowl. Cover and refrigerate for 6 hours. Drain the scallops; transfer to a large bowl.

Combine the remaining ingredients with the scallops; mix well. Adjust the seasoning with salt and additional black pepper, to taste. Serve immediately.

*See "Skinning a Tomato," page 72.

QUINOA CANO

Serves 4

When planning a side dish, quinoa makes a nice alternative to rice. Besides its nutritional value, quinoa has a pleasing taste and texture. Serve Quinoa Cano as an accompaniment to seafood or meat dishes; garnish each serving with a tablespoon of one of your favorite salsas.

- **1 tablespoon olive oil**
- **1 tablespoon minced garlic**
- **½ cup minced onion**
- **1 serrano chile, minced**
- **2 cups quinoa**
- **2 tablespoons of Rich Chicken Stock (page 48) dissolved in 2½ cups water (or use 2½ cups chicken stock)**
- **2 teaspoons salt**

Heat the oil in a medium-size saucepan. Add the garlic, onion, and chile; cook over medium heat until the onion begins to soften, about 3 to 5 minutes. Add the quinoa and stir well. Add the Chicken Stock and the salt; bring the mixture to a boil. Reduce the heat to low; simmer, covered and undisturbed, until all the liquid is absorbed, about 20 minutes. Serve hot.

Quinoa, The Super Grain

Quinoa, pronounced *keen'-wa*, has the highest protein content of any grain. It is also high in *lysine*, an amino acid that is scarce in the vegetable kingdom. One serving of this great grain—about one cup—will provide you with 6 grams of protein and 20 percent of your daily iron requirement, and it has only 138 calories and just 2 grams of fat. See the note on this page regarding washing quinoa.

Note

Make sure you rinse quinoa thoroughly before using it. The grain is coated with a natural insecticide, *saponin*, produced by the plant, which makes it taste bitter to insects (and us). Water easily removes it.

QUINOA SUMMER SALAD

Picnic size: Serves 12

This is a great dish to carry along to a family reunion, a summer picnic, a church social, or a school potluck. The recipe serves 12, but it can be halved to serve 6. Don't let the long list of ingredients deter you from trying this delicious salad; there is actually very little prep work, so the salad can be made quite easily from a well-stocked pantry.

1 teaspoon peanut or vegetable oil
¼ cup diced yellow onion
1 tablespoon minced garlic
Pinch crushed red pepper flakes
2½ cups water
3 teaspoons salt
½ teaspoon freshly ground black pepper
2 cups quinoa, well rinsed
½ cup diced red bell pepper
¾ cup diced jícama
¾ cup diced tomato
2 teaspoons minced serrano or jalapeño chiles
¾ cup julienned carrots
½ cup fresh sweet corn kernels, shaved from the cob (or used frozen corn, thawed)
¼ cup diced red onion
4½ teaspoons chopped fresh cilantro
1 tablespoon chopped fresh mint (or use fresh basil for a different taste)
2 tablespoons toasted canola or olive oil
3 tablespoons balsamic vinegar (make sure it's balsamic)
1 teaspoon salt
¼ teaspoon pepper

Heat the peanut oil in a medium saucepan. Add the yellow onion and garlic; cook over medium heat until the onion begins to soften, 3 to 5 minutes. Add the red pepper flakes; cook 1 minute more.

Add the water, 2 teaspoons of the salt, and ½ teaspoon of the pepper to the onion mixture; bring to a boil. Mix in the quinoa; reduce the heat to low and simmer, covered and undisturbed, 20 minutes. Remove from the heat, drain any remaining water, and transfer the mixture to a medium-size bowl. Set aside to cool.

Combine the cooled quinoa, the remaining salt and pepper, and the remaining ingredients in a large mixing bowl; mix well. Chill before serving.

SEAFOOD PASTA SALAD
WITH SCALLOPS AND BAY SHRIMP IN A LIGHT PESTO VINAIGRETTE

Serves 8 to 10

Serve this salad on a bed of lettuce leaves and garnish it with parsley and/or freshly grated Parmesan cheese. This salad makes an excellent luncheon or buffet dish. If you wish to cut calories, use a low-calorie mayonnaise or substitute 1 cup of your favorite low-calorie dressing for the vinaigrette.

- 1½ pounds fresh tri-color fusilli pasta (cork screw pasta)
- ¼ pound bay scallops
- 1 cup mayonnaise (or low-calorie salad dressing)
- ⅓ cup red wine vinegar
- 6 tablespoons prepared pesto
- ½ teaspoon dried oregano
- ½ teaspoon salt
- 1 teaspoon freshly ground black pepper
- 1 roasted red bell pepper*, deseeded, deveined, and diced
- 1 roasted green bell pepper*, deseeded, deveined, and diced
- ½ red onion, diced
- 1 cup grated carrots
- ¼ pound cooked bay shrimp**
- ½ cup freshly grated Parmesan cheese, for garnish

Place the pasta in a large pot of boiling water; cook it until it's *al dente*, 10 to 12 minutes. Drain; rinse with cool water. Transfer to a large bowl.

Place the scallops in 1 quart of boiling water; reduce the heat, and simmer until just cooked, about 2 to 3 minutes—they will turn white, opaque, and firm. Remove from heat, drain, and cool in cold water.

Combine the mayonnaise, vinegar, pesto, oregano, salt, and pepper in a small bowl; mix well.

Add the bell peppers, onions, and carrots to the cooked pasta. Add the mayonnaise mixture to the pasta mixture; blend well. Add the shrimp and the scallops; stir to blend. Chill the salad well before serving. Garnish with Parmesan cheese.

*See "Roasting Peppers," page 65.

**Precooked bay shrimp (small, pink, pre-peeled shrimp) can be found in the freezer section of most supermarkets; just make sure you don't cook them twice!

Pesto... Presto!

Pesto is available in the freezer section of many supermarkets, but it's very easy to make. Pesto is a wonderful way to save the flavor of fresh summer basil for winter meals. To preserve the color of pesto, stir in 1 tablespoon of freshly squeezed lemon juice during the final minute of blending.

- ½ **cup firmly packed fresh basil**
- **3 garlic cloves**
- ¼ **cup pine nuts or walnuts**
- ¼ **cup grated aged Parmesan cheese (optional)**
- ½ **cup olive oil**
- **Salt to taste**

Place the basil, garlic, pine nuts, and cheese in a food processor or blender; process until finely chopped. With the motor running, add the oil in a thin, steady stream until the mixture forms a smooth paste and is well blended, 2 to 3 minutes. Refrigerate, covered. You can also freeze pesto.

SWEET POTATOES CAROLINA

Serves 4

The flavors of smoky and sweet followed by a little chipotle "kick" combine to make this smooth, savory dish a great accompaniment to roasts and grilled meats. Serve it with your next turkey, a pork roast, ham, or grilled lamb chops.

> **2 pounds (about 3 medium) sweet potatoes**
> **2 tablespoons butter**
> **1 tablespoon honey (or add more to taste)**
> **1½ chipotle chiles en adobo (canned smoked jalapeño chiles in adobo sauce), minced (or add more to taste)**
> **1 teaspoon adobo sauce (from the can of chipotle chiles)**
> **4 tablespoons Rich Chicken Stock (page 48) dissolved in 6 ounces of water (or use 1 cup chicken stock)**

Scrub the sweet potatoes and pierce them twice with a knife. Place the sweet potatoes in a knotted or sealed plastic bag or in a bowl covered with plastic. Microwave on high until the potatoes are soft and yield to the touch, about 9 to 12 minutes. Cool for 10 minutes, then peel. Place the sweet potatoes in a medium-size bowl and, using an electric mixer or by hand, mash well. Add the butter, honey, and minced chipotle; mix well. Add ¾ cup of the chicken stock and mix well. If the mixture is stiff, continue mixing and add one tablespoon more at a time of the remaining chicken stock until the mixture is creamy. Taste and adjust honey and chipotles to taste. Salt is usually not necessary in this recipe. Serve immediately, or store in the refrigerator in an airtight container; reheat gently before serving.

- Fettuccine with Shrimp and Green Cashew Sauce
- Fettuccine with Shiitake Mushrooms and Fresh Tomato Sauce
- Rasta Pasta with Calypso Salsa,
served with Chicken Breast Criollo and Mango Salsa

Jamaican Curry Crab Cakes

Sautéed Shrimp Diablo

Peppered Salmon with Cilantro and Roasted Serrano Aïoli

Grilled Halibut with Yellow Pepper Beurre Blanc,
served with Salsa Fresca

• Chorizo Omelet,
served with Roasted Red Pepper Sauce and Black Beans

• Beef Fajita Platter,
with Fire-Roasted Red Tomato Sauce

Bahia Brochette

Amazon Catfish,
topped with Spicy Roasted Peanuts,
served on a bed of Costa Rican Rice

JAGUARS

Jaguars are the most powerful predatory animals of the Americas. Their heavily muscled bodies are equally adept at climbing in trees or swimming in rivers. They will chase prey into the water or swim looking for turtles, fish, and even crocodiles. Jaguars can survive in a variety of terrains—forests, mountains, grasslands, and even swamplands—and they can sustain themselves with a variety of foods—from large herd animals to small insects. While jaguars usually weigh between 100 to 250 pounds, these incredibly strong cats have been seen dragging full-grown horses for more than a mile.

Jaguars are master hunters. Their bodies are specialized for night hunting. The big cats have very sensitive ears that can turn in different directions to pick up sound. They have excellent night vision, quiet padded feet for moving silently through the forest, whiskers to act as sensors in the dark, and strong muscles for running quickly. While they swim and climb with ease, jaguars usually stalk their prey on the ground, creeping close then pouncing swiftly. Jaguars seize their prey with their strong forelegs and then kill it with one bite through the head or neck with their sharp canine teeth.

Jaguars are also known as clever hunters. Amazonian forest dwellers believe that the jaguar catches fish by deliberately dangling its tail in the water to lure the fish—then, when the fish rises to the surface, the jaguar will flick the fish onto the riverbank with its paws.

Jaguars are solitary and secretive; they mark their territory by scratching trees and leaving scent marks. The cats come together at mating time, and after about three months, the mother jaguar gives birth to two or three kittens. Like all cats, jaguar kittens are born blind and helpless. They will stay with their mother for more than a year, learning to hunt and fend for themselves. When they mature, they will move off of their mother's home range and stake out their own territory, where they will assume their important role in the ecosystem of the rain forest.

PANTHERA ONCA

Because jaguars are at the top of the food chain, they keep the herbivore population under control. Without predators like the jaguar, these vegetarian animals, such as tapirs and sloths, would reproduce unchecked and destroy the forest by over-eating it. Jaguars also help to control the numbers of smaller carnivores, such as opossums and foxes, which, if unchecked, would destroy many of the forest's smaller mammals and birds and upset the delicate balance of life in the rain forest.

Known as El Tigre in the myths and legends of Central and South America, jaguars have long played an important role in the religions of the New World. To the Aztec, the jaguar was the God of the Night, ruler of the underworld; its spotted coat represented the stars of the night sky. To the Canelos Quiche people, Amasangua, the spirit of the forest, appears as the elusive black panther. Jaguar skins were worn as symbols of power and prestige by priests, rulers, and nobles in the Inca, Aztec, and Maya worlds, and throughout Central and South America.

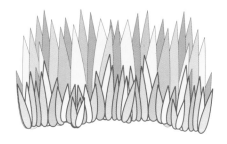

The jaguar still plays a very important role in the cultural and spiritual lives of many forest peoples today, but no group has identified with the animal to such an extent as have the Matses. The Matses are a tribe of hunter gatherers who inhabit the lowland jungles of northeastern Peru. This fiercely proud and independent people guard the spirit and customs of their ancestors. Their needs are supplied by the forest and they resist the intrusion of outsiders. The Matses admire the strength, guile, and hunting prowess of the jaguar. To embody the jaguar's spirit, the Matses tattoo their faces with markings that resemble those of a jaguar. The Matses men wear long, bamboo splints in their upper lips, and the women wear them in their noses—like jaguar whiskers.

Note

You can tell jaguars from leopards by their spots. The jaguar has small black spots arranged in rosettes, with usually one or two extra spots in the rosette's center; the leopard's rosettes are usually empty in the center.

Chapter 8

Entrees

ALAMBRE
STEAK AND BACON SCRAMBLE

Serves 4

This is a hard recipe to describe—it's a mixture of sautéed sliced steak and bacon with bell peppers, onions, chiles, and cheese. The name, alambre, means "wire" in Spanish, but we think it may be a corruption of *al hambre* "to the hunger." Alambre makes a great filling for wraps and burritos, and it will definitely fill you up—which is probably why it is very popular entrée in small restaurants and cafés throughout the Yucatán and Chiapas!

10 strips of bacon (about ½ pound)
2 pounds skirt steak, well trimmed
1½ medium onion, sliced in rings
  ⅛ inch thick
2 garlic cloves, peeled and sliced
4 serrano chiles, thinly sliced in
  rings
1 red bell pepper sliced in rings ⅛
  inch thick, then cut in half
1 green bell pepper sliced in rings ⅛
  inch thick, then cut in half
4 tablespoons water
2 teaspoons salt
2 tablespoons chopped cilantro
2 tablespoons freshly squeezed
  lime juice
¾ cup shredded Monterey Jack
  cheese (loosely packed)

In a large 12-inch skillet, over medium heat, cook the bacon until it is brown and crispy, about 8 to 10 minutes. Remove the bacon strips from the pan and place them on paper towels to absorb any excess grease. Discard all the fat in the skillet, but don't wash the skillet; set aside.

Slice the steak against the grain, cutting the strips 1½ to 1¼ inches thick. Over high heat, reheat the same skillet that the bacon was cooked in; when hot, place ⅓ of the steak strips in the pan and cook for 2½ to 3 minutes, stirring occasionally. Set the cooked meat aside in a small bowl. Repeat with the remaining meat. Place the onions in the same skillet, and cook over high heat, tossing frequently, until brown, about 3 to 4 minutes. Reduce the heat to medium low and add the garlic, chile, and bell peppers to the onions; stir; cook for 3 minutes. Add the meat, the water, and the salt; stir; cook over medium heat until the liquid in the pan has almost disappeared, about 3 minutes. Add the cilantro to the the meat and vegetable mixture; stir; remove the skillet from the heat; add the lime juice and stir well. Serve immediately, topped with the cheese.

APPLE-ROASTED DUCK WITH APPLE-JALAPEÑO CHUTNEY

Serves 4

This is a knockout dish: the chutney is spicy sweet with a bite, and it complements the flavor of the roasted meat. Instead of duck, try this recipe with a capon or even a pork loin (split it and stuff it)—the results will be equally delicious.

- 4 Granny Smith apples, cored and quartered
- 1 medium yellow onion, quartered
- 2 jalapeño chiles
- ¼ pineapple, cubed (about 1½ cups)
- ½ cup freshly squeezed lemon juice
- 1 teaspoon ground cinnamon
- 1 teaspoon freshly ground black pepper
- 2 (4-pound) ducks, split, with skin on and fat removed from body cavity (see note, next page)
- Apple-Jalapeño Chutney (see recipe, next page)

Preheat the oven to 350°F. Combine the apples, onion, chiles, pineapple, lemon juice, cinnamon, and black pepper in a food processor or blender; purée until smooth. Rub the apple mixture under the skin and inside the cavities of the ducks.

Place the ducks, breast side up, in a shallow roasting pan. Cover and roast for 30 minutes. Uncover the ducks and continue roasting until the skin becomes crispy and golden brown, about 30 minutes more.

Remove the birds from the oven. Carve the ducks. Place 1 thigh and 1 duck half on each plate. Top with warm Apple-Jalapeño Chutney and serve.

APPLE-ROASTED DUCK WITH APPLE-JALAPEÑO CHUTNEY, CONT.

APPLE-JALAPEÑO CHUTNEY

Makes about 6 cups

- 4 Granny Smith or Pippin apples, cored (don't peel), cut into $\frac{1}{2}$-inch cubes
- 2 jalapeño chiles, thinly sliced
- 1 medium yellow onion, cut into $\frac{1}{2}$-inch cubes
- $\frac{1}{2}$ red bell pepper, diced
- $\frac{1}{2}$ cup golden raisins
- 1 cup fresh or frozen cranberries
- $2\frac{1}{2}$ tablespoons chopped fresh cilantro
- 1 tablespoon lemon zest*
- 2 tablespoons freshly squeezed lemon juice
- $\frac{1}{2}$ cup honey
- $\frac{1}{2}$ cup apple cider vinegar
- $\frac{1}{4}$ cup packed dark brown sugar
- $\frac{1}{2}$ tablespoon ground cinnamon
- $\frac{1}{4}$ teaspoon freshly grated nutmeg
- $\frac{1}{2}$ teaspoon chopped ginger root

Combine all of the ingredients in a large saucepan. Bring the mixture to a boil. Reduce the heat to low, stir, and cover. Simmer just until the apple skins begin to turn pale, about 20 minutes (the apples should NOT be mushy). Remove the chutney from the heat, and set it aside. (Note: This flavorful chutney can be served either hot or cold.)

Defatting a Duck

To remove the fat from a duck, prick the breast with a fork four or five times. Parboil the bird for 3 minutes; then take the duck from the water and let it cool. Pick out the remaining fat deposits. This won't be difficult now, because the parboiling will have made the fat deposits very easy to see.

*The zest of the lemon is the outermost peel of the fruit without any of the pith (white membrane). To remove the zest, use a zester or the fine side of a vegetable grater.

FETTUCCINE with SHIITAKE MUSHROOMS and FRESH TOMATO SAUCE

Serves 4

This is a great vegetarian entrée—for vegan vegetarians, omit the Parmesan cheese.

1½ pounds fresh fettuccine
4 tablespoons olive oil
2 tablespoons minced shallots
4 teaspoons minced garlic
3 cups shiitake mushrooms, sliced
2 cups Fresh Tomato Sauce (page 88)
1 cup diced tomatoes
1 teaspoon salt
¼ teaspoon freshly ground black pepper
2 teaspoons minced fresh parsley
4 rounded tablespoons freshly grated Parmesan cheese
½ cup Salsa Fresca (page 67)

Cook the fettuccine according to the package's directions for *al dente*. (To check on the "doneness," cut one stand in half. The pasta is done when the center is cooked.) Toss the cooked, drained pasta with 2 tablespoons of the oil in a large bowl. Set aside.

Meanwhile, heat the remaining 2 tablespoons of oil in a 12-inch skillet.* Add the shallots, garlic, and shiitake mushrooms to the pan; cook over medium heat, stirring frequently, until the mushrooms soften, 3 to 4 minutes.

Add the Fresh Tomato Sauce, pasta, tomatoes, salt, pepper, and parsley to the pan; stir well. Add 2 tablespoons of the Parmesan cheese to the pasta mixture; mix well; cook until heated through. Remove from heat. Transfer to individual plates; serve immediately. Garnish each serving with ½ tablespoon of the remaining Parmesan cheese and 2 tablespoons of the Salsa Fresca.

*Note: If you are using a smaller skillet, make this recipe in two batches, or hold the pasta in the bowl, keep warm, and add the finished sauce with vegetables and the 2 tablespoons of Parmesan cheese to the bowl and toss well.

FETTUCCINE WITH SHRIMP AND GREEN CASHEW SAUCE

Serves 4

Green Cashew Sauce is a Latin American version of pesto; it uses cilantro instead of parsley and cashews instead of pine nuts. The result is a wonderful flavor combination that scores a hit with the pasta and shrimps.

- 1½ **pounds fresh fettuccine**
- 4 **tablespoons olive oil**
- 24 **large shrimp (21-25 size,* about 1 pound), peeled, cleaned, and deveined**
- 2 **teaspoons minced shallots**
- 1 **teaspoon minced garlic**
- ½ **cup heavy cream**
- 4 **tablespoons Green Cashew Sauce (page 81)**
- 1 **teaspoon salt**
- ¼ **teaspoon freshly ground black pepper**
- 4 **rounded tablespoons freshly grated Parmesan cheese**
- ½ **cup Salsa Fresca (page 67)**

Cook the fettuccine according to the package's directions for *al dente* (To check on the "doneness," cut a strand of pasta in half. It's cooked when the center is done.) Toss the cooked, drained pasta with 2 tablespoons of the oil in a large bowl. Set aside.

Meanwhile, heat the remaining 2 tablespoons of oil in a 12-inch skillet.** Add the shrimp; cook over medium heat until they begin to turn pink, 2 to 3 minutes. Add the shallots and garlic; cook until the shallots soften, 2 to 3 minutes more. Add the cream and the Green Cashew Sauce; stir well. Add the pasta, salt, and pepper to the pan; mix well; add 2 tablespoons of the Parmesan cheese; stir well. Remove the pasta from the heat; transfer to individual serving plates. Garnish each serving with ½ tablespoon of the remaining Parmesan cheese and 2 tablespoons Salsa Fresca.

*For shrimp sizes, see "Selecting Shrimp," page 113.

**Note: if you are using a smaller skillet, make this recipe in two batches, or hold the pasta in the bowl, keep warm, and add the finished sauce with shrimps and the 2 tablespoons of Parmesan cheese to the bowl and toss well.

RASTA PASTA with CALYPSO SALSA

~~~~~~

Serves 4

This is a tasty vegetarian pasta dish. The fresh citrus, mint, ginger, and pineapple in the Calypso Salsa compliment the coconut milk in the pasta for a real flavor treat. For variety, top each serving with a Chicken Breast Criollo (page 91) and a heaping spoonful of Mango Salsa (page 67).

- 1 cup shredded sweetened coconut
- 1½ cups water
- 1½ pounds fresh fettuccine
- 4 tablespoons olive oil
- 2 teaspoons minced garlic
- 4 teaspoons minced shallots
- ⅛ teaspoon crushed red pepper flakes
- ½ cup heavy cream
- 8 tablespoons freshly grated Parmesan cheese
- 2 teaspoons chopped fresh parsley
- ½ cup Calypso Salsa (page 66)

Combine the coconut and water in a small saucepan; bring the liquid to a boil. Reduce the heat; simmer 5 minutes. Place a small sieve over a small bowl. Strain the coconut mixture. Reserve the liquid; discard the solids. Set aside.

Cook the pasta according to the package's directions for *al dente*. Toss the cooked, drained pasta with 2 tablespoons of the oil in a large bowl. Set aside.

Heat the remaining 2 tablespoons of oil in a 12-inch skillet. Add the garlic, shallots, and the red pepper flakes; cook over medium heat until the shallots are transparent, about 2 minutes. Add the pasta mixture, coconut liquid, and cream to the garlic mixture in the pan. Simmer, stirring occasionally, until the pasta absorbs the liquid, 3 to 4 minutes. Add the cheese and parsley; toss well. Serve immediately, topped with Calypso Salsa.

COCONUT PECAN CHICKEN

Serves 4

This is a real favorite—a nutty, toasted coconut crust surrounding a tender, juicy chicken breast, topped with the lightly sweet taste of Mango Butter. It's irresistible!

- **8 skinless, boneless chicken breast halves**
- **2 eggs**
- **1 tablespoon water**
- **1 teaspoon salt**
- **1/2 teaspoon freshly ground black pepper**
- **1 cup pecans**
- **1 cup shredded sweetened coconut**
- **2 tablespoons olive oil**
- **4 tablespoons Mango Butter (page 92)**

Place the chicken breasts between two sheets of plastic wrap and lightly pound them with a small mallet to 1/4-inch thickness.

Beat the eggs with the water, salt, and pepper in a shallow bowl. Set aside.

Place the pecans in a food processor or blender, pulse the machine two or three times to lightly chop the nuts. Add the coconut to the pecans; pulse five to six times until crumbly and well combined (but not a paste). Transfer the pecan/coconut crumbs to a piece of waxed paper or a flat plate. Dip the chicken breasts in the egg mixture, then press into the crumb mixture, coating both sides well.

Heat the oil in a 12-inch skillet. Add the chicken. Cook over medium-low heat, turning once, until nutty golden brown, about 8 minutes. To serve, place two pieces of chicken on each plate and top each piece with 1/2 tablespoon Mango Butter (the heat from the chicken will melt the butter appropriately). Serve immediately.

LINGUINE WITH CHORIZO AND SHRIMP IN A FRESH TOMATO CREAM SAUCE

Serves 4

This dish is served in a small restaurant right off the beach in Playa del Carmen. It's pasta with a tropical twist. The fresh flavors of shrimp and tomatoes and the spicy tastes of chorizo and chile are melded together with cream. The result—a tango of flavor on your plate!

- ½ pound dried linguine (or spaghetti)
- 2 garlic cloves, peeled and crushed
- 3 tablespoons salt, for the pasta water
- 1 tablespoon + 1 teaspoon olive oil
- ¾ pounds large shrimp (21-25 size,* about 18 shrimp)
- 6 ounces chorizo,** removed from casing and crumbled
- 2 serrano chiles, minced
- 2 medium tomatoes, peeled,*** seeded, and diced (about 1 cup)
- ½ cup fresh cream
- 1 teaspoon salt
- 4 ounces (½ cup) freshly grated Parmesan cheese
- 3 green onions, chopped, for garnish

In a large pot bring 3 quarts of water to a boil; add the 2 crushed garlic cloves and 3 tablespoons of salt. Add the pasta and cook according to package instructions for *al dente*. Remove from heat; drain; toss with 1 tablespoon of oil, and set aside.

In a large 12-inch skillet, heat 1 teaspoon olive oil over medium heat; add the shrimp, the chorizo, and the chile; cook, while stirring, until shrimp are pink but still firm, 1½ to 2 minutes. Add the tomatoes, stir well, and cook 2 minutes more. Add the cream and the salt; mix well. Stir in the pasta; mix well. Continue cooking briefly to allow pasta to reheat, about 1 minute. Remove from heat; add the Parmesan cheese; toss well. Place the pasta in individual serving plates; garnish with green onions.

*For shrimp sizes, see "Selecting Shrimp," page 113.
**Saag's brand chorizo is the best we've found short of making our own (see our recipe page 148).
***See "Skinning a Tomato," page 72.

GRILLED FLANK STEAK WITH CHIPOTLE CHILE BUTTER

Serves 4

Quick and easy, this entrée takes just minutes to make. The steaks can be barbecued or broiled. Serve with a green salad and rice or quinoa.

- **1 tablespoon freshly squeezed lemon juice**
- **2 tablespoons olive oil**
- **4 (8-ounce) flank steaks, ¾ inch thick**
- **1 teaspoon salt**
- **¼ teaspoon freshly ground black pepper**
- **4 tablespoons Chipotle Chile Butter (page 93)**

Preheat the broiler. Spray the broiler pan rack with nonstick cooking spray.

Mix the lemon juice and oil in a small, shallow bowl. Coat each steak with the lemon mixture. Sprinkle pepper on each steak.

Place the steaks on the prepared rack; broil 4 inches from the heat, turning once, until cooked to the desired doneness: 4 minutes for rare, 6 minutes for medium rare, 8 minutes for medium, and 11 minutes for well done.

Serve each steak garnished with 1 tablespoon of Chipotle Chile Butter.

Note

These steaks can also be prepared in a 12-inch skillet. Cook over medium-high heat, turning once, for the same desired doneness as the broiling time.

BAHIA BROCHETTE

Serves 4

This is a very tasty, fun, and easy dish to prepare—most of the work can be done ahead of time. Bahia Brochettes are perfect entrées for summer barbecues or patio dinners.

MARINADE

Makes about 1 cup

- ½ cup rice vinegar
- 1 tablespoon light molasses
- 2 tablespoons freshly squeezed lime juice
- 3 tablespoons chopped fresh cilantro
- ½ teaspoon salt
- ½ teaspoon habanero chile hot sauce (or other hot sauce)
- 1 tablespoon light corn syrup

BROCHETTE

- ½ pound skinless, boneless chicken breast halves, cut into 8 pieces
- 8 large shrimp (21/25 size,* about 6 ounces), cleaned and deveined
- ½ pound swordfish or shark, cut into 8 cubes
- 1 green bell pepper, seeded and deveined, cut into 8 pieces
- 1 red bell pepper, seeded and deveined, cut into 8 pieces
- 1 large onion, cut into 16 pieces
- 4 cherry tomatoes

BROCHETTE GLAZE

Makes about 1½ cups

- 4 tablespoons dark molasses
- 2 tablespoons Jamaican Jerk Spices, wet or dry (page 74-75)
- 5 tablespoons apricot jam
- 7 tablespoons light corn syrup
- 2 tablespoons freshly squeezed lime juice
- 4 tablespoons + 1 teaspoon cider vinegar
- 2 tablespoons tamarind paste or mango chutney (see "Tamarind," page 229)

Combine all the ingredients for the marinade in a large plastic container with an airtight lid, or in a gallon-size plastic bag. Add the chicken, shrimp, and fish. Cover or seal; marinate refrigerated for 12 to 16 hours.

Meanwhile, place all the ingredients for the glaze in a food processor or blender; purée until smooth. Store the mixture in the refrigerator in an airtight container for 4 hours to allow the flavors to marry.

Preheat the grill using a medium-high heat. On four metal skewers, alternately thread equal amounts of the bell

* For shrimp sizes, see "Selecting Shrimp," page 113.

peppers, onion, and marinated meat and seafood. Cap each skewer with a cherry tomato.

Grill the brochettes over medium heat, brushing with the Brochette Glaze as the brochette cooks, and turning several times, until the chicken is firm, the shrimp have curled, and the fish is flaky, about 10 minutes. Serve immediately.

Before You Grill...

Before cooking, review "Barbecuing" on pages 54-55. If you are using wooden skewers instead of metal, soak them in water for 30 minutes so they won't burn on the grill.

BLACKENED SWORDFISH STEAKS WITH AVOCADO SALSA

Serves 4

The Cajun Spices and the tart and creamy Avocado Salsa complement the meaty flavor of the swordfish in this tasty dish.

> 4 (6- to 7-ounce) swordfish steaks
> 2 tablespoons Cajun Blackening Spices (page 76)
> 2 tablespoons peanut or vegetable oil
> 1 cup Avocado Salsa (page 72)

Pat the steaks dry with paper towels. Place the Cajun Blackening Spices in a plastic or paper bag; add one steak. Seal the bag and shake until the steak is well coated with the spice mixture. Repeat with the remaining steaks.

Heat the oil in a 12-inch skillet. Add the steaks; cook over medium heat, turning once, until the spices begin to caramelize and blacken, about 7 minutes. Serve each steak topped with 3 tablespoons of Avocado Salsa.

COCHINITAS PIBIL
MAYAN-STYLE PORK, BAKED IN BANANA LEAVES

Serves 4

This is a classic Mayan dish. "Cochinitas" means little pigs and a "pib" is an oven. In pre-Columbian times, when a hunter came home with a wild pig, the meat was spiced with achiote paste, wrapped in leaves, and roasted in earthen pits. Today, in a similar manner, pork roasts are marinated with Seville orange juice, covered with achiote, wrapped in banana leaves, and slow roasted. The tender, deliciously spiced meat is then served with fried plantains (page 111), rice, and Black Beans Otomí (page 147). If you have a lidded clay cooking pot, by all means use it for this recipe and ignore the instructions for the aluminum foil.

- 1¼ cups of freshly squeezed Seville orange juice (or the juice of 4 limes, 2 oranges, and 1 grapefruit)
- 4 ounces achiote paste (for substitute, see "Achiote Paste," page 227)
- 1 (3½-pound) pork shoulder
- 4 banana leaves, prepared (see note on following page)
- 1 teaspoon salt
- ¼ teaspoon pepper

Squeeze the juice into a large nonreactive bowl. Add the achiote paste; mix well. Add the pork, coating the entire roast with the marinade mixture. Marinate in the refrigerator for 2 to 4 hours (overnight would be better).

Preheat the oven to 350°F. Line a 14 x11-inch baking dish with aluminum foil. Lay 2 banana leaves cross-wise so that the bottom of the baking dish is covered. Place the pork roast on the banana leaves; pour the Pibil marinade over the meat; season with the salt and pepper. Cover the roast with the remaining 2 banana leaves. Cover the baking dish with aluminum foil, pressing the foil to the pan sides to form a mini-oven.

Bake for 2 hours, or more, until very tender. Remove the roast from the pan. Degrease the Pibil pan juices; correct the seasoning. Prepare individual servings of the Pibil; spoon 3 to 4 tablespoons of the Pibil sauce over each serving. Serve immediately. Refrigerate the remainder of the Pibil sauce in a covered container; use it for saucing Capered Pork Chops Pibil (page 77), or on grilled tilapia, sole, or halibut.

Preparing Banana Leaves for Cooking

Banana leaves are easier to use when they have been softened and made pliable. To prepare the leaves: Turn the stove burner on to high; place a banana leaf directly on the burner; move the leaf constantly so that all of the surface is exposed to the heat (about 10 seconds). Turn over and repeat on the opposite side (about 10 seconds). You will notice that the leaf softens and the color changes to a darker green. Be very careful not to burn the leaf. Set aside. Repeat procedure with next leaf.

BARRACUDA CHETUMAL

Serves 4

Imagine a sunny day on a tropical beach. Your host deep-fries fresh-caught barracuda and serves it *al fresco*, under a shady palm tree, with avocado and lime slices, fresh salsas, and hot tortillas. If you don't have barracuda steaks, use corvina.

5 ounces freshly squeezed lime juice
2 teaspoons coarse-ground salt
½ teaspoon black pepper
4 (6- to 8-ounce) barracuda steaks, 1 inch thick
¼ cup flour
½ cup peanut oil
1 avocado, sliced, for garnish
1 lime, sliced, for garnish

Mix the lime juice, salt, and pepper together in a small bowl. Place the barracuda steaks in a shallow bowl, pour the lime juice mixture over the steaks, turning them every 5 minutes for 20 minutes.

Place the flour on a large dinner plate and dredge each steak in the flour, coating well.

Heat the oil in a 10-inch skillet over medium-high heat. When the oil reaches 350°F, add the steaks and cook for 7 minutes, turning once. Remove the fish from the pan and drain on paper towels. Serve immediately, garnished with slices of avocado and lime, and accompanied by your favorite salsa and hot corn tortillas.

PECAN CRUSTED SNAPPER

Serves 4

This is a great way to serve snapper—the pecan crust adds a nutty flavor and a pleasing texture to the fish. It is important not to overcrowd the pan while you are cooking these fillets. If your pan cannot accommodate all the fish at one time, just cook the fillets in two batches. It doesn't take long. For an elegant look, shave the Mango Butter before topping the snapper fillets.

> **2 eggs**
> **1 tablespoon water,**
> **1 teaspoon salt**
> **½ teaspoon freshly ground black pepper**
> **1½ cups roasted pecans, finely chopped into crumbs (not into a paste!)**
> **4 (6-ounce) snapper fillets, deboned, skin removed**
> **2 teaspoons olive oil**
> **4 tablespoons Mango Butter (page 92)**

Beat the 2 eggs with the water, salt, and pepper in a shallow bowl. Spread the pecan crumbs on a plate or a piece of waxed paper. Pat the snapper fillets dry with paper towels. Dip the fillets in the egg mixture, then dredge them in the pecan crumbs, coating both sides well.

Heat the olive oil in a 12-inch skillet. Add the fillets; cook over medium heat, turning once, until the coating begins to crack and the juices run, about 7 to 8 minutes, depending on the thickness of the fillets. The fish is cooked when the crust on the second side begins to crack and a little white liquid begins to seep out. Remove from heat; serve immediately. Top each fillet with 1 tablespoon of shaved Mango Butter.

CAMARONES AL MOJO DE AJO
GARLIC SHRIMP

Serves 4

Garlic and shrimp are a favorite Latin seafood combination and this popular dish is found on many menus in beach-side cafés and restaurants throughout the Gulf of Mexico and the Caribbean coast. Our version comes accompanied by a head of roasted garlic, definitely a dish for garlic lovers. Serve Camerones al Mojo de Ajo with rice and a fresh green salad and, of course, a loaf of good French bread.

- **4 garlic heads**
- **2 tablespoons olive oil**
- **2 medium shallots, minced (about 5 tablespoons)**
- **2 pounds extra large shrimp (16-20 size;* about 36 shrimp)**
- **4 medium tomatoes, peeled** and chopped (about 1 cup)**
- **2 chile serranos, minced**
- **2 green onions, chopped**
- **2 tablespoons freshly squeezed lime juice**
- **1 teaspoon salt**
- **Sprig of cilantro**

Preheat the oven to 350°F. Place a garlic head side ways on a chopping board. Using a knife, slice off the bottom ⅓ of the head. Set the bottom portion aside.

Repeat with each of the remaining garlic heads. Heat 1 tablespoon of the oil in a 12-inch skillet over medium heat; place the four garlic heads cut end down in the pan so that the cut cloves make contact with the oil. Cook for 5 minutes on medium low; the cut end should look brown (don't let the garlic burn or it will develop a bitter taste). Remove the garlic heads from the pan; set the pan, and the garlic oil in it, aside. Place the garlic heads in a small baking dish; bake in the preheated oven for 20 to 25 minutes. Remove from oven and set aside.

Peel the bottom portions of the garlic heads; mince. Add 1 tablespoon oil to the skillet containing the garlic oil. Heat the oil over medium heat; add the minced garlic, shallots, and chile; cook until the mixture begins to sweat, 1½ minutes. Add the shrimp; toss; cook for 4 to 5 minutes, tossing so that they cook evenly. Add the tomatoes; cook 2 minutes more. Add the salt; toss and turn off the heat. Add the lime juice and the green onion; toss lightly. Place the shrimp in individual plates, garnishing each dish with one of the roasted garlic heads. Serve immediately.

*For shrimp sizes, see "Selecting Shrimp," page 113.
**See "Skinning a Tomato," page 72.

POLLO PIBIL
MAYAN–STYLE CHICKEN, BAKED IN BANANA LEAVES

Serves 4

Pollo Pibil is a classic Maya dish that is traditionally cooked in earthen pits. The combination of citrus and achiote give the dish a distinctive color and rich flavor. The banana leaves infuse additional flavor to the chicken as they steam, and they help keep the chicken moist and juicy. To make your feast complete, serve this dish with rice, Tostones (fried plantains) (page 111), Black Beans Otomí (page 147) , and a garnish of Spicy Pickled Onions (page 71). If you have a lidded clay cooking pot, use it for this recipe and ignore the instructions for the aluminum foil.

> 1¼ cups freshly squeezed Seville
> orange juice
> (or the juice of 4 limes, 2 oranges,
> and 1 grapefruit)
> 4 ounces achiote paste
> (for substitute, see "Achiote
> Paste," page 227)
> 1 (3½- to 4-pound) chicken, cut
> into 4 serving sections
> 4 banana leaves, prepared (see
> note on following page)
> 1 teaspoon salt
> ¼ teaspoon pepper

Squeeze the juice into a large nonreactive bowl. Add the achiote paste; mix well. Add the chicken pieces, stirring so that each piece is coated with the marinade mixture. Marinate in the refrigerator for at least 2 hours (overnight would be better).

Preheat the oven to 350°F. Line a 14 x 11-inch baking dish with aluminum foil. Lay 2 banana leaves cross-wise so that the bottom of the baking dish is covered. Place the chicken pieces on the banana leaves; pour the Pibil marinade over the chicken; season with the salt and pepper. Cover the chicken with the remaining 2 banana leaves. Cover the baking dish with aluminum foil, pressing the foil to the pan sides to form a mini-oven.

Bake for 1 hour. Remove the pan from the oven; remove the foil cover and the top banana leaves from the pan. Adjust the oven shelf to sit 6½ inches from the broiler heating element; change oven setting to "broil." Return chicken to oven; broil for 4 minutes. Remove the chicken from the pan. Place servings on individual plates. Degrease the Pibil pan juices; correct the seasoning. Spoon 3 to 4 tablespoons of the Pibil sauce over each serving. Serve immediately. Refrigerate the remainder of the Pibil sauce in a covered container; use it for saucing Capered Pork Chops Pibil (page 177), or on grilled tilapia, sole, or halibut.

CAPERED PORK CHOPS PIBIL

Serves 4

This is a great second-day recipe. It utilizes the remaining Pibil Sauce from Pollo Pibil. The sauce, flavored with the chicken juices and banana leaves from the Pibil pan, makes a rich topping for the capered pork chops.

- **½ cup flour (for coating)**
- **1 teaspoon salt**
- **¼ teaspoon freshly ground black pepper**
- **4 (6- to 8-ounce) T-bone pork chops**
- **2 tablespoons butter**
- **4 tablespoons minced garlic**
- **4 tablespoons capers with their juice**
- **⅔ cup Pibil Sauce**

Spread flour on a dinner plate. Sprinkle salt and pepper over one side of a pork chop, lightly press the seasoned side of the pork chop into the flour; sprinkle salt and pepper on the unseasoned side; turn over and press this side into the flour; set aside. Repeat the process with the remaining 3 chops.

Using a 12-inch skillet, heat the butter over medium heat until it starts to brown. Add the pork chops; cook over medium heat, turning several times, for 6 minutes. Add the garlic; let it soften but don't let it burn. Add the capers and their juice and the Pibil Sauce. Increase the heat to medium high and allow the sauce to boil for 30 seconds. Serve the pork chops on individual plates, topped with the Capered Pibil Sauce.

Preparing Banana Leaves for Cooking

Banana leaves are easier to use when they have been softened and made pliable. To prepare the leaves: Turn the stove burner on to high; place a banana leaf directly on the burner; move the leaf constantly so that all of the surface is exposed to the heat (about 10 seconds). Turn over and repeat on the opposite side (about 10 seconds). You will notice that the leaf softens and the color changes to a darker green. Be very careful not to burn the leaf. Set aside. Repeat procedure with next leaf.

LOMITO DE VALLADOLID
PORK CHOPS VALLADOLID

Serves 4

This uncomplicated dish uses a tangy roasted tomato sauce; it goes well with rice, quinoa, or pasta.

- **3 pounds pork loin chops**
- **1½ cup water**
- **3 teaspoons salt**
- **3 pounds tomatoes**
- **1 habanero chile, roasted**

Trim the pork chops of all excess fat; reserve the fat. Cut the meat into ½-inch cubes, set aside. Place the fat in an 8-quart saucepan. Cook the fat on medium low heat until it browns, about 3 to 4 minutes. Let the pot cool for 2 minutes, then discard the fat, but do not discard the fat drippings. Place the meat in the saucepan with the drippings, add the water and 2 teaspoons of salt, cover and cook over medium-low heat for 30 minutes. Remove the lid and raise the heat to medium; cook until the liquid evaporates.

Roast the tomatoes and the habanero chile (see this page or page 65). Rinse each tomato in cool running water for about 5 seconds, discarding the skin. It's OK to leave a little of the blackened skin on the tomatoes. Put the tomatoes and ½ of the roasted chile in a blender or food processor; purée. Add 1 teaspoon of salt to the mixture; blend. It should yield 5 to 6 cups of sauce.

When all of the liquid has evaporated from the saucepan containing the pork, add the tomato sauce. Cook, uncovered, over medium-low heat, stirring occasionally, until the tomato sauce has been reduced by half, about 20 minutes. Serve immediately.

Fire Roasting Tomatoes

A really quick way to roast a tomato—or a chile—is to use a small blowtorch; it takes 30 seconds to roast a tomato this way. Place the tomato on a grill rack on the stovetop or on another heavy-duty surface. Using the blowtorch, scorch the skin of the tomato evenly on all sides. Allow the tomato to cool, then remove the skin if desired.

Mini or micro torches (about 6 inches tall) are also available at hardware stores. They are easier to hold than the larger ones but they will require a little more time to roast a tomato—about 60 seconds. We have even used them on fresh ears of corn. The results are wonderful.

As always when using flame, be very careful. Blowtorches are not for use by children.

DEEP-FRIED WHOLE SNAPPER WITH FRESH TOMATO SALSA

Serves 2

Deep-fried whole fish is a popular dish throughout Latin America and the Caribbean. In fishing communities, the fish is often scaled and fried in little beach-side restaurants just as it comes in from the boat. Served with fried plantains, warm tortillas, and a cold beer, this dish captures the essence of Latin American coastal cuisine.

1 (1¼- to 1½-pound) whole snapper or rock cod, cleaned and scaled
1 egg
1 tablespoon water
½ teaspoon salt
⅛ teaspoon pepper
½ cup corn meal
1½ cup peanut oil, for cooking
½ medium red onion, diced
3 serrano chiles, minced
2 medium tomatoes, diced
1 tablespoon fresh cilantro, chopped
2 tablespoons freshly squeezed lime juice
1 lime, thinly sliced, for garnish

Using a paring knife, score* both sides of the fish, making the cuts ½-inch deep. In a wide, shallow bowl, mix the egg with the water; pass the fish through the egg mixture, coating it well. Sprinkle the salt and the pepper equally on both sides of the fish. Spread the corn meal on a dinner plate; roll the fish in the corn meal, coating it well.

Heat the oil in a large, 12-inch skillet over medium-high heat to 350°F. Do not let the oil smoke. Put the fish in the oil and cook it for 2 to 2½ minutes; turn and cook an additional 2 to 2½ minutes, until the fish is done. The fish will be done when the coating is crispy and the flesh separates easily from the bones. Set the fish aside on paper towels to drain.

Place the onion, chiles, tomatoes, cilantro, lime juice, and ¼ teaspoon salt in a medium-size bowl, mix well. Spoon half the tomato mixture onto a medium-size serving platter; place the fish on the platter; spoon the remaining tomato salsa over the fish. Place one lime slice over the fish's eye; garnish the rim of the serving platter with the remaining lime slices. Serve immediately.

*Make diagonal cuts from left to right and right to left, carving a diamond pattern into the skin of the fish.

AMAZON CATFISH

Serves 4

This dish is like a flavor carnival, combining the fruity Cayman Curry Sauce with the taste of fresh tomatoes and Spicy Roasted Peanuts. Try this recipe with other freshwater fish such as trout or tilapia.

Sauce

1 tablespoon peanut or
    vegetable oil
1 medium yellow onion, diced
1 cup Cayman Curry Sauce (page 87)
½ cup diced jícama
½ cup seeded, drained, and
    diced tomatoes (slice tomatoes
    in half first, then squeeze out the
    seeds and excess juice)

Fish

2 eggs
1 tablespoon water
1 teaspoon salt
½ teaspoon freshly ground black
    pepper
½ cup all-purpose flour
4 (6-ounce) catfish fillets,
    deboned, skin removed
1 cup Japanese* bread crumbs or
    other unseasoned dried bread
    crumbs
½ cup cornmeal
Peanut or vegetable oil, for frying
¼ cup Spicy Roasted Peanuts
    (page 105), for garnish

To prepare the sauce, heat 1 tablespoon of oil in a 10-inch skillet. Add the onion; cook over medium heat until the onion is golden brown, about 5 minutes. Add the Caiman Curry Sauce; bring the liquid to a boil. Add the jícama and the tomatoes to the sauce mixture. Reduce the heat to low; simmer about 2 minutes. Set aside; keep warm.

To prepare the fish, beat the eggs, water, salt, and pepper in a shallow bowl. Spread the flour on a flat plate or a piece of waxed paper. Combine the bread crumbs and cornmeal on another flat plate or piece of waxed paper. One at a time, dredge the catfish fillets in the flour, then dip them in the egg mixture, then dredge them in the cornmeal/bread crumb mixture, coating both sides well.

Heat ½ inch of oil to 350°F in a large, deep, heavy skillet. Carefully add 2 fillets; cook over medium heat, turning once, until golden brown, 6 to 8 minutes. Remove with a slotted spoon or spatula; drain on paper towels. Repeat with the remaining fillets. Top the fillets with the warm sauce; garnish with Spicy Roasted Peanuts. Serve immediately.

*Japanese bread crumbs (*panko*) can be found with other bread crumbs and batter mixes in most supermarkets and are available through mail order.

SAUTEED PRAWNS RIO COCO
SHRIMP IN LIME COCONUT SAUCE

Serves 4

This dish combines the flavors of the tropical coast—shrimp, coconut, lime, and a kiss of chile—in a savory dish that's hard to beat.

2 cups sweetened shredded coconut
1½ cups cold water
¼ cup heavy cream
1½ tablespoons olive oil
2 tablespoons finely chopped shallots
1 tablespoon finely chopped garlic
½ serrano or jalapeño chile, finely chopped
36 large shrimp (21-25 size,* about 1½ pounds), shelled, deveined, and patted dry
1 cup diced jícama
1 teaspoon chopped fresh parsley
2 tablespoons freshly squeezed lime juice

Preheat the oven to 350°F. Spread ½ cup of the shredded coconut on a baking pan, and bake for 7 minutes, stirring once while toasting. Remove the coconut from oven and reserve it for garnish.

Combine the remaining 1½ cups of coconut with the water in a small saucepan; bring the liquid to a boil. Reduce the heat; simmer for 15 minutes. Place a small sieve over a small bowl; strain the coconut mixture.

Reserve the liquid; discard the solids. You should have 1 cup of the coconut milk. (If you have too much, return the liquid to the saucepan; reduce to 1 cup over medium heat.) Refrigerate to cool the liquid down to room temperature. Add the heavy cream to the cooled coconut milk and set aside.

Heat ½ tablespoon of the oil in a 10-inch skillet. Add the shallots, garlic, and chile; cook over medium heat until the shallots are soft and transparent, 2 to 3 minutes. Remove from heat.

Meanwhile, heat the remaining oil in a 12-inch skillet. Add the shrimp; cook over high heat until they turn pink, 3 to 4 minutes. (Don't crowd the shrimp—if you're using a smaller skillet, cook the shrimp in two batches.) Add the shallot mixture to the shrimp; mix well. Add the coconut cream mixture to the shrimp, and continue cooking over high heat until the sauce in the pan is reduced by one-third, about 4 minutes. Add the jícama, parsley, and finally the lime juice to the shrimp; mix well and remove the pan from the heat immediately. Garnish with the reserved toasted coconut. Serve immediately.

*For shrimp sizes, see "Selecting Shrimp," page 113.

PASTA PAELLA

Serves 4

This dish is a Spanish classic done with pasta instead of rice; it combines seafood, chicken, and linguiça in a saffron cream sauce. Pasta Paella makes a wonderful main course. Serve it with a green salad and a loaf of French bread.

PASTA

- $\frac{1}{2}$ pound dried linguine
- 2 quarts water
- 2 tablespoons salt
- 1 tablespoon olive oil

Bring two quarts of water to a boil in a large pot; add salt and linguine. Cook the pasta according to the package's directions for *al dente*, about 7 to 8 minutes. (To check on the "doneness," cut one stand in half; the pasta is done when the center is cooked.) Drain off hot water from pot; place the pot of pasta under cold running water until pasta is cool; drain in a colander. Place the pasta in a large bowl; add 1 tablespoon of olive oil, and toss the pasta so that all the strands are coated and won't stick together. Set aside.

PAELLA SAUCE

- 2 tablespoons olive oil
- $\frac{3}{4}$ pound linguiça sausage, sliced into $\frac{1}{2}$-inch pieces
- $\frac{3}{4}$ pound chicken breast meat, cut into $\frac{1}{4}$-inch cubes
- 2 tablespoons butter
- 2 teaspoons chopped garlic
- 2 tablespoons chopped shallots
- 1 pound prawns, cleaned and deveined
- 1 pound calamari, sliced into 1-inch x $\frac{1}{2}$-inch strips
- $\frac{1}{2}$ pound fresh fish (mahi mahi, monkfish, or halibut), cut into $\frac{1}{4}$-inch cubes
- 12 green-lipped mussels, cleaned and debearded
- 2 cups white wine
- 1 large pinch of saffron
- $\frac{1}{2}$ cup julienned carrots
- $\frac{1}{2}$ cup julienned jícama
- 2 tablespoons flour
- 1 cup cream (for a lower-calorie version, use 1 cup milk)
- Salt and pepper to taste
- 1 cup fresh diced tomatoes
- 1 cup freshly grated Parmesan cheese
- 2 tablespoons freshly chopped parsley

Heat 1 tablespoon of olive oil in a large 14-inch skillet over a low fire; add the linguiça; cook until done. Set the sausage aside. Drain the grease from the skillet (do not wash skillet). Heat the remaining oil in the same skillet over low heat; add the chicken; cook until done, about 3 to 4 minutes. Set chicken aside with linguiça. Without cleaning the pan, add butter, garlic, and shallots. Cook over low heat until the garlic sweats, about 1 minute. Add the prawns and calamari; cook over medium heat for four to five minutes. Add the fish, the mussels, white wine, saffron, julienned carrots, and jícama. Bring the liquid to a boil; cover the skillet; continue cooking until the mussels open, about 2 minutes. Remove the mussels from the pan (leaving the rest of the ingredients); set mussels aside with chicken and linguiça. Add 2 tablespoons of flour to the ingredients in the pan; mix well. Cook the contents of the pan over medium low heat until the sauce is reduced by half, about 5 minutes. Add the cream (or the milk) to the sauce; season with salt and pepper to taste. Add the diced tomatoes; stir. Remove from heat.

Put the desired portion of pasta in each plate; warm in a microwave about 30 seconds each. When pasta is warm, add the pieces of chicken, sausage, and three mussels to each plate. Pour the sauce (with the fish and calamari) over the pasta, dividing it evenly between the plates. Serve immediately, garnished with the cheese and parsley.

PORK CHOPS BRAISED IN TOMATILLO SAUCE

Serves 4

This is one of our favorite ways to do pork—the rich and tangy tomatillo sauce complements the browned, diced pork. While this dish doesn't make a really great visual presentation, it more than makes up for this shortcoming with flavor. Try garnishing it with a dollop of Crème Fraîche (page 51) or sour cream, and a sprig of cilantro. Serve it accompanied by rice, quinoa, or pasta. *Sabroso!*

> **3 pounds T-bone pork chops**
> **2 cups of Tomatillo Sauce (page 88)**
> **1 teaspoon salt**

Remove the bone and excess fat from the pork chops; reserve. Heat a 10-inch skillet over medium heat. Place the bones and the trimmed fat in the pan and cook, stirring occasionally, until browned, about 5 minutes. Remove the bones and fat from the skillet; reserve the skillet and its drippings. Cut the meat into $\frac{1}{2}$-inch cubes. Place the meat in the skillet with the drippings, cook over high heat until brown, stirring frequently; about 5 minutes. When the meat has browned, turn off the heat; allow the skillet to cool for 1 to 2 minutes. Add the Tomatillo Sauce, stir, cover the skillet with a lid, cook over medium low heat for 30 minutes. Add salt, stir, and serve immediately.

SAUTÉED SHRIMP DIABLO

Serves 4

Shrimp Diablo means shrimp "the Devil's way" or, in other words, hot! These are really spicy, flavorful shrimp. If you want them to taste of the inferno, add more chile to the sauce as you cook it. Be careful not to overcook the sauce; it's supposed to be rich and chunky. Rice makes a nice accompaniment to this dish and will absorb every remaining bit of the tasty sauce.

> **2 tablespoons olive oil**
> **2 tablespoons minced shallots**
> **2 teaspoons minced garlic**
> **¼ teaspoon crushed red pepper flakes**
> **32 large shrimp (21-25 size,* about 1½ pounds), peeled and deveined**
> **1 cup Fresh Tomato Sauce (page 88)**
> **1 cup Salsa Fresca (page 67)**
> **¾ cup roasted cashew nuts**
> **2 tablespoons chopped fresh cilantro**

Heat the oil in a 12-inch skillet. (It's best not to crowd the shrimp when cooking. If you are using a smaller skillet, make this recipe in 2 batches, dividing the ingredients equally). Add the shallots, garlic, red pepper flakes, and shrimp; cook over medium heat until the shrimp begin to turn pink, about 3 minutes.

Add the Fresh Tomato Sauce to the shrimp mixture; cook until the sauce begins to simmer, about 1 minute. Add the Salsa Fresca, cashew nuts, and cilantro; mix well. Remove from the heat. Serve immediately, spooning extra sauce over the shrimp.

*For shrimp sizes, see "Selecting Shrimp," page 113.

SNAPPER MARDI GRAS

Serves 4

This dish is like a party in your mouth! The Cajun Blackening Spices and Roasted Red Pepper Sauce dance with the fresh tomatoes and cilantro to make this a memorable seafood dish.

- 4 (6-ounce) snapper fillets, deboned, skin removed
- 3 tablespoons olive oil
- ¼ cup Cajun Blackening Spices (page 76)
- 1 cup Roasted Red Pepper Sauce (page 83)
- ½ cup seeded, drained, and diced tomatoes (slice the tomatoes in half first, then squeeze out the seeds and excess juice)
- 2 tablespoons chopped fresh cilantro

Rinse the the snapper fillets under cool running water; pat dry with paper towels. Rub the fillets lightly with 1 tablespoon of the oil (or less) so that the spices will adhere. Place the Cajun Blackening Spices in a plastic or paper bag; add one fillet. Seal and shake until the fillet is well coated with the spice mixture. Repeat with the remaining fillets.

Heat the remaining 2 tablespoons of oil in a 12-inch skillet. Add the fillets (don't crowd the fillets, if using a smaller skillet, cook the fillets in two batches). Cook over medium heat, turning once, until the fillets begin to blacken (about 3½ minutes on the first side, 2 minutes on the second side). Don't worry about the blackened color of the spices—that's what you're looking for in this dish. Add the Roasted Red Pepper Sauce and the diced tomatoes; cook 1 minute more. Transfer the fillets to a serving platter, leaving the sauce in the pan. Simmer the sauce for 2 minutes more, then spoon the sauce over the fillets. Serve the fillets garnished with the chopped cilantro.

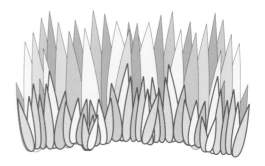

TURKEY YUCATECA

Serves 10 to 12

This is a bird you won't forget. The meat is juicy and tender; the dressing is sweet, fruity, and spicy, combining the flavors of tropical fruits and liqueur, with the smoky bite of chipotle chiles and achiote. The sauce is fantastic! To prepare this dish, you'll need an oven cooking bag, which can be found in any supermarket in the plastic-wrap section. The bag makes the turkey extra moist and cleanup a snap!

- 3 Granny Smith or Pippin apples (about 1 pound), cored and chopped, with peels left on
- 1½ pounds dried fruit mix—apricot, mango, pineapple, and papaya
- ½ cup frozen orange juice concentrate
- ½ cup pineapple juice
- ½ cup chipotle chiles in adobo (canned, smoked jalapeño chiles)
- 2 cups tequila or rum
- 2 cups orange liqueur (e.g. Curaçao, Grand Marnier, Triple Sec)
- 5 tablespoons sweet butter, softened
- 1 (10- to 12-pound) fresh young tom turkey
- 2 tablespoons salt
- 2 tablespoons freshly ground black pepper
- 2 tablespoons achiote paste (for substitute, see "Achiote Paste," page 227)
- 2 tablespoons minced fresh garlic

In a medium-size bowl, combine the apples, dried fruits, orange juice concentrate, and pineapple juice. Set aside.

Combine the chiles, tequila, and orange liqueur in a food processor or blender; purée until it becomes a liquid paste. Pour the liquid over the fruit mixture; stir; let sit for 30 minutes.

Place a small sieve over a small bowl. Strain the fruit mixture; reserve both the liquid and the fruit solids. Add 2½ tablespoons of the butter to the fruit mixture. Set aside.

Preheat the oven to 350°F. Rinse the turkey inside and out, and pat it dry with paper towels. Combine the salt, pepper, achiote paste, and garlic in a small bowl; mix well. Rub the body and the cavities, outside and in, with the salt/achiote mixture.

Press 3 cups of the solid fruit mixture into the body cavity of the turkey, and 2 cups into the front cavity (wishbone area). Insert a cooking thermometer into the thickest part of the breast, not touching the bone.

Place the bird into an oven cooking bag, breast side up; pour the reserved liquid and remaining fruit mixture over the turkey. Melt the remaining butter and pour it over the bird. Tie the bag, not quite closing it, gathering it on top to form a natural "chimney." Placed the bagged turkey into a large roasting pan, making sure that the bag is not hanging over the sides.

Roast the turkey until the meat thermometer registers 180°F, about 3 hours.

Remove the turkey from the oven; let it rest for 45 to 60 minutes. Remove the fruit mixture from the cavities. Pour the sauce into a cup and skim off any excess fat. Serve the carved turkey with the fruit dressing and sauce.

IN PRAISE OF THE OVEN COOKING BAG

Use a cooking bag to save on cleanup and keep your bird constantly basted in the cooking juices. This is effortless cooking: put the stuffed turkey in a preheated oven and go about your daily routine. Open the oven door a few hours later, and you've got a tender, juicy bird ready for your table.

Place the turkey in the cooking bag so that the bag will close to form a "chimney."

CALAMARI STEAK WITH ROASTED RED PEPPER SAUCE

Serves 4

This is a great way to serve calamari. The delicate, somewhat sweet flavor of the squid is enhanced by the rich, tangy Roasted Red Pepper Sauce.

2 eggs
1 tablespoon water
1 teaspoon salt
½ teaspoon freshly ground black pepper
½ cup all-purpose flour
4 (4½- to 5-ounce) calamari steaks
2 tablespoons peanut oil
1 cup Roasted Red Pepper Sauce (page 83)
½ cup diced tomatoes
1 teaspoon chopped fresh parsley
Salt and pepper to taste

Beat the eggs with the water, salt, and pepper in a shallow bowl. Spread the flour on a flat plate or piece of waxed paper. Set aside.

Using a small mallet, lightly pound the calamari steaks between 2 sheets of plastic wrap or waxed paper to tenderize them. Dip the steaks in the egg mixture, then dredge in the flour, coating both sides well.

Heat the oil in a 12-inch skillet. Add the steaks (don't crowd the steaks in the skillet—if using a smaller skillet, cook them in two batches). Cook over medium heat until the first side is golden brown, about 4 minutes. Turn the steaks; cook 2 minutes more. Add the Roasted Red Pepper Sauce, tomatoes, and parsley; cook until heated through, 1 minute.

Sprinkle salt and pepper to taste. Transfer the calamari to a serving plate. Spoon the sauce remaining in the pan over the steaks (it should have a chunky texture), and serve immediately.

WHAT? NO CALAMARI?

Chicken breasts can be substituted for the calamari: Use 8 skinless, boneless chicken breast halves (1¼ pounds), pounded to a ¼-inch thickness and soaked overnight in 2 cups of clam juice.

PEPPERED SALMON WITH CILANTRO AND ROASTED SERRANO AIOLI

Serves 4

This is a savory way to serve fresh salmon; perfect for a summer evening meal *al fresco*. This recipe makes almost 2 cups of the Cilantro and Roasted Serrano Aïoli. If you are going to make the Aïoli ahead of dinner, or if you have leftover sauce—especially if you use raw eggs in the recipe, the Aïoli needs to be kept refrigerated.

- 3 egg yolks or 3 tablespoons mayonnaise
- 1 teaspoon salt
- ¼ cup freshly squeezed lime juice
- 1 garlic clove
- 4 serrano or jalapeño chiles, roasted* and seeded
- 1 teaspoon balsamic vinegar (do not substitute)
- 5 tablespoons chopped fresh cilantro
- 1 cup high-quality extra-virgin olive oil
- 4 (6-ounce) salmon fillets
- 1 teaspoon freshly ground black pepper
- 2 tablespoons peanut oil
- 4 cilantro sprigs, for garnish

To prepare the sauce, place the yolks, salt, lime juice, garlic, roasted chiles, vinegar, and cilantro in a food processor or blender. Blend until smooth, about 1 to 2 minutes. With the motor running, add the oil in a thin, steady stream until all of the oil has been incorporated into the sauce. Transfer the sauce to an airtight container; refrigerate until ready to use.

To prepare the fish, season both sides of the fillets with the black pepper. Heat the peanut oil in a 12-inch skillet. Add the fish, cook over medium heat, turning once, until the fish is cooked through, 7 to 8 minutes. Serve the salmon with a dollop the Roasted Serrano Aïoli and a sprig of cilantro as garnish.

*See "Roasting Peppers," page 65.

FILETE A LA YUCATECA
FILLET TAILS YUCATÁN STYLE

Serves 4

This steak makes an elegant main course for a special dinner, or a quick one for a casual dinner—very versatile! Much of the work can be done ahead (and there's really not much prep work). Serve this steak with a baked potato (the salsa goes well with sour cream), or rice.

2 (1-pound) beef fillet tails
3 cups water
2 tablespoons salt, for brine
1 bunch scallions (green onions), well rinsed
2 medium sweet white onions, such as Walla Walla or Visalia, thinly sliced
½ cup freshly squeezed Seville orange juice
(or use the freshly squeezed juice of 2 limes, 1 orange, and ½ grapefruit)
2 cups diced tomatoes (about ¼ x ¼-inch cubes)
1 teaspoon salt
3 tablespoons chopped fresh cilantro
¼ habanero chile, finely minced
4 garlic cloves, each sliced lengthwise into 4 pieces
8 green onions
1 teaspoon olive oil

Trim the excess fat off of the meat; reserve the fat. Butterfly* each steak (cut it horizontally through the center), then separate each steak into 2 pieces. Mix the water and salt in a medium-size nonreactive bowl; add the meat to the brine and set aside for 30 minutes. (If you are not planning to cook it now, after 30 minutes, drain the meat and store it, covered, in the refrigerator.)

Cut the bottom 2 inches (the heads) off of the scallions, set the heads aside; chop the green section and place it in a medium-size nonreactive bowl. Add the sweet onion slices, the Seville orange juice, the diced tomatoes, 1 teaspoon of salt, the chopped cilantro, and the habanero chile to the bowl; mix well and set the Sweet Onion and Tomato Salsa aside. (Refrigerate, covered, if you are preparing ahead.)

Heat a 12-inch skillet over medium heat; add the fat and cook, tossing occasionally, until the fat has been browned, about 4 minutes. Turn off the heat and allow the pan to cool. Remove and discard the fat. Place the garlic slices in the same pan with the fat drippings; over medium heat cook the

*To butterfly a piece of meat or seafood, cut lengthwise through its center, stopping when the piece is almost split in half; leave the two sections connected. Open the two sections so they lay flat; they will open out like two butterfly wings.

EIGHT

190

garlic slices, turning twice, until they are browned, about 2½ to 3 minutes. Remove the garlic from the pan, set aside on a plate. Add the reserved scallion heads to the same pan with the drippings and brown, 1½ minutes on each side. Turn off the heat; let the scallions rest in the pan for an additional 2 minutes. Place the scallions on the plate with the garlic. Using the same pan with the drippings, add the olive oil and heat over high heat for 1 minute. Put the meat in the skillet, cook, turning once, 6 minutes for medium rare. (To cook medium, let the meat rest in the pan, with the heat off, for an additional 3 minutes.) Place the steaks on individual serving plates; serve the Sweet Onion and Tomato Salsa in small ramekins next to the steak, about ½ cup in each.

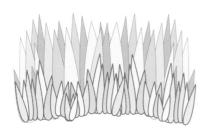

GRILLED CHICKEN BREAST CRIOLLO WITH MANGO SALSA

Serves 4

This chicken makes for great grilling, and topped with Mango Salsa, it's quite a hit! Leftovers can be shredded and used in tacos and enchiladas, and as a filling for Tostaditas (page 109).

> 1 cup Criollo Marinade (page 90)
> 4 (7-ounce) boneless, skinless chicken breasts, pounded to a ¼-inch thickness
> 1 tablespoon peanut oil
> 1 cup Mango Salsa (page 67)

Put the Criollo Marinade into a sealable plastic bag or nonreactive bowl; add the chicken. Make sure each breast is well coated with the liquid. Seal or cover and refrigerate for 2 hours, allowing the chicken to marinate.

Remove the chicken from the marinade. Heat the oil in a 12-inch skillet. Add the chicken and cook over a medium heat, turning once, until browned and the juices run clear, about 6 minutes. Remove from heat, garnish with 4 tablespoons of Mango Salsa per chicken breast, and serve.

MAYAN CLAY POT CHICKEN

Serves 3 to 4

This is a delicious, country-style way to prepare chicken. Serve the chicken topped with the savory clay pot juices, accompanied by rice or potatoes.

1 (3½- to 4-pound) broiler chicken
4 tablespoons achiote paste
   (for substitute, see "Achiote
   Paste," page 227)
½ cup freshly squeezed Seville
   orange juice
   (or use the freshly squeezed
   juices of ¼ grapefruit,
   ½ orange, and 1 lime)
½ medium red onion, sliced
6 garlic cloves, halved
1 jalapeño chile, sliced
1 red bell pepper, sliced
4 leafy sprigs of fresh spearmint
½ teaspoon freshly ground black
   pepper
½ teaspoon salt

Preheat the oven to 350°F. Soak the clay pot and its lid in water for 10 minutes. Drain.

Rinse the chicken in cool water; pat dry with paper towels. Place it in a bowl. Dissolve the achiote paste (or substitute) in ¼ cup of Seville orange juice. Brush the achiote mixture on the chicken while in the bowl (be careful, achiote stains!).

Combine the onion, garlic, jalapeño chile, bell pepper, and mint in a medium-size bowl; mix well. Place three-quarters of this vegetable mixture into the bottom of the prepared clay pot. Place the remaining vegetable mixture into the cavity of the chicken. Place the chicken into the clay pot, on the vegetable mixture, breast side up. Combine the remaining ¼ cup Seville orange juice with the remaining achiote mixture; pour it around (not over) the chicken. Season with the pepper and salt.

Cover the clay pot with the lid. Bake until a meat thermometer, when placed in the center of the thickest part of the breast, but not touching the bone, registers 180°F, about 1 hour 15 minutes.

Remove the pot from the oven; let stand 10 minutes. Transfer the chicken to a platter; carve. Pour the liquid from the pot into a cup; skim off any excess fat. Serve the chicken topped with the savory clay pot juices.

Clay Pot Cooking

Clay pot cooking is an ancient technique. Baking meats in the lidded pot creates the benefits of pit cooking—the cooking juices are sealed in to keep the meat moist and tender. Clay cooking pots can be found in the cookware section of major department stores, in cookware specialty stores, and through cookware mail-order catalogs. If you don't have a clay pot, use a heavy, lidded casserole.

JAMAICAN-STYLE BBQ CHICKEN BREASTS WITH PINEAPPLE SALSA

Serves 4

This recipe combines the Caribbean flavors of jerk seasoning with fresh pineapple. It's a knockout dish!

4 chicken breasts (with skin on)
2 tablespoons + 2 teaspoons peanut oil
2 tablespoons Jamaican Jerk Spices, Dry (page 74)

PINEAPPLE SALSA
Makes about 2½ cups

1 cup diced fresh pineapple
½ cup diced jícama
½ cup diced tomato
1 serrano or jalapeño chile, minced
¼ cup diced red bell pepper
2 tablespoons freshly squeezed lime juice
2 tablespoons chopped fresh cilantro
Salt and freshly ground black pepper to taste

To prepare the chicken, rub the chicken with 2 tablespoons of the oil. Sprinkle the Jamaican Jerk Spices over both sides of the chicken; lightly rub the mixture into the meat and skin. Place the chicken in a plastic bag or sealable container; refrigerate for 4 hours to let the jerk flavors "penetrate" the meat.

Meanwhile, combine the salsa ingredients together in a nonreactive bowl; cover and refrigerate.

Heat the remaining 2 teaspoons of oil in a 12-inch skillet. Add the chicken; cook over high heat, skin side down, until the skin begins to crackle and crisp, about 3½ minutes. Lower the heat to medium, turn the chicken, and continue cooking until the juices run clear when cut in the thickest part of the breast, about 5 minutes.

Serve the chicken garnished with 2 or 3 tablespoons of the Pineapple Salsa.

TO GRILL: Review "Barbecuing" on page 54. Cook the chicken on the grill, skin side down, until the skin becomes crisp and brown, 3 to 4 minutes. Turn the chicken and move it to a cooler part of the grill; continue cooking until the juices run clear when cut in the thickest part of the breast, about 5 to 7 minutes.

TO BROIL: Preheat the broiler. Place the chicken in a shallow roasting pan; broil the chicken 4 to 6 inches from the heating element, skin side up, until the skin becomes crisp, about 6 minutes. Turn the chicken and continue to cook for 5 to 6 minutes. Turn the oven from broil to bake and continue cooking at 350°F until the juices run clear when cut in the thickest part of the breast, about 5 minutes.

FAJITAS

Serves 4

Fajita means "little belt" in American Spanish. Originally, fajitas were made from a cut of meat such as flank steak or skirt steak—but now everything from chicken to lamb and even seafood is being used. The meat is first marinated in a mixture of lime juice and spices, then it is cooked at a high temperature on a grill—a mesquite grill gives a particularly rich taste. If you do not have a grill, a very hot cast iron skillet will do. When the meat is cooked to medium rare or medium, it's removed from the grill and sliced into strips—"little belts" or *fajitas*.The fajitas are then thrown back onto the grill (or back into the pan) and tossed quickly with onions, bell peppers, chile peppers, and garlic. As the meat and vegetables cook together, their juices intermingle, giving the combination a savory flavor. The fajitas and veggies are then removed from the heat and served up with hot tortillas and salsa. A wedge of lime, sour cream, shredded cheese, and guacamole are often served as accompaniments.

This is a fun dish for a group meal. Serve the fajitas on a platter, along with hot tortillas and a variety of salsas and accompaniments, and let everyone compose their own plate. Be creative; vary the spices and the meat.

1½ **pounds flank or skirt steak, divided into four portions**
2 **tablespoons freshly squeezed lemon juice**
1 **tablespoon salt**
1 **teaspoon pepper**
1 **tablespoon peanut oil**
1 **medium red bell pepper, cut into strips ¼ inch wide**
1 **medium green bell pepper, cut into strips ¼ inch wide**
1 **medium onion, halved then cut into strips ¼ inch wide**
3 **serrano chiles, minced (about 2 tablespoons)**
1 **tablespoon freshly minced garlic**
1 **teaspoon cumin**
¼ **teaspoon oregano**
½ **teaspoon chile powder**
2 **medium tomatoes, diced**
3 **tablespoons chopped cilantro**

Place the four pieces of steak on a small platter. Mix the lime juice, 1½ teaspoons of the salt, and ½ teaspoon of the pepper together; pour over the steaks; allow to marinate for 15 minutes, turning the steaks once.

In a heavy 12-inch skillet, heat 2 teaspoons of the oil over high heat; before the oil smokes, add the meat, reserving the marinade juice, and cook for 6 minutes, turning once. Remove the meat from the skillet; set aside on a platter. In the same skillet, add the remaining teaspoon of oil, the bell peppers, onion, serrano chiles, and garlic; cook on high heat until the vegetables are soft, about 3 minutes. Reduce the heat to low; add the cumin, oregano, chile powder, the remaining salt and pepper, and the diced tomatoes; stir well; cook for two minutes. Cut the steak into ¼-inch strips. Add the steak and the reserved marinade juice to the skillet; toss well; cook for 1 minute. Remove from the heat; add the cilantro. Serve immediately with hot tortillas, salsa, and slices of avocado.

CARIBBEAN SPICED MAHI MAHI WITH HABANERO-PEACH BUTTER

Serves 4

This dish is a tasty way to prepare saltwater fish; try it with halibut or thresher shark. The Habanero-Peach Butter adds a lightly spicy, fruity accent that complements the flavor of the fish. Grill the fish to make this dish extra special.

> 2 medium garlic cloves, minced
> ½ medium red onion, minced
> ½ tablespoon ground red (Cayenne) pepper
> 1 tablespoon freshly ground black pepper
> 1½ tablespoons mild paprika
> ½ teaspoon dried thyme
> ½ teaspoon dried oregano
> ½ teaspoon dried basil
> 4 (6- to 8-ounce) mahi mahi fillets, boned
> 4 tablespoons Habanero-Peach Butter (page 94)

Preheat the broiler. Combine the garlic, onion, red pepper, black pepper, paprika, thyme, oregano, and basil in a shallow bowl; mix well.

Dredge the mahi mahi fillets in the spice mixture, coating both sides well. Place the fillets into a foil-lined baking sheet. Broil 4 inches from the heat, turning once, until the juices begin to run, about 7 minutes. Garnish each fillet with 1 tablespoon of the Habanero-Peach Butter (the heat from the fish will melt the butter appropriately). Serve immediately.

SUGAR REEF CHICKEN

Serves 8

This dish is sweet, spicy, and tangy all at the same time, but not overwhelmingly so. Barbecued or grilled, the chicken is tender and flavorful and makes a great company dish. Serve it over a bed of Costa Rican Rice (page 145) accompanied by sautéed vegetables, or try it with tortillas and your favorite salsa. Take this chicken with you on your next picnic.

1 quart + ½ cup water
½ tablespoon + 1 teaspoon Jamaican Jerk Spices, Wet or Dry (pages 74-75)
1 tablespoon chopped fresh ginger root
1 tablespoon chopped garlic
1 cup unsweetened pineapple juice
1 cup peanut or vegetable oil
16 chicken thighs or breast halves (about 4 pounds)
7 tablespoons tamarind paste or mango chutney (see "Tamarind," page 229)
7 tablespoons light corn syrup
6 tablespoons + 2 teaspoons cider vinegar
8 tablespoons light molasses
1 teaspoon habanero hot sauce (or other hot sauce)

To Make the Marinade:

In a large saucepan, combine 1 quart of the water with ½ tablespoon of the Jamaican Jerk Spices, the ginger, and the garlic. Cook over medium heat until the liquid begins to simmer. Remove the saucepan from the heat; allow the liquid to cool. Add the pineapple juice and the oil to the cooled liquid; mix well.

Transfer the marinade to a nonreactive bowl or a large sealable plastic bag; add the chicken, making sure each piece is well coated with the marinade. Cover or seal, and refrigerate for 4 hours, allowing the chicken to marinate.

To Make the Glaze:

Place the remaining ingredients in a food processor or blender; purée until smooth. (If you make extra glaze, it can be kept covered and refrigerated in an airtight container for several weeks).

To Bake:

Preheat the oven to 350°F. Remove the chicken from the marinade. Discard the marinade. Place the chicken in a large, shallow baking dish.

Bake the chicken until the juices run clear and a meat thermometer placed in the center of the thickest pieces, not touching the bone, registers 180°F, 30 to 40 minutes. Brush on the glaze twice during the last 5 minutes of cooking. Serve immediately.

To Grill:

Before starting, review "Barbecuing" on page 54. Barbecue the chicken, turning once, for 10 to 20 minutes, depending on the size of the piece. Generously brush on the glaze after the chicken has begun to brown.

SPIDER MONKEYS

Spider monkeys—like all New World monkeys—have prehensile tails that they use as extra arms. This fifth limb helps them swing effortlessly through the forest canopy as they go about searching for fruits. A pad of "nonskid" skin at the tip of their tails improves the tail's grip, allowing the monkeys to use their tails to grasp objects, hang from trees, hold an infant, explore tree crevices, and brush away insects. The tails also help them keep their balance as they leap from tree to tree. Hanging by their tails, with all other limbs free, the acrobatic monkeys appear to be "spiders" suspended from their webs.

Long, muscular arms and legs, and light, slender bodies enable these monkeys to move easily through the canopy. Restless and agile, the spider monkeys move like trapeze artists, leaping or dropping twenty-five feet at a time through the tree tops, which tower as high as one hundred feet above the forest floor.

High in the canopy, the monkeys eat, sleep, and raise their young. Spider monkeys feed solely on fruit—and they are very finicky eaters. They sniff fruit to see if it is ripe, and they will drop the fruit to the ground after just one bite if it is not to their taste. These monkeys are social animals; they live in groups, often helping each other with child care, grooming each other, chattering together, and standing guard. They sleep in large troops—sometimes made up of a hundred monkeys—but they break up into smaller bands during the day.

The usual social grouping consists of females and their young—with or without an adult male. Males, who are dominate to females, often wander by themselves. The mother spider monkey has just one baby, and she tends this little one attentively, carrying it with her through the trees as it clings to the fur on her belly. The baby monkeys are playful and they soon learn to ride on their mothers' backs or take off on their own for a swing through the trees.

Spider monkeys are gentle, unaggressive animals and there are few fights within their groups. When males are present in the group, they threaten intruders with barks, and by breaking branches and dropping them onto the trespassers; they may also threaten these interlopers by defecating on them. The spider monkeys' natural enemies are hawks and eagles; these birds of prey are among the few rain forest dwellers who have access to the lofty world of the spider monkey.

ATELES GEOFFROYI

Chapter 9

Desserts

SUN-DRIED CRANBERRY-APPLE PIE

Makes two 9-inch pies

Sun-dried cranberries add a nice twist to apple pie. Serve this pie warm, accompanied by a scoop of vanilla ice cream.

> 2 Pie Shells (below)
> ½ cup sun-dried cranberries
> 10 Red Delicious apples, peeled, cored, and coarsely chopped
> ½ cup sugar
> ½ teaspoon ground cinnamon
> Crumbly Topping (see recipe, this page)

Preheat the oven to 350°F. Prepare the Pie Shells, as directed.

Combine the cranberries, apples, sugar, and cinnamon in a large bowl; mix well. Place half of the filling evenly in each prepared pie shell. Sprinkle the Crumbly Topping equally over both pies. Bake until the pastry crust is golden brown, 50 to 60 minutes.

PIE SHELLS

> 2 cups all-purpose flour
> 4 tablespoons sugar
> ⅛ teaspoon salt
> 1 cup cold unsalted butter, cut into small pieces
> 6 tablespoons cold water

Combine the flour, sugar, and salt in a small bowl. Cut the butter* into the flour

mixture until the mixture is crumbly. Add the water, 1 tablespoon at a time, until the dough just holds together. Shape the pastry into a ball; chill for 30 minutes. Cut the dough in half; roll each half out onto a lightly floured board. Fit the pastry into two 9-inch pie pans; refrigerate the prepared pie shells for 30 minutes.

CRUMBLY TOPPING

> ½ cup unsalted butter, cut into small pieces
> 1 cup all-purpose flour
> ⅔ cup packed light brown sugar

Using your fingertips, combine the butter and flour in a small bowl, breaking the butter pieces into smaller, pea-sized pieces. Mix in the brown sugar. The mixture will be crumbly.

*See note on "Cutting In," page 217.

INCA NUT TORTE

Makes one 10-inch torte

This is a very rich white chocolate brownie—dense and chewy. The hidden bit of chile adds a barely perceptible zing to the chocolatey treat. For an elegant presentation, serve each slice garnished with a dollop of fresh whipped cream, chopped Brazil nuts, and a sprig of mint. To serve the torte warm, microwave each portion on medium for 20 seconds, then garnish.

- ¼ **cup graham cracker crumbs**
- 1 **pound white chocolate, shaved or cut into small pieces**
- 3 **eggs**
- ½ **teaspoon vanilla**
- ¼ **teaspoon crushed red chile flakes**
- ¾ **cup light corn syrup**
- ¼ **cup butter, melted**
- ½ **cup chopped Brazil nuts**
- ½ **cups chopped cashews**

Preheat the oven to 280°F. Grease a 10-inch springform pan. Sprinkle the graham cracker crumbs in the pan. Tap the pan, making the crumbs stick to the bottom and side; discard the excess crumbs.

Melt the white chocolate in the top of a double boiler over medium heat, stirring often. Don't let the temperature of the chocolate exceed 110°F on a candy thermometer. Set aside.

Combine the eggs, vanilla, red pepper flakes, and corn syrup in a medium-size bowl; beat together. Add the melted chocolate, butter, Brazil nuts, and cashews to the egg mixture; mix well.

Pour the batter into the prepared pan. Bake until golden brown and the sides pull away from the pan, about 1 hour and 15 minutes. Let stand for 1½ hours; remove the side from the pan. Serve chilled or warm.

Deep-Fried Whole Snapper,
served on a bed of Salsa Brava,
with Tostones and Avocado Slices

Cochinitas Pibil,
Mayan-style Pork Roast, baked in banana leaves, served with Black Beans,
Rice, Pico de Gallo, and Plantains

Filete a la Yucateca,
Fillet Tail Yucatan Style, served with Sweet Onion and Tomato Salsa

Steamed Mussels in Cilantro and Serrano Cream Sauce,
topped with Salsa Fresca

• Aruba Lime Custard Bowl

• Key Lime Pie

- Pumpkin Cheesecake

- Mocha Cheesecake

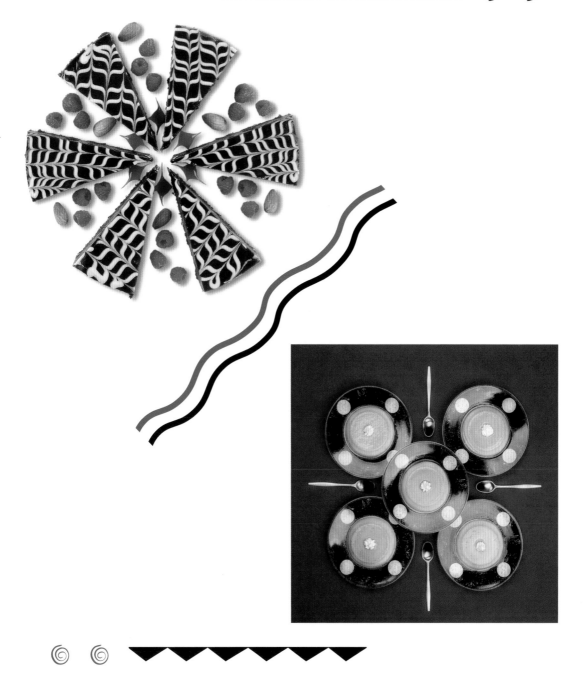

- Coconut Flan

- Chocolate Truffle Torte

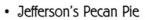

• Jefferson's Pecan Pie

• Chocolate Brazil Nut Pie

JAMAICAN BREAD PUDDING

Makes 12 puddings

Garnish these individual puddings with confectioner's sugar, drizzles of raspberry Melba sauce, fruit syrup, Passionfruit Glaze (page 229), or Apricot-Lime Glaze (page 212).

½ cup raisins
4 tablespoons rum
3 eggs
1 cup sugar
1 teaspoon vanilla
Pinch of freshly grated nutmeg
2 cups whole milk
¼ cup butter, melted
4 cups cubed bread (½-inch cubes)
1½ cups diced fresh fruit (oranges, mangos, cherries, pineapple, etc.) or fruit cocktail, drained (Do not use bananas)

Preheat the oven to 325°F. Grease 12 muffin cups well.

Combine the raisins and rum in a small microwavable bowl; microwave on high for 20 seconds. Set aside.

Cream the eggs and the sugar in large bowl. Add the vanilla, nutmeg, and milk; mix well. Add the melted butter to the milk mixture; mix well.

Combine the bread and the raisin mixture in a large bowl; mix well. Add the milk mixture to the bread mixture; mix well. Stir in the mixed fruit; mix gently (do not mash the fruit).

Divide the batter evenly among the muffin cups. Bake until golden brown, 35 to 40 minutes. Remove from muffin tin. Place in individual serving plates; garnish, if desired; serve warm.

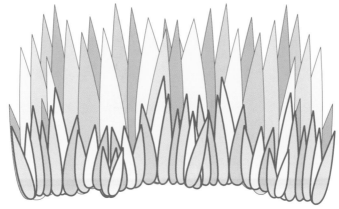

CARIBBEAN-STYLE RICE PUDDING

Serves 6

For an elegant presentation, serve this pudding in Buttercrunch Cookie Baskets (page 211), topped with a dollop of whipped cream and a sprinkle of cinnamon.

1 cup long grain white rice
1¼ cups whole milk
⅓ cup cajeta or sweetened condensed milk
1 cup sugar
½ stick cinnamon, crushed (about ½ tablespoon)
1 teaspoon lemon zest*
½ teaspoon vanilla
Whipped cream, to garnish
Cinnamon, to garnish

Bring 6 cups of water to boil in a 3-quart saucepan. Add the rice. Simmer, uncovered, until tender and the grains are split, 35 to 40 minutes. Drain.

Transfer the drained rice to a medium saucepan; add the remaining ingredients. Cook over low heat until the rice mixture is thick, 15 to 20 minutes. Remove the mixture from the heat.

Divide the mixture among 6 individual serving dishes; serve warm or refrigerate until chilled. Garnish with whipped cream and a dash of cinnamon.

Cajeta is a sweetened caramelized goat's milk that is sold in jars in Latin groceries. If unavailable, substitute sweetened condensed milk.

*The zest of the lemon is the outermost peel of the fruit without any of the pith (white membrane). To remove the zest, use a zester or the fine side of a vegetable grater.

ARUBA LIME CUSTARD BOWL

Makes 8 servings

This sweet-tart lime custard, served in Buttercrunch Cookie Baskets and topped with fresh fruit, makes an elegant and refreshing dessert.

- 2 (14-ounce) cans sweetened condensed milk
- 8 egg yolks
- 1 cup freshly squeezed lime juice (fresh only!)
- Zest from 4 limes*
- 1 cup diced fruit (mangos, papayas, berries, or other fresh fruit)
- Juice of ½ lime
- 1 teaspoon sugar
- 1 cup whipping cream
- 8 Buttercrunch Cookie Baskets (see page 211)
- 8 sprigs of mint, for garnish

Combine the condensed milk and the egg yolks in a medium-size nonreactive bowl; mix well. Add the lime juice and zest; blend well. Cover and refrigerate. Chill for 4 hours to set.

In a small bowl, combine the fruit with the juice of ½ lime and the sugar; mix well. In a medium-size bowl, whip the cream until soft peaks form.

Fill each Buttercrunch Cookie Basket with ½ cup of the chilled lime custard filling. Top each basket with 2 tablespoons of the fresh fruit mixture. Garnish each with a small dollop of fresh whipped cream and a sprig of mint. Serve immediately.

Note

To make sure the Buttercrunch Cookie Baskets will be crisp, wait until just before you are planning to serve the dessert before filling them; meanwhile, keep the Lime Custard, whipped cream, and fruit refrigerated.

*The zest of the lime is the outermost peel of the fruit without any of the pith (white membrane). To remove the zest, use a zester or the fine side of a vegetable grater.

SAMMY'S IBARRA CHOCOLATE CAKE

Makes one 9-inch layer cake

This rich, flavorful cake bakes up beautifully and makes a great presentation. It tastes good warm with just a scoop of vanilla ice cream. Or, stack the layers and use a rich chocolate frosting as a filling, topping the towering cake with Melba sauce and fresh whipped cream. Garnish it all with fresh raspberries—make it as decadent as possible.

> **3 pounds Ibarra chocolate (see note, this page), shaved or cut into small pieces**
> **1 tablespoon ground cinnamon**
> **2 cups sour cream**
> **8 eggs**
> **2 tablespoons vanilla**
> **1 cup butter**
> **4½ cups all-purpose flour**
> **1 cup sugar**
> **2 teaspoons baking powder**
> **2 teaspoons baking soda**
> **1 tablespoon salt**
> **1½ cups heavy cream**
> **2 cups sliced almonds (optional)**

Preheat the oven to 325°F. Grease and flour two 9-inch cake pans or two 10-inch springform pans.

Melt the chocolate in the top of a double boiler over simmering water. Do not let the temperature of the chocolate exceed 110°F on a candy thermometer.

Combine the cinnamon, sour cream, eggs, vanilla, and the melted chocolate in a medium-size bowl; mix well. Add ½ cup of the butter, mix well. Set aside.

Sift together the flour, sugar, baking powder, baking soda, and salt in a large bowl. Mix in the remaining ½ cup of butter. Add the chocolate mixture to the flour mixture; mix well. Add the cream and almonds; mix well.

Pour the batter evenly into the prepared pans. Bake until a toothpick inserted into the center comes out clean, about 1½ hours.

Note

This cake is best kept at room temperature; refrigeration tends to toughen it.

Ibarra Chocolate

Ibarra is the brand name of a Mexican-style chocolate. It comes in 3-ounce cakes formed of cacao nibs, sugar, cinnamon, and almonds. Sold in boxes of six, it's available in some supermarkets, in Latin markets, and through mail order.

AARON'S SLIGHTLY-MORE-SINFUL FLOURLESS IBARRA CHOCOLATE CAKE

Makes one 10-inch layer cake

Frost and stack the layers, or serve them in small slices garnished with powdered sugar. These cakes are excellent topped with whipped cream and Ibarra chocolate shavings.

> **8 egg whites**
> **¾ cup sugar**
> **1 pound + 2 ounces Ibarra chocolate (see note, page 206), shaved or cut into small pieces**
> **½ pound unsalted butter**
> **1 tablespoon freshly squeezed lemon juice**
> **4 tablespoons orange liqueur (e.g. Grand Marnier, Cointreau, Triple Sec)**
> **1 teaspoon vanilla**

Adjust the oven rack to the lower third of the oven. Preheat the oven to 250°F. Grease and flour two 10-inch springform pans or two 9-inch cake pans.

Using a hand mixer or beater, whip the egg whites in a small bowl. When they begin to form small peaks, slowly add the sugar, a little at a time. Continue beating until the egg whites become stiff and glossy, about 7 minutes. Set aside.

Place the chocolate and butter in the top of a double boiler; melt over simmering water, stirring constantly.

Transfer the chocolate mixture to a large bowl. Add the juice; with a wire whisk, beat until well combined. Add the liqueur, whisking to combine. Add the vanilla; beat together.

Gently fold the egg white mixture, one-quarter at a time, into the chocolate mixture, using a rubber spatula. Pour the batter evenly into the prepared pans. Bake, on the lower rack, until a toothpick inserted into the center of the cake comes out clean, about 1½ hours. Cool the layers before removing them from the pans. Frost and stack to make a layer cake, or garnish with fresh whipped cream and chocolate shavings.

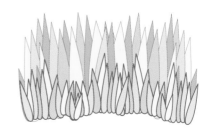

WALNUT PIE

Makes 2 pies

This is a great dessert to make in autumn when the fresh walnut harvests are in. Serve these pies, hot or at room temperature, with a scoop of vanilla ice cream alongside each slice.

> **2 Pie Shells (see recipe, this page)**
> **2½ cups coarsely chopped walnuts**
> **1½ cups granulated sugar**
> **½ cup packed light brown sugar**
> **6 eggs**
> **2 teaspoons vanilla**
> **4 tablespoons butter**
> **2 cups dark corn syrup**

Preheat the oven to 350°F. Prepare the Pie Shells, as directed.

Combine the walnuts, granulated sugar, brown sugar, eggs, vanilla, butter, and corn syrup in a medium-size bowl; mix well.

Pour half the mixture into each prepared pie shell. Bake until the pastry crust is golden brown, 45 to 50 minutes. Cool slightly before serving.

PIE SHELLS

> **2½ cups all-purpose flour**
> **Pinch of salt**
> **⅔ cup vegetable shortening**
> **⅔ cup very cold water**

Combine the flour and salt in a small bowl. Cut the shortening* into the flour mixture until the mixture is crumbly. Add the water, 1 tablespoon at a time, until the dough just holds together. Shape the pastry into a ball; chill for 30 minutes.

Cut the dough in half; roll each half out onto a lightly floured board. Fit the pastry into two 9-inch pie pans; refrigerate the prepared pie shells for 30 minutes.

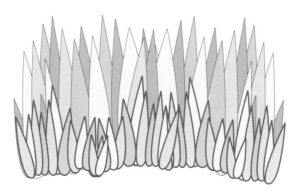

*See note on "Cutting In," page 217.

COCONUT FLAN

Flans are Spanish-style baked custards. This delicious dessert is popular throughout Latin America. Usually made with heavy cream, this equally delicious recipe calls for half-and-half (and about half the calories!) The coconut adds a definite tropical twist.

> **7 egg yolks**
> **6 tablespoons sugar**
> **Pinch of salt**
> **2$\frac{1}{2}$ cups half-and-half**
> **$\frac{1}{4}$ vanilla bean or 1 teaspoon pure vanilla extract**
> **$\frac{1}{2}$ cup + 2 tablespoons shredded coconut**

Preheat the oven to 350°F. Place the egg yolks in a medium-size nonreactive bowl; mix in $\frac{1}{2}$ of the sugar (3 tablespoons) and the tiny pinch of salt; stir until well mixed, about 2 minutes. In a medium saucepan, over low heat, heat the half-and-half, the vanilla (if using extract), the remaining sugar, and the coconut. Bring the mixture to scald (do not allow to boil), between 190° and 200°F. If using vanilla bean, scrape the inside of the bean into the mixture. When half-and-half mixture reaches scald, remove from heat. Add the hot half-and-half mixture to the egg mixture, stirring well.

Place 8 six-ounce ramekins into a baking pan. Pour the coconut flan mixture in equal amounts into the 8 ramekins. Add water to the pan until the level reaches two-thirds the way up the sides of the ramekins. Bake the flans for 50 minutes.

When cooked, remove the ramekins from the pan; place on a counter top until they have cooled enough to be touched, then refrigerate. Serve chilled. For garnish, top each flan with a sprig of mint.

PECAN TURTLE BROWNIES

Makes 18 large/36 small brownies

These brownies are unbelievably popular—maybe because they're so delicious! The caramel adds just the right amount of gooeyness to the brownie's chocolatey richness. Good for eating right out of your hand—or for a more formal presentation, top with chocolate syrup or caramel sauce and serve with a scoop of vanilla ice cream.

- 1 cup unsweetened cocoa powder
- 1⅓ cups sugar
- 1 cup all-purpose flour
- 4 eggs
- 1 cup butter, melted
- 6 ounces caramel candy (e.g. Kraft), about 19 pieces
- 4 tablespoons caramel topping (or 2 additional ounces of caramel candy, about 6 pieces)
- ¼ cup whipping cream
- 1 cup semisweet chocolate chips
- 1 cup coarsely chopped pecans
- 32 pecan halves

Preheat the oven to 350°F. Grease and flour a 9 x 13-inch baking dish with butter (a glass baking dish is preferable).

In a medium-size mixing bowl, combine half of the brownie's cake ingredients: ½ cup cocoa, ⅔ cup sugar, ½ cup flour, and 2 eggs; mix well. (Don't make the second half of the cake mixture ahead of time, or it will be difficult to spread.) Add ½ cup of the melted butter; mix well. Spread the mixture* over the bottom of the prepared baking dish.

Bake for 15 minutes; remove from oven, and place on a rack to cool until the top is firm, about 15 minutes.

Meanwhile, place the caramel, caramel topping, and cream into a small microwave-safe mixing bowl; cover and microwave for 15 seconds; stir and repeat the process until the mixture is smooth and well mixed, about 1 to 1½ minutes. Pour the melted caramel mixture over the cooled brownie layer. Distribute the chocolate chips and the chopped pecans evenly over the top of the caramel layer.

In a medium-size mixing bowl, combine the remaining cocoa, sugar, flour, and eggs; mix well. Add the remaining melted butter; mix well. (Again, don't make this mixture ahead, or it will not spread well.) Pour the mixture evenly over the chocolate chip layer.* Distribute the pecan halves evenly over the top of the brownie layer.

Bake until a toothpick inserted into the center comes out clean, about 25 to 35 minutes. Cool and cut into serving-size pieces. Serve at room temperature.

*If the mixture is too thick to pour or spread, heat slightly in a double boiler, about 2 to 3 minutes, to soften.

BUTTERCRUNCH COOKIE BASKETS

Makes 8

These crunchy baskets make elegant and tasty containers for Aruba Lime Custard (page 205), Chocolate Ecstasy (page 215), and Caribbean-Style Rice Pudding (page 204), or use them for serving ice cream or sorbets.

- ½ **cup butter, softened**
- ½ **cup light corn syrup**
- ⅔ **cup packed dark brown sugar**
- 1 **cup old-fashioned oats (not the quick-cooking kind)**
- ¾ **cup all-purpose flour**
- 1 **teaspoon vanilla**

Preheat the oven to 375°F. Line baking sheets with parchment paper, waxed paper, or use nonstick baking sheets.

Combine the butter, corn syrup, and brown sugar in a medium-size saucepan; cook over medium heat, stirring constantly, until the sugar dissolves, about 4 to 5 minutes. Increase the heat and bring the mixture to a boil; remove from the heat. Stir in the oats, flour, and vanilla. Mix well.

Drop 1 tablespoon of the cookie dough onto each end of the prepared baking sheets (bake only 2 baskets per sheet). Bake until the dough becomes bubbly, spreads, and begins to turn a rich brown, about 12 minutes.

Remove the cookies from the oven; let stand for about 1 minute. Remove the cookies from the sheet with a spatula, and let cool over inverted custard cups (the cookies will harden in the shape of the cups). Remove the baskets from the cups. When completely cool, store in an air-tight container to keep them from getting soggy.

MAKING COOKIE BASKETS:

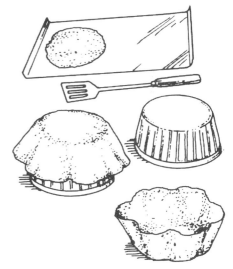

After letting cookies cool for about 1 minute, drape each one over an inverted custard cup.

MANGO CHEESECAKE

Makes one 10-inch cake

For a tangy complement to this dessert, serve individual slices garnished with a drizzle of Passionfruit Glaze (page 229) or Apricot-Lime Glaze (see note this page).

Graham Cracker Crust (see recipe, this page)
2 (8-ounce) packages cream cheese, at room temperature
1 cup sugar
1½ cups sour cream
3 eggs
1½ cups mango purée
(made from fresh ripe mangos or frozen mangos, thawed)
½ teaspoon vanilla
1 teaspoon freshly squeezed lemon juice
Sour Cream Topping (see recipe, this page)

Preheat the oven to 300°F. Prepare the Graham Cracker Crust, as directed.

Combine the cream cheese and sugar in a food processor or blender; blend until well combined. Slowly add the sour cream , eggs, mango purée, vanilla and lemon juice; blend well. Pour the mixture into the prepared crust. Bake until set, about I hour. Be careful not to over cook.

Remove the cake from the oven; let cool until cake surface is room temperature, about 1 hour. Raise the oven temperature to 350°F. Top the cake with the Sour Cream Topping; bake 4 minutes

more. Remove from oven. Chill for at least 4 hours, garnish, and serve.

GRAHAM CRACKER CRUST

1¼ cups graham cracker crumbs
¼ cup finely chopped cashews
¼ cup sugar
3 tablespoons butter, melted

Grease the sides of a 10-inch springform pan with butter.

Combine the graham cracker crumbs, cashews, and sugar in a small bowl; stir to mix. Add the melted butter; mix well. Press the mixture into the bottom of the prepared pan.

SOUR CREAM TOPPING

1½ cups sour cream
½ cup sugar

Combine the sour cream and sugar in a food processor or blender; blend well.

Apricot-Lime Glaze

If you cannot find passionfruit glaze in your supermarket, use this Apricot-Lime Glaze.

Purée 2 tablespoons apricot jam, 2 tablespoons corn syrup, 1 teaspoon freshly squeezed lime juice, and 1 teaspoon cider vinegar in a food processor or blender. This makes approximately ⅓ cup.

LEMON CHEESECAKE

Makes one 10-inch pie

Garnish this cheesecake with sprigs of mint and thin slices of fresh lemon.

Graham Cracker Crust (see recipe, this page)
2 (8-ounce) packages of cream cheese, at room temperature
1 cup sugar
3 eggs
1½ cups sour cream
3 drops vanilla
¼ cup freshly squeezed lemon juice
Zest of 2 lemons*
Sour Cream Topping (see recipe, this page)
1 lemon, thinly sliced, for garnish

Preheat the oven to 300°F. Prepare the Graham Cracker Crust, as directed.

Combine the cream cheese and the sugar in a food processor or blender; blend until well combined. Add the eggs, one at a time, mixing well after each addition. Add the sour cream, vanilla, lemon juice, and zest, in that order, to the cheese mixture; mix well. Pour the cheesecake mixture into the prepared crust.

Bake 50 to 60 minutes. If the cake is not set by then (firm in the middle when slightly shaken), reduce the heat to 250°F, and bake 10 minutes more. Be careful not to over cook. Remove from oven; let cool until cake surface is room temperature, about 1 hour. Top with Sour Cream Topping. Chill for at least 4 hours. Garnish with thinly sliced lemon before serving.

GRAHAM CRACKER CRUST

1 cup graham cracker crumbs
¼ cup finely chopped cashews
2 tablespoons sugar
3 tablespoons butter, melted

Grease the sides of a 10-inch springform pan with butter.

Combine the graham cracker crumbs, cashews, and sugar in a small bowl; stir to mix. Add the melted butter; mix well. Press the mixture into the bottom of the prepared pan.

SOUR CREAM TOPPING

1¾ cups sour cream
Zest of 1 lemon*
½ cup sugar

Combine the sour cream and zest in a food processor or blender; blend well. Add the sugar; mix thoroughly.

*The zest of the lemon is the outermost peel of the fruit without any of the pith (white membrane). To remove the zest, use a zester or the fine side of a vegetable grater.

BANANA CHEESECAKE

Makes one 10-inch cake

Graham Cracker Crust (see recipe, this page)

2 (8-ounce) packages cream cheese, at room temperature

1 cup sugar

3 eggs

½ pound ripe bananas, puréed

1½ cups sour cream

1 teaspoon vanilla

2 tablespoons finely chopped cashews

Sour Cream Topping (see recipe, this page)

Preheat the oven to 300°F. Prepare the Graham Cracker Crust, as directed.

Combine the cream cheese and sugar in a food processor or blender; blend until well combined. Add the eggs, one at a time, mixing well after each addition. Add the puréed bananas, sour cream, and vanilla, in that order, to the cheese mixture; mix well. Pour the mixture into the prepared crust.

Bake until set (firm in the middle when slightly shaken), 50 to 60 minutes. If the cake is not set by then, reduce the oven temperature to 250°F; bake 10 minutes more. Be careful not to overcook. Remove cake from the oven; let cool until the cake surface is room temperature, about 1 hour. Raise the oven temperature to 350°F. Top cake with the Sour Cream Topping; bake 4 minutes more. Remove from oven. Chill for at least 4 hours before serving.

GRAHAM CRACKER CRUST

1¼ cups graham cracker crumbs

¼ cup finely chopped cashews

2 tablespoons sugar

3 ounces melted butter

Grease the sides of a 10-inch springform pan with butter.

Combine the cracker crumbs, cashews, and sugar in a small bowl; stir to mix. Add the butter; mix well. Press the mixture into the bottom of the prepared pan.

SOUR CREAM TOPPING

1¾ cups sour cream

½ cup sugar

Combine the sour cream and sugar in a food processor or blender; blend well.

Some Tasty Variations

Chocolate Lover's Crust

Substitute 1¼ cups of chocolate wafer cookie crumbs (e.g. Oreo or Hydrox, with cream filling removed) for the graham crackers, cashews, and sugar in the Graham Cracker Crust recipe (above). This crust is excellent with the Banana Cheesecake.

Mocha Cheesecake

Substitute 4 tablespoons coffee liqueur (e.g. Kahlúa, Tía María), 2 tablespoons brewed espresso coffee, and ¼ cup shaved semisweet chocolate for the banana purée in the Banana Cheesecake recipe (previous page). Pour the filling into a Chocolate Lover's Crust (above); the chocolate compliments the flavor of the Mocha Cheesecake nicely. Garnish with shaved semisweet chocolate.

Pumpkin Cheesecake

Substitute 8 ounces of pumpkin purée for the banana purée in the Banana Cheesecake recipe (previous page). Substitute ⅛ teaspoon freshly grated nutmeg for the vanilla. Garnish with chopped pecans.

CHOCOLATE ECSTASY

Serves 10 to 12

This dish is the essence of chocolate decadence. Use an ice cream scoop to spoon it from the baking pan, as its consistency is similar to a gooey brownie. Serve the scoops in Buttercrunch Cookie Baskets (page 211) and garnish with a dollop of fresh whipped cream, chopped cashew nuts, and a sprig of mint. It's wonderful served warm: simply reheat it in the microwave for 20 seconds before putting it in the cookie basket; then garnish and serve.

- ¼ cup butter, softened
- 1½ cups unsweetened cocoa powder
- 1 cup sugar
- 4 eggs
- 1¾ cups light corn syrup
- 2 teaspoons vanilla
- 2 tablespoons brewed espresso coffee, cold
- 1 cup chopped Brazil nuts

Preheat the oven to 280°F. Generously grease a 9 X 13-inch baking dish.

Beat the butter, cocoa, and sugar in a large bowl. Stir in the eggs; blend well. Mix in the corn syrup. Combine the vanilla and espresso in a small bowl; add to the cocoa mixture and mix well. Stir in the Brazil nuts.

Pour the mixture into the prepared baking dish; bake until a toothpick inserted in the center comes out clean, about 1 hour and 15 minutes. Cool 1 hour before serving.

CHOCOLATE BRAZIL NUT PIE

Makes two 9-inch pies

Meaty Brazil nuts, rich chocolate, and fragrant vanilla combine to make this pie a sweet celebration of tropical American flavors.

> Pie Crust (below)
> 4 tablespoons butter
> 3 eggs
> 2 cups coarsely chopped Brazil nuts
> 1 cup sugar
> 1 cup light corn syrup
> 2 teaspoons vanilla
> Chocolate Truffle Topping (see recipe, this page)

Prepare the pie crust. Preheat the oven to 350°F.

Combine the butter, eggs, nuts, sugar, corn syrup and vanilla in a medium-size bowl; blend well. Pour the filling into the chilled Pie Crusts. Bake until firm, about 40 minutes. Chill. Top with Chocolate Truffle Topping.

PIE CRUST

> 1 cup all-purpose flour
> Pinch of salt
> 6 tablespoons vegetable shortening
> 1/3 to 1/2 cup cold water

Combine the flour and salt in a small bowl. Cut the shortening* into the flour mixture until the mixture is crumbly. Add the water, 1 tablespoon at a time, until the dough just holds together.

Gather the pastry into a ball; chill for 30 minutes. Cut the dough in half; roll each half out onto a lightly floured board. Fit each half into a 9-inch pie pan. Refrigerate the pie crusts.

CHOCOLATE TRUFFLE TOPPING

> 1/4 cup heavy cream
> 1 1/4 cups shaved semisweet chocolate, about 6 ounces
> 6 tablespoons butter, softened, and cut into small pieces
> 2 tablespoons raspberry Melba sauce or seedless raspberry jam
> 2 tablespoons orange liqueur (e.g. Triple Sec, Curaçao)
> Shavings of white chocolate, optional, for garnish

Slowly warm the cream in a saucepan over low heat or in the top of a double boiler over simmering water, until it reaches 180°F degrees on a candy thermometer. Do not let the cream boil. Remove from the heat; cool down to 120°F, about 3 minutes. Add the semisweet chocolate, a little at a time, stirring constantly, until the chocolate is melted and the mixture is well blended. Slowly blend in the butter. Add the Melba sauce and liqueur; mix well. Spread the chocolate mixture evenly over both cooled pies. Garnish with white chocolate shavings, if desired.

*See note on "Cutting In," page 217.

JEFFERSON'S PECAN PIE

Makes two 9-inch pies

This is a Southern favorite and a popular Thanksgiving dessert. Serve it warm with a dollop of fresh whipped cream.

> **2 Pie Shells (see recipe, this page)**
> **6 eggs**
> **2 cups light corn syrup**
> **1 teaspoon vanilla**
> **6 tablespoons butter, melted**
> **2 cups sugar**
> **3 cups pecan halves**

Preheat the oven to 350°F. Prepare the Pie Shells, as directed.

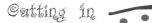

Cutting in

The process of cutting in is the mixing of a solid fat (such as butter or shortening) with a dry ingredient (such as flour) until the mixture forms small particles. Using a fork, press the shortening into the flour, continuously cutting until the mixture forms coarse little grains. Cutting in can also be accomplished by using a tool called a pastry blender, two knives, or even your fingertips (if you make sure your hands are cool and you don't handle the dough so much that the fat melts). A food processor can also be used, just be careful not to overwork the ingredients and make a paste. A few short pulses should do the trick.

Combine the eggs, corn syrup, vanilla, butter, and sugar in a medium-size bowl; mix well. Set aside.

Spread one-half of the pecans evenly over the bottom of each prepared pie shell. Pour half of the egg mixture into each of the pie shells.

Bake until the pastry crust is golden brown, about 45 to 50 minutes. Cool and serve.

PIE SHELLS

> **2½ cups all-purpose flour**
> **Pinch of salt**
> **⅔ cup vegetable shortening**
> **⅔ cup very cold water**

Combine the flour and salt in a small bowl. Cut the shortening into the flour mixture until the mixture is crumbly. Add the water, 1 tablespoon at a time, until the dough just holds together. Shape the pastry into a ball; chill for 30 minutes.

Cut the dough in half; roll each half out onto a lightly floured board. Fit the pastry into two 9-inch pie pans; refrigerate the prepared pie shells for 30 minutes.

KEY LIME PIE

Makes two 9-inch pies

This sweet-tart pie is fantastic by itself and the perfect end note to a seafood dinner. It is imperative that the lime juice you use in this recipe be fresh; don't be tempted to use bottled lime juice. Mini-food processors make quick work of juicing fresh limes.

> Graham Cracker Crust (see recipe, this page)
> 2 (14-ounce) cans sweetened condensed milk
> 8 egg yolks
> 1 cup freshly squeezed Florida Key lime juice (see note, next page)
> Zest from 4 limes*
> Whipped Topping (see recipe, this page)

Preheat the oven to 350°F. Prepare and bake the Graham Cracker Crust as directed.

Combine the condensed milk and the egg yolks in a medium-size bowl; mix well. Add the lime juice and zest; blend well. Pour the pie filling into the 2 cooled pie shells. Bake until set, about 12 minutes. Allow the pies to cool before adding the Whipped Topping.

GRAHAM CRACKER CRUST

> 2½ cups graham cracker crumbs
> 6 tablespoons sugar
> 1 teaspoon cinnamon
> 8 tablespoons melted butter

Preheat the oven to 350°F.

Combine the graham cracker crumbs, sugar, and cinnamon in a medium- size bowl; stir to mix. Add the butter; mix well. Press the mixture into two 9-inch pie plates. Bake 12 minutes; set aside to cool.

WHIPPED TOPPING

> 2 cups whipping cream
> 6 tablespoons sugar
> Fresh mint, for garnish
> Lime, thinly sliced, for garnish

Whip the cream and the sugar together in a small bowl until soft peaks form. Spread the cream mixture evenly over the tops of the cooled pies. Garnish each slice with a mint leaf and a slice of lime.

*The zest of the lime is the outermost peel of the fruit without any of the pith (white membrane). To remove the zest, use a zester or the fine side of a vegetable grater.

THE FISHWIFE'S PECAN PRALINES

Makes 18 candies

These popular candies are evocative of the French Quarter in New Orleans. Eat them whole as a sweet treat—or crumble them to use as a topping for ice cream or other desserts.

- **$2\frac{1}{2}$ cups sugar**
- **1 teaspoon baking soda**
- **$\frac{1}{8}$ teaspoon ground cinnamon**
- **1 cup buttermilk**
- **$\frac{1}{4}$ cup butter**
- **2 cups pecan halves**

Place parchment or waxed paper over 2 baking sheets. Set aside.

Combine the sugar, baking soda, cinnamon, buttermilk, and butter in a large, heavy saucepan; cook, over medium-high heat, without stirring, until the mixture reaches 238°F on a candy thermometer (or when a small amount of this mixture dropped in very cold water forms a soft ball). Immediately remove the mixture from the heat. Stir in the pecans. Using a wooden spoon, beat vigorously, until the mixture turns cloudy, about 1 minute.

Immediately drop the mixture by tablespoonfuls onto the prepared baking sheets to form 2- to $2\frac{1}{2}$-inch diameter pralines. Cool until firm. Store in an airtight container.

KEY LIME MERINGUE PIE

If you prefer, top the pie with a cloud of meringue. Use the egg whites leftover from making the key lime pie filling!

- **5 egg whites**
- **$\frac{1}{2}$ cup sugar**

Place the egg whites in a medium-size, clean, dry bowl. Whip the egg whites until they begin to get frothy. Slowly add the sugar, 1 tablespoon at a time, until the mixture forms stiff white peaks. Spread the meringue over the cooled pies.

To lightly brown the meringue peaks, place the pie under the broiler for 1 minute. Watch carefully to avoid burning.

Note on Key Limes

Key limes are different from the common green limes found in the supermarket. Key limes are smaller, tarter, and more yellow. By definition, a Key Lime Pie should be made with Key limes, but since they are almost impossible to find outside of Florida, regular limes can be substituted in this recipe. Your pies will still taste wonderful.

CHOCOLATE TRUFFLE TORTE

Makes one 10-inch torte

This torte is a very elegant, rich dessert. It is the perfect ending note for a special luncheon or dinner.

- **Chocolate Pie Crust (see recipe, this page)**
- **1 cup heavy cream**
- **12 ounces shaved semisweet chocolate**
- **10 tablespoons unsalted butter, at room temperature**
- **$\frac{1}{4}$ cup of raspberry Melba sauce or seedless raspberry jam**
- **$\frac{1}{8}$ cup orange liqueur (e.g. Triple Sec, Grand Marnier, Cointreau)**
- **$\frac{1}{8}$ cup raspberry liqueur (e.g. Chambord)**
- **1 cup shaved white chocolate, for garnish**

Prepare the Chocolate Pie Crust

Cook the cream in the top of a double boiler over simmering water, until it reaches 180°F on a candy thermometer. Remove from heat; cool to 120°F. Slowly add the semisweet chocolate, stirring constantly, until well blended. (If the mixture becomes lumpy, return the pan to the top of the double boiler over hot water; stir constantly until smooth.) Add the butter, 1 small piece at a time, blending it well into the cream mixture. Stir in the Melba sauce and the liqueurs.

Pour the mixture into the prepared crust. Chill 1 hour. Garnish with the white chocolate.

Serve the torte garnished with the shaved white chocolate.

CHOCOLATE PIE CRUST

- **1 cup crushed chocolate wafer cookies (e.g. Hydrox or Oreo, fillings removed)**
- **2 tablespoons butter**
- **$\frac{1}{2}$ cup crushed toasted almond slivers**

Combine the cookie crumbs and butter in a small bowl; mix well. Add the almonds; mix. Press the mixture into the bottom and sides of one 10-inch springform pan.

IGUANAS

Green iguanas are vegetarians; they are the only reptiles who both live in and feed on trees. These bright, almost fluorescent, green lizards can grow to be six feet in length and weigh up to thirty pounds; they look very much like miniature dinosaurs. Ornamental spikes crest down their spines from their heads to their tails, and a dewlap (an extendible throat pouch) hangs beneath their chins. Males display their dewlaps to other iguanas to warn them off of occupied territory and avoid real fighting.

Iguanas are fast runners, good climbers, and excellent swimmers and divers. Living in the trees along the riverbanks of tropical America, green iguanas spend their days basking in the sun and grazing on leaves. At the first hint of danger, they don't hesitate to throw themselves into the river. Diving to the bottom for protection, the lizards can stay submerged for several minutes until danger has passed. While they do prefer flight to fight, when cornered, iguanas can strike out with their tails, using them as lashing whips. The lizards can also bite. As an extreme measure, iguanas can shed their tails to escape capture; the tails will grow back, only without the decorative serrated edges. When not sunning themselves or eating, iguanas retreat to their burrows in deep hollows along the riverbanks. After mating, iguanas lay their soft-shelled eggs in holes dug in the sand at the bases of trees.

Iguanas are considered a delicacy in Mexico and Central America, where they have been eaten for thousands of years. Columbus reported seeing "a dragon about six-feet long which we killed with lances …the meat is white and tastes like chicken." One method of hunting iguanas involves a team effort. Young boys walk along riverbank looking for their prey; when they spot an iguana, one boy will frighten it so that it will drop into the water to hide. The other boys, who are waiting along the riverbank, then jump into the river to capture it.

Iguanas hold a religious and spiritual significance for many forest peoples. To many Maya, the four aspects of the sky and earth were represented by the double-headed iguana dragon. A huge temple built to honor the giant iguana, Itzam-Ye, has been recently excavated in Honduras. Among the Cuña of Panama, the iguana is renown for its clever ways: according to myth, he tricked El Tigre into giving fire to mankind.

Because iguanas are efficient converters of plant matter to protein, they have become the focus of a project by Dr. Dagmar Werner on an experimental farm in Costa Rica. Dr. Werner has proposed raising iguanas as a meat source in the tropics—a sort of "chicken of the trees". This would help save the rain forest since cattle ranching destroys the trees and soil and the delicate balance of the tropical ecosystem.

IGUANA IGUANA

MAIL ORDER SOURCES

Mail order can be fun. The prices are often quite reasonable, and ordering at home will save you lots of time searching for uncommon ingredients in specialty food stores in your area. The catalogs are fun to peruse and they will also introduce you to a world of foods and flavors you may not otherwise experience. Many mail order companies are now on line so you can access their catalogs on the net. So, go ahead and order what you need. You won't be sorry.

Mo Hotta-Mo Betta

465 Pacific Street
San Luis Obispo
800-462-3220
www.mohotta.com

Our favorite mail order catalog for salsas and hot sauces. Their web page is a great source of chile, salsa, and hot sauces as well as jerk and Cajun seasonings, achiote paste, gumbo filé, masa harina, cajeta, chipotle chiles in adobo, and more. Look under "provisions" in the catalog on their web page.

Old Southwest Trading Company

P.O. Box 7545
Albuquerque, NM 87194
305-836-0168

Dried chiles, hot sauces, and Southwestern foods

Melissa's World Variety Produce

P.O. Box 21127
Los Angeles, CA 90021
800-533-1870
www.melissas.com

Exotic produce, including cassava, tomatillos, jícama, plantains, fresh habaneros and other fresh and dried chiles, beans, and grains. Minimum case purchase required on fresh fruits and vegetables. Look under "product information" on their web site.

MAIL ORDER SOURCES

Frieda's

4465 Corporate Center Drive
Los Alamitos, CA 90720-2561
714/826-6100

www.friedas.com

Fresh exotic produce, spices, ethnic baskets

Penderly's

1221 Manufacturing
Fort Worth, TX 75207
800-533-1870

Spices, condiments, and seasonings

Dean and Delucca

560 Broadway
New York, NY 10012
800-221-7714

www.deananddelucca.com

A wide variety of imported and specialty foods

Los Chileros de Nuevo Mexico

P.O. Box 6215
Santa Fe, NM 87501
505-4716967

Fresh and dried chiles, and Southwestern food items

www.asiamex.com

A wide variety of spices and products from both sides of the Pacific, including *panko*, and Mexican chocolate

 # FOOD NOTES

ACHIOTE PASTE
A mixture of ground achiote seeds, vinegar, garlic, and spices. Available in Latin food stores, sometimes called *recado colorado*. There is really no substitute for the smoky flavor of achiote, but if necessary, mix 2 tablespoons of mild paprika with 2 teaspoons garlic powder, 1 teaspoon of cumin, 1/2 teaspoon black pepper, 1/2 teaspoon salt, 1/4 cayenne pepper, and 2 tablespoons of distilled white vinegar. This will give the color and some of the "zing" of achiote.

AVOCADOS
The dark, rough-skinned Haas avocados have a buttery, rich, creamy taste and texture. The larger, shiny avocados with the thin, light green skins tend to be watery tasting with little flavor. Choose the Haas.

CACTUS PEARS
Fruit of the Nopal cactus. These are seasonal. Available in some supermarkets and in Latin markets.

CAJETA
Caramelized goat's milk and sugar sold in jars. A delicious specialty of central Mexico. Available in Latin markets. Sweetened condensed milk is an acceptable substitute.

CAJUN SPICES / CAJUN BLACKENING SPICES
Used to coat seafood before pan searing or grilling. With heat, the spices become caramelized and turn black. If you can't find any in the supermarket spice section, mix your own—it's not difficult. See recipe on page 76.

CAYENNE PEPPER / GROUND RED CHILE PEPPER
Not to be confused with chili powder, which is a mixture of chile and spices used to make chili beans. Cayenne pepper or red chile pepper is finely ground, dried red chile peppers. Available in the spice section at supermarkets.

CHIPOTLE CHILES (en adobo)
Chipotles are large, dried, smoked jalapeños sold canned in a spicy tomato sauce (adobo). Available in some supermarkets, in Latin food stores, and through mail order.

CILANTRO
Also known as Chinese parsley, cilantro is the fresh, green leaves of the coriander plant; the dried seeds are the spice called coriander. Fresh cilantro is available in many supermarkets as well as in Asian and Latin markets.

CRÈME FRAÎCHE / CREMA MEXICANA
Thick cultured milk used as a garnish on many Latin dishes. Make your own (see recipe page 51), or find it sold under various names in Latin markets. If you must, you can substitute sour cream—but it's not the same!

FOOD NOTES

HABANERO CHILES

The hottest chile known, habaneros have a distinctive fruity fragrance and flavor. Available in some supermarkets and in Latin markets. If necessary, fresh jalapeños can be substituted for habaneros, usually at a ratio of two jalapeños to one habanero.

IBARRA CHOCOLATE/MEXICAN-STYLE CHOCOLATE

There is really no substitute for the flavor of Mexican-style chocolate. This chocolate is a mixture of cacao nibs—the heart of the cocoa bean—sugar, cinnamon and almonds. Ibarra is one of the brand names most commonly available in the United States. Ibarra Chocolate comes in 3-ounce cakes that are sold in boxes of six. Mexican chocolate is available in some supermarkets, in Latin food stores, and through mail order.

JERK SEASONING / SPICES

Flavorful Jamaican spice mixture used as seasoning for chicken, pork, and even seafood. If you can't find jerk in the spice section of the supermarket, mix your own. It isn't difficult to make—especially the dry mix (see recipe on page 74).

JICAMA

Plump tubers with dark brown skins and crisp, white flesh. They can be found in the produce section with potatoes and yams in many supermarkets, as well as in Latin and Asian markets.

KEY LIMES

Native to Florida, and almost impossible to find on the market, especially outside of that state. Substitute fresh lime juice from limes available in your supermarket.

LEMON JUICE / LIME JUICE

There is no substitute for the fresh lemon or lime juices called for in these recipes—you will not get the desired results with substitutions, especially when using bottled lemon or lime preparations.

NONREACTIVE

A material that doesn't react to the acid in foods—a good choice for a nonreactive container would be plastic, aluminum, Corning Ware, or stainless steel. Avoid cast iron.

MASA HARINA

Specially ground cornmeal made from dried corn soaked in lime and used for making tortillas and tamales. Quaker makes a masa harina available in many supermarkets in the flour and sugar section; masa harina is also available in Latin markets and through mail order.

FOOD NOTES

PASSIONFRUIT / PASSIONFRUIT GLAZE

A wonderfully fragrant fruit which is very difficult to find on the market in most of the United States. Some companies are now making tropical juice combinations which include passionfruit along with orange and pineapple or peach juice.

Apricot-Lime Glaze can be substituted for Passionfruit Glaze:

Purée 2 tablespoons apricot jam, 2 tablespoons corn syrup, 2 teaspoons concentrated frozen orange juice, 1 teaspoon fresh lime juice, and 1 teaspoon cider vinegar. Makes approximately $1/3$ cup.

PLANTAINS / PLATANOS

Large cooking bananas, used as a starch in soups and stews and for frying when green, or baked as a dessert when sweet and ripe. Available in Latin and Asian markets.

QUINOA

An Andean grain (pronounced "keen'-wah") very high in protein. Available in natural food stores, some supermarkets and through mail order.

SERRANO CHILES

Small tapered chiles with a snappy, fresh bite. If necessary, fresh jalapeños can be substituted one for one.

SEVILLE ORANGES

The "bitter orange" used in Mayan marinades and cooking. The juices of $1/2$ grapefruit, 1 orange, and 2 limes, mixed together, will produce a reasonable substitute.

SHRIMP SIZES

Shrimps are marketed by size (number per pound). You will pay more per pound for larger sizes. Please note: in some regions of the United States, the bigger shrimp, the large through colossal sizes, are also called prawns; in other regions, only the very largest shrimp, the jumbos and colossals, are called prawns.

ROCK SHRIMP

These are small, plump, hard-shelled shrimp, with a very pleasing flavor and texture.

TAMARIND

Sweet-sour pulp contained in the large pods of a tree native to Asia and North Africa. Extensively used as flavoring in East Indian and Middle Eastern cuisine, and popular in Caribbean cooking, tamarind paste can be found in Latin and Asian markets. Mango Chutney, available in the condiment section of supermarkets, can be used as a substitute for tamarind.

For Tamarind Glaze: purée 2 tablespoons Mango Chutney, 2 tablespoons corn syrup, and 2 teaspoons cider vinegar. Makes about $1/4$ cup.

BIBLIOGRAPHY & REFERENCES

For those of you who wish to explore the rain forest and its denizens, or the culinary, technical, or historical aspects of New World cuisine in greater depth—read on:

Alper, Joseph.
"Hot and Healthy."
Self (Jan. 1992), 86-89.

"Animals in Your Zoo."
Portland, OR: Metro Washington Park Zoo, 1990.

Ayersu, Edward S., ed.
Jungles.
Washington, DC: Smithsonian Institution, 1980.

Batterbury, Michael, and Ariane Batterbury.
"Columbus Makes Waves."
Food Arts (Oct. 1991), 28-35.

Behler, John L.
"That's a Croc."
Wildlife Conservation (Sept.-Oct. 1993), 70-71.

Brown, Dale M., ed.
Aztecs: Reign of Blood and Splendor.
Alexandria, VA: Time-Life Books, 1992.

Brown, Dale M., ed.
Incas: Lords of Gold and Glory.
Alexandria, VA: Time-Life Books, 1968.

Brown, Dale M., ed.
The Magnificent Maya.
Alexandria, VA: Time-Life Books, 1993.

Carcione, Joe, and Bob Lucas.
The Green Grocer.
San Francisco: Chronicle Books, 1972.

Caufield, Catherine.
In the Rain forest.
Chicago: University of Chicago Press, 1984.

Crosby, Alfred W. Jr.
The Columbian Exchange.
Westport, CT: Greenwood Press, 1972.

Crump, Donald J., ed.
National Geographic Book of Mammals, Vols. 1-2.
Washington, DC: National Geographic Society, 1981.

De Beer, Sir Gavin, et al., eds.
Encyclopedia of the Animal World. 21 vols.
Lausanne, Switzerland: Elsevier International Projects Ltd., 1972.

Fisher, Ron et al.
Emerald Realm: Earth's Precious Rain forests.
Washington, DC: National Geographic Society, 1990.

Forsyth, Adrian, and Ken Miyata.
Tropical Nature.
New York: Charles Scribner's Sons, 1984.

Gray, Ralph, ed.
Secrets of Animal Survival. Books for Young Explorers.
Washington DC: National Geographic Society, 1983.

Hale, William Harlan.
Horizon Cookbook and Illustrated History of Eating and Drinking Through the Ages.
New York: American Heritage, 1968

BIBLIOGRAPHY & REFERENCES

Herbst, Sharon Tyler.
The Food Lover's Companion.
Hauppauge, NY: Barron's Educational Series, Inc., 1990.

Hunt, Joni Phelps.
A Chorus of Frogs.
San Luis Obispo, CA: Blake Publishing, 1992.

Hyatt, Darril A.
Foods America Gave the World.
Boston: L.C. Page and Co., 1937.

Jennings, Gary.
Aztec.
New York: Avon Books, 1980.

Johnson, William Weber.
The Andean Republics.
New York: Time-Life Books, 1965.

Larousse Encyclopedia of Animal Life.
London: Hamlyn, 1972.

Leonard, Jonathan Norton.
The First Farmers.
Alexandria, VA: Time-Life Books, 1973.

Leonard, Jonathan Norton.
Latin American Cooking.
Alexandria, VA: Time-Life Books, 1968.

Mitchner, James A.
Caribbean.
New York: Ballentine Books, 1989.

National Fish and Seafood Promotional Council.
"Fish and Seafood Made Easy."
U.S. Department of Commerce, Washington, DC, 1989.

Olaya, Clara Ines.
"Caju / Marañón / Merey / Acaiu / Cashew Nut."
Américas 42, no. 3 (1990), 52-53.

Orr, Robert T.
Animals in Migration.
New York: Macmillan, 1970

Popescu, Petru.
Amazon Beaming.
New York: Viking, 1991.

Quintana, Patricia.
Feasts of Life.
Tulsa, OK: Council Oaks Books, 1989.

Rhoades, Robert E.
"Corn, The Golden Grain."
National Geographic (June 1993), pp. 93-117.

Robertiello, Jack.
"Desert Fruits Prick Appetites."
Américas 47, no. 4 (1995), 58-59.

Robertiello, Jack.
"Peanut / Mani / Cacahuete."
Américas 43, no. 4 (1991), 58-59.

Robertiello, Jack.
"Piña / Ananas / Pineapple / Abacaxi."
Américas 42, no. 4 (1990), 54-55.

BIBLIOGRAPHY & REFERENCES

Robertiello, Jack.
"Xitomatle / Tomato / Tomate / Jitomate."
Américas 42, no. 5 (1990), 54-55.

Ross, Charles A., ed. *Crocodiles and Alligators.*
New York: Facts on Filé. 1989.

Rudloe, Jack.
Time of the Turtle.
New York: Random House, 1979

Rudloe, Anne, and Jack Rudloe.
"Sea Turtles in a Race for Survival."
National Geographic 185, no. 2 (1994), 94-121.

Schneider, Elizabeth.
"Spotlight on Tropical Tubers and Other Starchy Staples."
Food Arts (Jan.-Feb. 1992).

Schneider, Elizabeth.
Uncommon Fruits and Vegetables, a Commonsense Guide.
New York: Harper and Row, 1986.

Schweid, Richard.
Hot Peppers.
New Orleans: New Orleans School of Cooking, 1987.

Sokolov, Raymond.
Why We Eat What We Eat.
New York: Summit Books, 1991.

Swartz, John.
"The Great Food Migration."
Newsweek 118 (Special issue: Fall/Winter 1991), 58-62.

Tannahill, Reay.
Food in History.
New York: Stein and Day, 1973.

Thorbjarnarson, John.
"Crocodile Lakes of Hispanola."
Wildlife Conservation, (Jan.-Feb. 1990), 42-47.

Viola, Herman J., and Carolyn Margolis.
Seeds of Change.
Washington, DC: Smithsonian Institution Press, 1991.

Von Welanetz, Diana, and Paul Von Welanetz.
Guide to Ethnic Ingredients.
Los Angeles: J.P. Tarcher, 1982.

Wexo, John Bonnett.
Zoobooks: Alligators and Crocodiles.
San Diego: Wildlife Education, Ltd., December 1990.

Wexo, John Bonnett.
Zoobooks: Endangered Animals.
San Diego: Wildlife Education, Ltd., January 1984.

Wilson, Edward O.
"Rainforest Canopy, The High Frontier."
National Geographic (Dec. 1991), 78-106.

INDEX

INDEX

INDEX

INDEX

INDEX

To Order
Additional Cookbooks

If you would like additional copies of
THE TURTLE BAY COOKBOOK A Feast of Flavors from Latin America and the Caribbean
CALL 831/ 375-7108
or complete the coupon that follows and mail to:
Chef's Pride
1996-1/2 Sunset Drive
Pacific Grove, CA 93950

THE TURTLE BAY COOKBOOK
A Feast of Flavors from Latin America and the Caribbean

I am ordering_____quantity (number of books) @ $17.95 each = _____

Tax, mailer, and postage: add $5.50 per book = _____

TOTAL ENCLOSED: _____

I am paying by:　　　Check_____　　Money Order_____　　Credit Card_____

MasterCard____VISA____Discover____American Express____

Card#: _____　　Expiration date: _____/_____

Signature (required): _____

Name: _____

Address: _____

City: _____ State: _____ Zip Code: _____

Phone: (_____) _____-_____

Mail to (if different from above):

Name: _____

Address: _____

City: _____ State: _____ Zip Code: _____

NOTES

 # NOTES

 # NOTES